Frommer's®

BRITAIN'S
BEST-LOVED
DRIVING
TOURS

Wiley Publishing, Inc.

Written by Roy Woodcock, John McIlwain

Revised eighth edition published 2008
Revised seventh edition published 2006
Revised sixth edition published 2004
Revised fifth edition published 2002
Revised second edition 1995, published in this format 1997
First published January 1991
Reprinted December 1997
Second edition of revised format 1999

Edited, designed and produced by AA Publishing.

Published by AA Publishing

Published in the United States by
Wiley Publishing, Inc.
111 River Street, Hoboken, NJ 07030

Find us online at Frommers.com

Frommer's is a registered trademark of Arthur Frommer.
Used under license.

ISBN 978-0-470-22696-4

Cataloging-in-Publication Data is available from the Library of
Congress.

Color separation: Daylight Colour Art, Singapore

Printed and bound by G. Canale & C. S.P.A., Torino, Italy

Right: *Woolsack Races, Tetbury, Gloucestershire*

A03367

CONTENTS

ABOUT THIS BOOK

This book is not only a practical touring guide for the independent traveller, but is also invaluable for those who would like to know more about Britain.

It is divided into 6 regions, each containing between 4 and 6 tours which start and finish in major towns and cities which we consider to be the best centres for exploration.

Each tour has details of the most interesting places to visit en route. Panels catering for special interests follow some of the main entries – for those whose interest is in history, wildlife or walking, and those who have children. There are also panels which highlight scenic stretches of road and which give details of local events, crafts and customs.

The simple route directions are accompanied by an easy-to-use map at the beginning of each tour, along with a chart showing how far it is from one town to the next in miles and kilometres. This can help you to decide where to take a break and stop overnight, for example. (All distances quoted are approximate.)

Before setting off it is advisable to check with the information centre at the start of the tour for recommendations on where to break your journey and for additional information on what to see and do, and when best to visit.

Tour Information
See pages 167–80 for addresses, telephone numbers and opening times of the attractions mentioned in the tours, including telephone numbers of tourist offices.

Accommodation and Restaurants
See pages 160–66 for a list of recommended hotels and restaurants for each tour.

Business Hours
Banks generally open 9am to 4 or 5pm weekdays. Some open on Saturdays until noon. In Scotland, opening times differ and some close for lunch.

Post offices open from 9am to 5.30 or 6pm Monday to Friday and 9am to 12.30pm on Saturdays.

Shops are open from 9am to 5.30pm, Monday to Saturday. Some are also open from 10am to 4pm on Sunday.

Credit Cards
All major credit cards are widely accepted in Britain.

Currency
The unit of currency is the pound (£), divided into 100 pence. Coins: 1, 2, 5, 10, 20 and 50 pence; £1 and £2. Notes: £5, £10, £20 and £50.

Customs Regulations
Visitors from EU countries are governed by EU regulations and can bring in items for their own personal use without paying duty. Visitors resident outside Europe are limited to certain duty-free allowances; check at time of purchase.

Electricity
240 volts, 50 cycles AC. Plugs are three-pin style. Most hotels are fitted with special razor sockets which will take both 240 or 110 volts. Visitors from the US will need a transformer for other appliances and a plug adaptor. Visitors from Europe, Australia and New Zealand will need an adaptor.

Embassies
Australia: Australian High Commission, Australia House, Strand, London WC2B 4LA, tel: 020-7379 4334.
Canada: Canadian High Commission, 38 Grosvenor Street, London W1X 0AA, tel: 020-7258 6600.
New Zealand: New Zealand High Commission, New Zealand House, 80 Haymarket, London SW1Y 4TQ, tel: 020-7930 8422.
US: American Embassy, 24 Grosvenor Square, London W1A 1AE, tel: 020-7499 9000.

Emergency Telephone Numbers
Police, fire and ambulance tel: 999.

Entry Regulations
Passports are required by all visitors except citizens of EU countries, who must have suitable identity documents. Visas are not required for entry into Britain by American citizens, nationals of the British Commonwealth and most European countries.

Health
Inoculations are not required by visitors for entry to Britain. Health insurance is recommended for non-EU citizens.

Motoring
For information on all aspects of motoring in Britain, see page 158.

Public Holidays
1 January – New Year's Day
2 January – holiday in Scotland only
Good Friday
Easter Monday (not Scotland)
1st Monday in May – May Day
Last Monday in May – Spring Bank Holiday
1st Monday in August – Bank Holiday in Scotland only
Last Monday in August – August Bank Holiday (not Scotland)

25 December – Christmas Day
26 December – Boxing Day

Route Directions

These abbreviations are used for British roads:

A – main road;
B – local road;
unclassified roads – minor roads

Telephones

Insert coins after lifting the receiver; the dialling tone is a continuous tone.
Useful numbers:
Operator – 100
Directory Enquiries – 118 500
International Directory
Enquiries – 118 505

To make an international call, dial 00 (the international code), then the country code, followed by the area code, minus the first 0, and the local number.

Country codes are
Australia 61
Canada 1
New Zealand 64
Republic of Ireland 353
UK and Northern Ireland 44
US 1

Time

The official time is (GMT) Greenwich Mean Time.

British Summer Time (BST) begins in late March when the clocks are put forward an hour. In late October, the clocks go back an hour to GMT. The official date is announced in the national newspapers and is always at 2am on a Sunday.

Tourist Offices

England: VisitBritain, Black's Road, Hammersmith, London W6 9EL (tel: 020-8846 9000). Scotland: VisitScotland, 23 Ravelston Terrace, Edinburgh EH4 3TP (tel: 0131–332 2433).
Wales: Wales Tourist Board, 2 Fitzalan Road, Cardiff CF24 0UY (tel: 029-2049 9909).

Hever Castle, Kent: Anne Boleyn's childhood home

THE WEST

The rich, rural lands of the counties from Dorset and Wiltshire westwards contain some spectacular scenery. Soft chalklands around Salisbury give way to harder and older rocks, which create the steep and dramatic hills of the Quantocks, Exmoor and Dartmoor.

An alternating sequence of cliffs and beaches form the western coastline: there are the precipitous granite cliffs near Land's End, and stupendous sandstone cliffs on the northern fringe of Exmoor. Steep roads are an indication of the resistance of the rocks. As a contrast to hills and cliffs, the flat fenlands of the Somerset Levels stretch away from the coast. The Levels are dotted with dairy cattle grazing on lush green meadows, many of which, thanks to conservation techniques, still contain buttercups and other wild flowers.

The pretty village of Selworthy in Somerset stands on the side of a wooded hill

West Country towns are situated round the edges of the high ground and in the river valleys. Many coastal towns which grew up as fishing ports have become holiday resorts, and traffic tends to be congested during the summer. Even the M5 motorway can become crowded at peak holiday weekends.

Early settlements left their mark on this area, too: Dartmoor probably has the greatest number of relics, but more famous and popular are the sites at Glastonbury, Stonehenge and Avebury. More recent evidence of human activity can be seen in many areas of mining, which is still practised near St Austell, where china clay is obtained for the paper industry.

Copper and tin were important minerals in Cornwall from the time of the Romans until earlier this century, when richer and larger deposits in other countries made the British mines uneconomic. The history of mining can be traced in the mining museums which are among the increasing number of the southwest's indoor attractions, complimenting the scenic splendour of this part of Britain.

St Michael's Mount – a place of mystery and magic

Penzance

The end of the railway line and the most westerly major town of England enjoys a mild climate which enables palm trees to grow along the coastline. Penzance was immortalised by Gilbert and Sullivan in *The Pirates of Penzance*. The National Trust's Trengwainton Gardens, just inland, contain magnolias and many delicate shrubs. Penlee House Gallery and Museum is among the cultural attractions, and there is plenty of activity in the little harbour. The *Scillonian* makes regular sailings to the Isles of Scilly.

St Austell

Originally noted for tin mining, St Austell has become associated with the china clay industry, which is why the landscape to the north is scarred with hollows overlooked by lunar mounds of white debris. The China Clay Country Park includes a fascinating depiction of mining history. This regional market centre grew up around the Market Hall, one of many local buildings constructed from granite, and other buildings of architectural interest include the parish church, the White Hart Hotel and the Quaker Meeting House.

Lynton

Steep, tree-covered cliffs make up the northern edge of Exmoor, with Lynton at the top of the slope and Lynmouth down by the sea below. The Catholic church is an outstanding building with decorative marble work, and the Lyn and Exmoor Museum has interesting displays about the area. Joining Lynton with Lynmouth is the dramatic cliff railway, built by the Victorian lawyer Sir George Newnes and funded by the fortune he made by publishing the famous *Sherlock Holmes* stories.

Bridgwater

Situated on the edge of Sedgemoor, where James II defeated the Duke of Monmouth's rebellion in 1685 in the last battle fought on English soil, Bridgwater grew up as a port and still has a tidal river linking it to the sea. The church is a fine and imposing building, well worth a visit; Monmouth used the tower as a look-out while trying to locate the King's infantry. Another famous figure in the Bridgwater area was Admiral Blake, and his birthplace is now a museum which contains exhibits of his life, as well as a history of the town.

Salisbury

This ancient town was originally at Old Sarum, 2 miles (3km) to the north, where there was an Iron-Age settlement. In 1220 the foundations of the new cathedral were laid at New Sarum, now called Salisbury, and gradually the new town developed. The cathedral is beautiful, built in the shape of a double cross, with a graceful spire rising to 404 feet (123m). Among many features of interest are the Poultry Cross, St Thomas's Church, the Playhouse and the delightful River Avon.

Bays,Cliffs
& Granite

Small bays, sandy beaches and steep rugged cliffs alternate around the Cornish coast on this tour, which then heads inland across undulating countryside, dotted with relics of the mining industry. Granite is everywhere, in the walls and in the villages.

3 DAYS • 158 MILES • 256KM

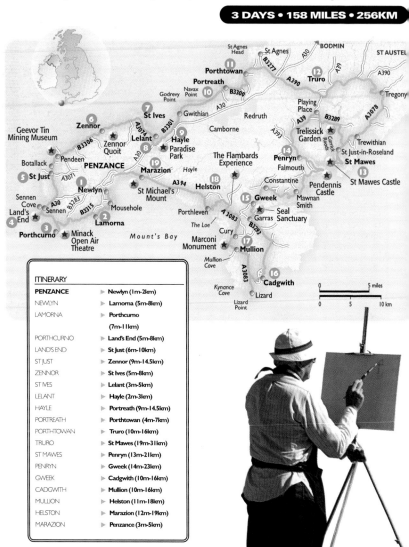

ITINERARY		
PENZANCE	▶	**Newlyn (1m-2km)**
NEWLYN	▶	**Lamorna (5m-8km)**
LAMORNA	▶	**Porthcurno (7m-11km)**
PORTHCURNO	▶	**Land's End (5m-8km)**
LAND'S END	▶	**St Just (6m-10km)**
ST JUST	▶	**Zennor (9m-14.5km)**
ZENNOR	▶	**St Ives (5m-8km)**
ST IVES	▶	**Lelant (3m-5km)**
LELANT	▶	**Hayle (2m-3km)**
HAYLE	▶	**Portreath (9m-14.5km)**
PORTREATH	▶	**Porthtowan (4m-7km)**
PORTHTOWAN	▶	**Truro (10m-16km)**
TRURO	▶	**St Mawes (19m-31km)**
ST MAWES	▶	**Penryn (13m-21km)**
PENRYN	▶	**Gweek (14m-23km)**
GWEEK	▶	**Cadgwith (10m-16km)**
CADGWITH	▶	**Mullion (10m-16km)**
MULLION	▶	**Helston (11m-18km)**
HELSTON	▶	**Marazion (12m-19km)**
MARAZION	▶	**Penzance (3m-5km)**

ⓘ *Station Road, Penzance*

The end of England – the haunting majesty of Land's End

SPECIAL TO...

A 20-minute helicopter flight from Penzance takes you to St Mary's, the largest of the Isles of Scilly. There is also a summer service to Tresco, the second largest island. Tresco has several miles of deserted golden beaches, but no roads and cars.

▷ *From Penzance, drive south along the coast for a mile (1.6km) to Newlyn, and a little further to Mousehole.*

❶ Newlyn, Cornwall
Really a suburb of Penzance, this is a lively and colourful fishing port, once famous for its artist colony. The Newlyn Art Gallery shows contemporary work.

Further along the coast is Mousehole. Pronounced 'mowzel', this delightful old fishing village consists of a semi-circle of colour-washed and granite houses round its harbour. Some of the roofs are specially weighted down to combat strong sea winds. Dolly Pentreath, supposedly the last person to speak Cornish as her native language, died here in 1777.

▷ *Continue on an unclassified road to Lamorna.*

❷ Lamorna, Cornwall
Lamorna is a holiday centre. The tempting golden sand of its spectacular cove is surrounded by steep blocks of granite cliffs and rocky outcrops.

▷ *Join the B3315, then at Trethewey turn left on to an unclassified road to Porthcurno.*

❸ Porthcurno, Cornwall
Porthcurno's beach of almost-white sand is overlooked by a remarkable theatre in the cliffs. The Minack is Britain's equivalent to an ancient Greek theatre, set 200 feet (60m) above the waves. It was created by Miss

Rowena Cade, who cut it out of the cliffs in 1931. The theatre has a 16-week season, and can seat 750 on its granite terraces.

▷ *Return to the B3315 and continue for another 4 miles (6km), then join the A30 to Land's End.*

❹ Land's End, Cornwall
England's most westerly point, Land's End is 873 miles (1,405km) from John O'Groats, Scotland's most northerly town. On a fine day the Isles of Scilly, 28 miles (45km) away, can be seen, along with Wolf Rock Lighthouse and the Longships Lighthouse, only 1½ miles (2km) offshore. Land's End is the setting for wild coastal walks and amazing rock formations.

Further along is the small village of Sennen, the battle-ground of the last Cornish fight against invading Danes. Sennen Cove has a good sandy beach and excellent bathing.

▷ *Continue with the A30, then left on to the B3306 for 5 miles (8km) to St Just.*

FOR CHILDREN

The legendary Last Labyrinth at Land's End is a major attraction using electronic equipment and including a life-size galleon with scrambling nets and cabins. You can also watch the glass-blower or woodcarver at work, and there is a fascinating collection of shells.

St Ives' golden beaches attract many holidaymakers in summer

off the road before entering Hayle, is a conservation theme park with otters and endangered species of birds. There is also a first-class falconry display.

Just south of the town at St Erth is the Cheney Mill Farm Park, an all-weather attraction with animals, birds and a large play barn.

▶ *The B3301 runs along the coast to Portreath.*

> ### RECOMMENDED WALKS
>
> From the B3301 it is possible to walk to Godrevy Point and Navax Point on a circular walk of 3 miles (5km).

5 St Just, Cornwall
This enchanting village and its neighbourhood are rich in antiquities. St Just is noted for the contents of its large medieval church: a stone of the 5th or 6th century inscribed with XP, the first two letters of the Greek word for Christ, and the shaft of a 9th-century Hiberno-Saxon cross. Abandoned and ruined mines litter the countryside north of the town.

At Botallack, along the B3306, is a deep mine which extended out beneath the sea, and at the Geevor Tin Mining Museum at Pendeen, a little further on, you can take an underground tour of this working mine.

▶ *Keep going along the B3306 to Zennor.*

6 Zennor, Cornwall
Zennor, named after St Senara, is a grey stone village huddled round its restored 12th-century church in a wild, bleak landscape. The Wayside Folk Museum, the oldest private museum in Cornwall, recaptures the flavour of this area from 3000 BC onwards, with displays on archaeology, tin mining and many other aspects of Cornish life. The writers D H Lawrence and Virginia Woolf both lived here in the 1920s. Zennor Quoit, to the southeast, is a chambered tomb dating from about 2000 BC.

▶ *A further 5 miles (8km) along the B3306 is St Ives.*

7 St Ives, Cornwall
St Ives was a prosperous pilchard port in the 19th century, but is now more noted for tourism, with its two fine sandy beaches and many excellent museums and galleries. The town has managed to preserve its old-world charm: quaint houses and narrow streets cluster round the 15th-century church. Be sure to visit the wonderful Tate Gallery, the Barbara Hepworth Museum and Sculpture Garden, and the Leach Pottery, if reopened.

ⓘ *The Guildhall, Street-an-Pol*

▶ *Take the main A3074 for 3 miles (5km) to Lelant.*

8 Lelant, Cornwall
Lelant has a fine Norman and Perpendicular-style church with a 17th-century sundial.

▶ *Follow the A3074, then the B3301 to Hayle.*

9 Hayle, Cornwall
During the 18th century Hayle developed as a port for the copper trade, but now it is a small industrial town with a good sandy beach, though there are still a few boats to be seen in the harbour. Paradise Park, just

10 Portreath, Cornwall
Portreath's tiny harbour cottages cluster around the port and the 18th-century pier, at the foot of windswept cliffs. It is a marvellous place to go walking along the coast path and there are spectacular views from Reskajeage Downs, above.

▶ *Turn inland along the B3300, then left on unclassified roads for Porthtowan.*

11 Porthtowan, Cornwall
Porthtowan is a pleasant little place with a sandy beach and magnificent cliffs to north and south. If you have time, walk up on to the cliffs for fantastic views inland and over the Atlantic.

▶ *Follow unclassified roads, then the B3277 and A390 to Truro.*

12 Truro, Cornwall
Truro is a quiet town with a blend of old and new buildings. Lemon Street has many fine Georgian structures, and Walsingham Place is a beautiful early 19th-century crescent off Victoria Place. The whole town is dominated by the cathedral,

which has three spires and was built on the site of a 16th-century church. The Royal Cornwall Museum in River Street is considered the finest in Cornwall and there is also a fine art gallery and concert hall.

i *Pydar House, Pydar Street*

▶ *Follow the A39 eastwards, then turn right along the A3078 for St Mawes.*

13 St Mawes, Cornwall
Smart shops and houses and many narrow old streets make this an interesting place to wander round. You should try to visit St Mawes Castle, built by

Henry VIII in the 1540s to guard the mouth of the Fal estuary. The views across Carrick Roads, a stretch of sea, to Falmouth are particularly impressive.

Trelissick Garden, north of St Mawes, boasts a fine collection of exotic plants from all over the world.

▶ *Turn north on the A3078 then the B3289, using King Harry ferry, which closes before dusk, then join the A39 and follow signs to Penryn.*

14 Penryn, Cornwall
Almost everything in Penryn is built of granite – granite buildings, a granite port and granite

blocks lying around everywhere waiting to be shipped out. The narrow streets of this old town stretch up the sides of the valley in an untidy but appealing way.

Further on is Falmouth, set on one of the finest natural harbours in the world. There are beaches to the south of the town, and on the northern side of the peninsula are the docks and 18th- and 19th-century buildings. Pendennis Castle was built at the same time as its twin, St Mawes Castle, to guard the harbour entrance.

i *Prince of Wales Pier, Falmouth*

▶ *Leave Falmouth on unclassified roads passing through Mawnan Smith, Porth Navas, Constantine and Brill to Gweek.*

15 Gweek, Cornwall
This lovely little stone village with two stone bridges across the channels of the Helford River is now better known for its seal sanctuary. Along the picturesque and tranquil banks of the Helford, sick and wounded seals and birds are treated. There are displays which show the work of the centre, and a safari bus will take you round the park to see the convalescent pool, nursery and exercise areas.

▶ *Travel to Garras on unclassified roads. Then take the B3293 and unclassified roads across Goonhilly Downs, south to Cadgwith and on to Lizard Point on an unclassified road and the A3083.*

16 Cadgwith, Cornwall
Attractive thatched cottages clustered round the small beach and harbour create a beautiful setting for local fishermen and tourists. Sandy coves alternate with rugged cliffs along this stretch of coast, but the most dramatic feature is the noisy, swirling water of the Devil's Frying Pan, created when a vast sea cave collapsed.

Truro's cathedral was built on the site of a 16th-century church

Cadgwith, a busy fishing harbour
Opposite: Sir Francis Drake

Further on, Lizard Point is the southernmost point in England with dramatic 180-foot (55m) cliffs and a lighthouse, open to the public.

▷ *Head north from Lizard Point for 4 miles (6km) along the A3083, then the B3296 to Mullion.*

RECOMMENDED WALKS

Among the most dramatic walks is the path from Cadgwith towards Landewednack. On the west coast of the Lizard, the coast near Kynance Cove can look most romantic and appealing.

17 Mullion, Cornwall
The village of Mullion boasts a fine 14th- and 15th-century church, which contains carved oak bench-ends, well worth

inspecting. The church tower is partially built of the local multi-coloured serpentine. Nearby Mullion Cove is surrounded by steep cave-pocked cliffs and has splendid views.

▷ *Drive on unclassified roads via Poldhu and Cury to the A3083 and on to Helston.*

18 Helston, Cornwall
Radio buffs should visit Poldhu Point before entering Helston, to see the Marconi Monument, which commemorates the first transatlantic transmitting station. The ancient Furry Dance takes place in Helston on 6 May, when there is dancing in the streets all day. In the past this town was a port, before the Loe Bar, a 600-foot (183m) ridge of shingle, blocked it off from the sea. Behind Loe Bar is The Loe, a pretty lake, into which, according to legend, Sir Bedivere threw King Arthur's sword, Excalibur.

Nearby The Flambards Experience provides entertain-

ment for the whole family. It features an award-winning Victorian village, a simulation of the World War II blitz, awesome rides and other themes.

▷ *Take the B3304 through Porthleven, then along the A394 to Marazion. Take an unclassified road before the bypass, into the village.*

19 Marazion, Cornwall
This ancient port is famous for St Michael's Mount, the granite island located offshore, but is a remarkable place in its own right. Cornwall's oldest chartered town, it has the safest beach in Cornwall and some of the best windsurfing in Europe. Henry III granted the town a charter in 1257 and for hundreds of years tin and copper ores were exported from here. The small town still attracts plenty of visitors, in spite of the bypass which has reduced the amount of through-traffic.

▷ *Return to Penzance via an unclassified road to the A394.*

FOR HISTORY BUFFS

St Michael's Mount is accessible by foot at low tide, and you should make time to get across to see the castle and priory, both founded by Edward the Confessor in the 11th century. This was the legendary home of the giant Cormoran, who was slain by Jack the Giant Killer.

BACK TO NATURE

The bird-watching hot spot of Marazion Marsh lies close to the sea just behind the coast road at Marazion. Autumns in previous years have produced regular sightings of aquatic warblers and spotted crakes, as well as occasional records of transatlantic vagrants, such as white-rumped sandpipers and lesser yellowlegs.

Mining,
Moorland &
Legends

This tour leads through granite scenery, market towns and green river valleys, before crossing the moorland expanse of Dartmoor, famous for its ponies and notorious prison, and finally descending to the farmlands around Tavistock.

ITINERARY

ST AUSTELL	▶ Bodmin (12m-19km)
BODMIN	▶ **Camelford (15m-24km)**
CAMELFORD	▶ Tintagel (6m-10km)
TINTAGEL	▶ **Boscastle (4m-6.5km)**
BOSCASTLE	▶ Launceston (14m-23km)
LAUNCESTON	▶ **Lydford (13m-21km)**
LYDFORD	▶ Okehampton (9m-14.5km)
OKEHAMPTON	▶ **Moretonhampstead (13m-21km)**
MORETONHAMPSTEAD	▶ **Princetown (14m-23km)**
PRINCETOWN	▶ Tavistock (7m-11km)
TAVISTOCK	▶ **Morwellham Quay (4m-6.5km)**
MORWELLHAM QUAY	▶ Liskeard (17m-27km)
LISKEARD	▶ Dobwalls (3m-5km)
DOBWALLS	▶ Lostwithiel (9m-14.5km)
LOSTWITHIEL	▶ St Austell (10m-16km)

3 DAYS • 150 MILES • 242KM

[i] *Southbourne Road, St Austell*

▶ *Leave St Austell on the B3274 to the China Clay Country Park. Drive north on the A391, then cross the A30 and follow the A389 to Bodmin.*

❶ Bodmin, Cornwall

The only Cornish town recorded in the Domesday Book, Bodmin lies on the steep southwestern edge of Bodmin Moor, which overlooks the town. The Celts, Romans and King Arthur have all had links with the town, and the parish church, the largest in Cornwall, is dedicated to St Petroc, the greatest of all Celtic saints.

Further north, just off the A389, is Pencarrow House, begun in the 1700s by Sir John Molesworth. In the grounds is an ancient Iron-Age encampment, and there are walks through the flower gardens, a play area and a pets' corner.

[i] *Shire Hall, Mount Folly*

▶ *From Pencarrow return to the A389. Turn left, then after half a mile (0.8km), left again on to the B3266 to Camelford.*

❷ Camelford, Cornwall

Camelford is thought by some to have been Camelot, the fabulous city of King Arthur, and Slaughter Bridge, one mile (1.6km) to the north, is said to have been Arthur's last battleground. The North Cornwall Museum contains many items of Cornish rural life, with sections on agriculture and slate and granite quarrying.

[i] *North Cornwall Museum, The Cleave*

▶ *From Camelford continue on the B3266, turning left on to the B3314 and then almost immediately right to join the B3263 to Tintagel.*

❸ Tintagel, Cornwall

Romance and legends connect this area strongly with King

Tintagel: the Old Post Office (left); weathered cliffs (below)

Arthur. The dramatic cliffs of slate on 'the Island', which is really a peninsula, have caverns and a waterfall. The 12th-century ruins of Tintagel Castle are in a spectacular setting on a wild, wind-lashed promontory. In the small town the highlight for most visitors is the Old Post Office, a small 14th-century manor house built of local slate. Excellent and beautiful walks can be found along the coast paths nearby and in the Rocky Valley, a few miles further north.

▶ Follow the **B3263** along the coast to Boscastle.

RECOMMENDED WALKS

Trethevy carpark, north of Tintagel, is a good starting point for walks in the Rocky Valley, especially to St Nectan, for beautiful woodland scenery.

❹ Boscastle, Cornwall

Boscastle is a picturesque harbour at the head of a deep S-shaped inlet between high cliffs. A few houses are actually built into the side of the road, and oak woods, river valleys and the sea combine to make this a classic beauty spot. The river and the tide occasionally meet with explosive collisions just beyond the outer breakwater.

▶ From Boscastle take the **B3266** and unclassified roads east across the **A39** to join the **A395**. Turn left on to the **A395** and follow it for 3 miles (5km) before branching left on to unclassified roads again through Tresmeer and Egloskerry to Launceston.

❺ Launceston, Cornwall

Launceston is an ancient town standing on the hilltop around the ruins of a castle. This was the only walled town in Cornwall and the South Gate, a narrow arch, remains.

St Thomas's Church has the largest font in Cornwall, and the Church of St Mary is famed for the carvings completely covering its external walls. A nostalgic steam railway runs into the Kensey Valley through 3 miles (5km) of glorious countryside. At the station there is a model railway and a small museum. The Tamar Otter and Wildlife Centre has peacocks and golden pheasants strutting about, and deer roam the woods.

▶ Continue eastwards on the old **A30**, now unclassified, then just past Lobhillcross turn right on to unclassified roads to Lydford.

❻ Lydford, Devon

Formerly a major centre for tin, this secluded village nestled on the edge of Dartmoor is dominated by the haunting remains of its 12th-century castle. Its old prison, a visible reminder of the harsh conditions endured by prisoners in the past,

Okehampton Castle, now in ruins but open to the public

was described as 'one of the most heinous, contagious and detestable places in the realm'. Lydford Gorge, scooped out by the River Lyd is approximately one mile (1.6km) to the south-west, where the 90-foot (27m) high tumbling White Lady Falls and the Devil's Cauldron are to be found.

RECOMMENDED WALK

Follow the River Lyd into the famous Lydford Gorge, and you will see the whirlpools and tumbling water of the Devil's Cauldron.

▶ Follow the **A386** north from Lydford, then after a short stretch east on the **A30** take the **B3260** to Okehampton.

One of England's finest clapper bridges can be seen at Postbridge

7 Okehampton, Devon

Okehampton is at the foot of the highest part of Dartmoor, accessible to walkers when the army is not using the firing range. An old ruined castle, one of Devon's largest, is located on a wooded hill to the west of town. The Museum of Dartmoor Life is an innovative museum portraying life in the area over hundreds of years.

Southeast of the town is Okehampton Camp, the remains of an Iron-Age hill-fort on a steep ridge.

i 3 West Street

▶ Return to the old **A30** (now an unclassified road) past Sticklepath and South Zeal. Just before Whiddon Down turn right on to the **A382** for Moretonhampstead.

8 Moretonhampstead, Devon

Before reaching this town you will pass the remarkable Castle Drogo, a massive granite castle designed by Edward Lutyens, to the left of the road near Drewsteignton. Drive on across the heart of Dartmoor to Moretonhampstead, a small market town with some fine old buildings. At Postbridge you can see the finest of the clapper bridges. One of England's oldest man-made bridges, it was used by pack-horses to carry ore from the mines.

RECOMMENDED WALKS

From Castle Drogo a circular tour leads through the delightful village of Drewsteignton, down to Fingle Bridge and then back along the wooded valley of the River Teign.

▶ Drive across Dartmoor for 14 miles (23km) along the **B3212** to Princetown.

9 Princetown, Devon

Princetown, the highest town in England, is noted for its prison, which was built for French captives of the Napoleonic Wars, brought to Dartmoor to work for Sir Thomas Tyrwhitt, who built a magnificent house near by.

FOR CHILDREN

The Miniature Pony Centre at Moretonhampstead encourages visitors to touch the animals, and rides can be arranged on the tiny ponies. The ponies have been pure-bred in pedigrees stretching back to about 1890, and other miniature animals here include bulls, pigs, goats and harvest mice.

there are many older buildings – the remains of a Benedictine abbey founded in the 10th century and 15th-century St Eustace's Church. The statue of Francis Drake is a reminder that the Elizabethan sailor was born at nearby Crowndale Farm.

☐i☐ *Town Hall, Bedford Square*

▷ *Leave Tavistock on the **A386** and just before crossing the river bridge, turn right along an unclassified road for 4 miles (6km) to Morwellham Quay.*

⑪ **Morwellham Quay,** Devon

Formerly a port, Morwellham, at 350 feet (107m) above sea level, is linked to the river by a remarkable inclined plane. It was the greatest copper port in Victorian times, and the old harbour and quays have been repaired by the Morwellham Trust. Crafts and costumes of 100 years ago are on show and there are underground reconstructions of working conditions and early mining techniques.

▷ *Return to the **A390** and head westwards to Liskeard.*

⑫ **Liskeard,** Cornwall

Liskeard is a small, lively town with attractive buildings including Webb's Hotel and Stuart House, where Charles I stayed for a week during 1644. Relics of the past can be found at St Keyne Station on the B3254 just outside town. Fair organs, street organs and a mighty Würlitzer are on show here in Paul Corin's musical collection.

▷ *A short drive along the **A390** brings you to Dobwalls.*

⑬ **Dobwalls,** Cornwall

The remarkable family theme park has eight adventure areas, with ropewalks, towers to climb and two railroads on a gauge of 7¼ inches (18cm). You can roar through tunnels and canyons on the *Queen of Wyoming*, or one of the other engines pulling the mini trains.

▷ *Continue with the **A390** to Lostwithiel.*

⑭ **Lostwithiel,** Cornwall

Lostwithiel sits at the highest point reached by the tide on the River Fowey. The old bridge dates from the 14th century, and Restormel Castle, which proudly overlooks the River Fowey, is even older, having first been built as a wooden fort in the 11th century.

At Charlestown, a few miles along the road, is the Shipwreck and Heritage Centre, which displays an interesting assortment of treasures from the sea bed. Outside the museum is the picturesque, unspoilt harbour, which still looks much as it did in the 1790s.

▷ *Return to St Austell on the **A390**.*

BACK TO NATURE

The wilds of Dartmoor have a surprising variety of wildlife. Cottongrass, sundew, bog asphodel and bog bean grace many of the wetter areas, and birdlife includes curlews, dunlin, lapwings, kestrels and buzzards.
In winter, look for short-eared owls, merlins and hen harriers.

SPECIAL TO...

Dartmoor and Bodmin Moor are great expanses of granite covered with boggy vegetation, heather and grasses, all of which can thrive on the acidic soils. When the minerals of granite are weathered, kaolin or china clay is often left behind. China clay has been quarried in this area for many years.
The China Clay Country Park, at Carthew, near St Austell, has a historic trail through the 19th-century clay workings.

▷ *Head west along the **B3357** to Tavistock.*

FOR HISTORY BUFFS

Dartmoor is rich in prehistoric remains; Bronze-Age coffins are beside the road a mile (1.6km) northeast of Princetown, along with a row of standing stones.
Two miles (3km) northwest, at Merrivale, are hut circles and one of Dartmoor's finest burial cists, while another group of Bronze-Age hut circles overlooks the River Walkham at Great Mis Tor, a mile (1.6km) further northeast of Merrivale.

---

⑩ **Tavistock,** Devon

Famous for its October Goose Fair, Tavistock is also of considerable interest for its association with tin and copper mining. The town is largely Victorian, but

Where Exmoor
Meets the Sea

Bright bays, steep coasts, low coastlines, lonely moorland and delightful stone villages combine to make this a memorable and varied tour.

3 DAYS • 133 MILES • 214KM

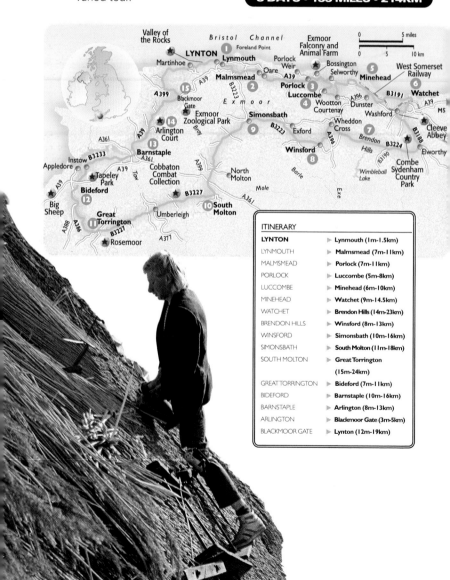

ITINERARY

LYNTON	▶ Lynmouth (1m-1.5km)
LYNMOUTH	▶ Malmsmead (7m-11km)
MALMSMEAD	▶ Porlock (7m-11km)
PORLOCK	▶ Luccombe (5m-8km)
LUCCOMBE	▶ Minehead (6m-10km)
MINEHEAD	▶ Watchet (9m-14.5km)
WATCHET	▶ Brendon Hills (14m-23km)
BRENDON HILLS	▶ Winsford (8m-13km)
WINSFORD	▶ Simonsbath (10m-16km)
SIMONSBATH	▶ South Molton (11m-18km)
SOUTH MOLTON	▶ Great Torrington (15m-24km)
GREAT TORRINGTON	▶ Bideford (7m-11km)
BIDEFORD	▶ Barnstaple (10m-16km)
BARNSTAPLE	▶ Arlington (8m-13km)
ARLINGTON	▶ Blackmoor Gate (3m-5km)
BLACKMOOR GATE	▶ Lynton (12m-19km)

Where Exmoor Meets the Sea

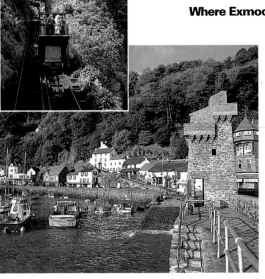

Top: Lynton's Cliff Railway
Above: the harbour at Lynmouth

Robber's Bridge further along the road there is a picturesque spot by the East Lyn, now only a tiny stream called Oare Water.

▶ *Take the unclassified road, then join the A39 to Porlock and eventually on to Selworthy.*

RECOMMENDED WALKS

Starting from Malmsmead, walk upstream along Badgworthy Water, where you might see a dipper or a kingfisher. From the memorial in Blackmore, walk on to the waterslide and Lank Combe, the probable location of Doone Valley.

---

i Town Hall, Lee Road, Lynton

RECOMMENDED WALK

Many footpaths lead from Lynton, notably a coastal walk into the Valley of the Rocks. Take the narrow road between the parish church and the Valley of the Rocks Hotel and follow a path carved out of solid rock on Hollerday Hill.

▶ *Take the B3234, dropping very steeply down into Lynmouth.*

❶ **Lynmouth,** Devon

Lynmouth is at the confluence of the East and West Lyn rivers. The 1890 cliff railway still provides a link with Lynton by means of two railcars; the top car uses water ballast to haul the other one up from the bottom. The River Lyn is very strongly embanked now and on leaving the town you will see the gorge down which the flood water came with such devastation in 1952. The poet Shelley lived in Lynmouth for a time.

▶ *Leave on the A39 towards Barnstaple, turn left on to the B3223 signed Simonsbath and then immediately left again up a narrow steep road which leads through Rockford and Brendon to Malmsmead.*

BACK TO NATURE

The wooded valley of Watersmeet, near Lynmouth, is safeguarded by the National Trust. Along the paths, look for the bright yellow flowers of the Welsh poppy, sometimes growing alongside clumps of the rare Irish spurge. Woodland birds are common and dippers and grey wagtails have become accustomed to human visitors.

❷ **Malmsmead,** Somerset

This isolated village is set in idyllic scenery, and is reached along narrow roads with gradients of 1 in 4. The East Lyn is a rocky stream, and if you walk up the valley of the tributary, Badgworthy Water, you will see some of the best of Exmoor. This is popularly assumed to be Doone country, though R D Blackmore, who wrote *Lorna Doone*, always refused to say where his tale of bandits was actually set. Blackmore, grandson of a 19th-century rector of Oare, further on from Malmsmead, named his characters after local people. The 500-year-old church here was the setting for Lorna Doone's violent wedding. At the

❸ **Porlock,** Somerset

Once down the notorious steep hill, and a descent of 1,350 feet (411m), pause to admire Porlock Weir, a small village of thatched cottages fringing a tiny harbour. Culbone Church is possibly the smallest surviving medieval church in England, and can only be reached on foot.

Exmoor Falconry and Animal Farm at Bossington is a must for family outings, with donkey rides and a hay bounce. Just off the A39 is Selworthy. Much of this pretty village is owned by the National Trust.

▶ *Return to the A39 and turn left towards Minehead. Shortly, turn right on an unclassified road to Luccombe.*

❹ **Luccombe,** Somerset

Pause in this secluded village to visit the fine church and churchyard, entered through a charming lychgate, and have a gentle stroll past the thatched cottages. At Wootton Courtenay, on the road to Minehead, the magnificent church has a saddleback roof.

▶ *From Wootton Courtenay, turn north to rejoin the A39 and continue to Minehead, then further to Dunster, just south of the A39, up the A396.*

5 Minehead, Somerset

A large expanse of sand and an attractive harbour area have lured visitors to this bright and breezy town. Take a ride on the West Somerset Railway, which runs through 20 miles (32km) of superb scenery from the coast to the Quantocks. Just outside Minehead is Butlins, a large holiday camp with a cable-car, monorail and funfair.

A little further on, Dunster's Norman castle looks out over the village and at the opposite end of the main street is the Conygar Tower, built in 1775 as a landmark for shipping. There is a 16th-century yarn market, and you can see the working water mill, on the River Avill, which dates from 1680 and still produces flour for local bakeries. Blenheim Gardens are fine to sit and relax in.

i 17 Friday Street

SPECIAL TO...

The Minehead Hobby Horse (or 'Obby 'Oss) procession takes place on the eve of May Day, and is said to have originated off an attempt to frighten off Danish invaders, using a strange, multicoloured beast accompanied by musicians to create a fearsome sight and sound. There is also an 'Obby 'Oss procession in Padstow, Cornwall.

▶ Follow the **A39**, then the **B3191** towards Blue Anchor and Watchet.

6 Watchet, Somerset

Much of Watchet's early growth was due to iron mining in the Brendon Hills; paper-making is now the main industry. The poet Coleridge found the main character for his epic poem *The Rime of the Ancient Mariner* in this historic seaport.

Just outside Washford, 3 miles (5km) south of Watchet, is Tropiquaria, which has displays of fish and animals. South of Washford is Cleeve Abbey,

founded by Cistercian monks in 1198, with a well-preserved refectory, gate house and chapter house. Further along the road is Combe Sydenham Country Park, in a hidden valley on the edge of the Brendons, where there is a restored 11th-century corn mill and a deer park.

▶ From Washford, follow the unclassified road southwards to join the **B3188** via Monksilver to Elworthy, then take the **B3224** west through the Brendon Hills.

7 Brendon Hills, Somerset

These undulating slopes, where Exmoor merges into the distinctive patchwork of the Brendon Hills, are not high enough for moorland, but have lush fields and trees and long views across the countryside. In earlier times small mining towns grew up to work the local deposits of iron ore, but the last one closed down in 1883. You can still see Bronze Age round barrows along the Ridgeway.

▶ Continue along the **B3224**, turn left on the **A396** and then follow an unclassified road to Winsford.

8 Winsford, Somerset

Winsford is one of the best centres for tourism on Exmoor, with its church standing over the village. The mysteriously inscribed Caractacus Stone, a mile (1.6km) to the south, probably dates from between the 5th and 7th centuries.

▶ From Winsford take the unclassified road to join the **B3223** and continue to Simonsbath.

9 Simonsbath, Somerset

Situated 1,100 feet (335m) above sea-level, Simonsbath is the highest village in Exmoor, in the centre of what used to be the Royal Exmoor Forest. Climb steeply out of the hamlet and on to the moors. In places the traditional old Exmoor hedges block the fabulous views.

▶ Use unclassified roads to cross the moor southwards, and join the **A399**, then the **B3226** for South Molton.

10 South Molton, Devon

Formerly important for the wool trade, but now a cattle market town and tourist centre, South Molton is known to have existed as a Saxon colony. The square is given grandeur by the Guildhall and Assembly Rooms which overlook it, and the splendid church has a magnificent tower and a remarkable stone pulpit. On the road west, the Cobbaton Combat Collection recalls World War II with tanks, artillery and radio equipment.

i 1 East Street

▶ Follow the **B3227** for 15 miles (24km) to Great Torrington.

11 Great Torrington, Devon

Great Torrington was a market town in Saxon times and the scene of fierce fighting in the Civil War. The original church was used as a gunpowder store but an explosion blew it to pieces. At Dartington Crystal you can watch fine crystal glass being blown, and just outside the town the Royal Horticultural Society has a garden at Rosemoor. The Gnome Reserve at West Putford has the world's largest population of gnomes.

i Castle Hill

▶ Take the **A386** to Bideford.

12 Bideford, Devon

This interesting little town was a major port in the 16th and 17th centuries. There is a new high bridge for the main road, but ships still move upstream to the old stone bridge across the estuary. The Royal Hotel, which dates from 1688, was where Charles Kingsley wrote part of his novel *Westward Ho!* Follow the old road to Barnstaple and you will pass Instow, a resort by the dunes with colourful views across to the port of Appledore.

Tapeley Park, on the way to Instow, has Italian terraced gardens and a traditional kitchen garden.

[i] *Victoria Park, The Quay*

▶ *Follow the coast road along the B3233 for around 10 miles (16km) to Barnstaple.*

FOR CHILDREN

At Abbotsham, 2 miles (3km) west of Bideford, is the Big Sheep, where you can watch the free demonstration of sheep milking and sheep shearing, and have a go at spinning. Other attractions include sheep racing, a nature trail and an adventure playground.

FOR HISTORY BUFFS

Like most towns on Devon's north coast, Bideford has strong maritime traditions. It was a busy port in England in the 16th century, with many links to the East Indies and the Americas. Smuggling as well as legal trading were part of the life in this area, and some of this history can be seen in the North Devon Maritime Museum in Appledore, north of Bideford.

13 Barnstaple, Devon
Barnstaple is one of North Devon's major market towns. It was once a busy ship-building town and a port trading with America, but the River Taw

Quince Honey Farm, South Molton

became too silted in the 19th century. There are many fine examples of Georgian architecture. Queen Anne's Walk is a pleasant colonnade, and you can still see the Tome Stone, where merchants used to set their money to make their contracts binding. The Museum of Barnstaple and North Devon is here, at The Square. The fine long bridge over the River Taw has 16 arches and dates from the 13th century.

[i] *The Square*

▶ *Continue northwards on the A39 for Arlington.*

14 Arlington, Devon
Arlington Court is one of the few great houses of North Devon. Formerly the home of the Chichester family, it has been owned by the National Trust since 1949. Sir Francis Chichester, the yachtsman, is the most famous descendant of this old family. The house contains a rich collection of model ships and there are walks in the park and woods. During the summer there are horse-and-carriage rides between the house and the collection of old carriages kept in the stables.

▶ *Continue along the A39 to Blackmoor Gate.*

15 Blackmoor Gate, Devon
Blackmoor Gate is really a road junction, but the Exmoor Zoological Park is near by along the A399 and provides entertainment for all the family. For the next few miles the road is narrow, winding and very steep in places, with dramatic views of coastal cliffs.

There is a short stretch of toll road, before entering the Valley of the Rocks, a gorge littered with enormous slabs of granite. Walk up to the top of Castle Rock, where the vertical drop is 800 feet (244m).

▶ *Take the A399 and then an unclassified road via Trentishoe and Martinhoe back to Lynton.*

Somerset's
Hamstone Towns

Wooded hills and rich valleys combine with the mellow dignity of country towns in golden stone to make South Somerset and Dorset one of the least spoiled parts of England. Add to this a splendid sea view and you have a tour to linger long in the memory.

3 DAYS • 130 MILES • 210KM

ITINERARY

BRIDGWATER	▶	**Taunton** (16m-26km)
TAUNTON	▶	**Ilminster** (15m-24km)
ILMINSTER	▶	**Chard** (5m-8km)
CHARD	▶	**Crewkerne** (8m-13km)
CREWKERNE	▶	**Beaminster** (7m-11km)
BEAMINSTER	▶	**Bridport** (6m-10km)
BRIDPORT	▶	**Abbotsbury** (10m-16km)
ABBOTSBURY	▶	**Dorchester** (9m-14.5km)
DORCHESTER	▶	**Cerne Abbas** (8m-13km)
CERNE ABBAS	▶	**Sherborne** (11m-18km)
SHERBORNE	▶	**Yeovil** (6m-10km)
YEOVIL	▶	**Montacute** (5m-8km)
MONTACUTE	▶	**Westonzoyland** (20m-32km)
WESTONZOYLAND	▶	**Bridgwater** (4m-6.5km)

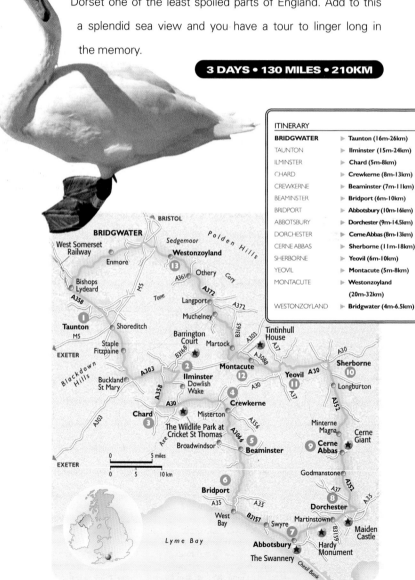

i Bridgwater House, Kings Square

▶ *Leave Bridgwater on an unclassified road to Enmore. Continue to Bishops Lydeard then turn left on to the A358 to Taunton.*

❶ Taunton, Somerset

As you drop steeply down from the Quantock Hills, a stunning view of the Vale of Taunton Deane opens up, with the undulating ridge of the Blackdown Hills in the distance. Taunton lies in the heart of this rich vale. The largest town between Bristol and Exeter, it has one of the biggest livestock markets in the southwest. In the Great Hall of Taunton Castle, the infamous Judge Jeffreys sent over 500 rebels to their deaths at his 'Bloody Assize'. A walk down Hammet Street gives the best view of the Perpendicular tower of 15th-century St Mary's Church. The town is a mecca for cricket lovers, and next to the County Ground is Somerset's Cricket Museum, in the 13th-century Priory Barn.

i Paul Street

SPECIAL TO...

The West Somerset Railway is the longest preserved line in Britain, running through some of the finest scenery in the West Country. Starting off at Bishops Lydeard, at the foot of the Quantocks, it runs 20 miles (32km) down to the coastal plain and beaches of the Bristol Channel.

▶ *Leave Taunton on the B3170 heading south. Shortly after crossing the M5, turn left for Staple Fitzpaine. Continue on unclassified roads towards Buckland St Mary and the A303. Turn left on to the A303, then right on to the B3168 to Ilminster.*

❷ Ilminster, Somerset

Dabinetts, Brownsnouts, Kingston Blacks and Red Streaks are all local varieties of apples. Somerset is real cider

Leaving Bishops Lydeard on the West Somerset Railway
Opposite: Abbotsbury swan

country, and near Ilminster, at Dowlish Wake, are Perry's Cider Mills, where this powerful apple brew has been made for centuries. Visitors can wander through the farm to see how it is done and afterwards sample some 'scrumpy' for themselves.

Ilminster has a lovely little shopping centre, built in the local hamstone (a golden limestone). Of particular note are the pillared market house and the 15th-century minster Church of St Mary. Herne Hill is a local beauty spot and vantage point to the southwest of the town. One of the earliest National Trust properties, Barrington Court, lies to the north – an intriguing model estate with Tudor manor house and gardens.

▶ *From Ilminster go south on an unclassified road, turning left on to the A358 for Chard.*

3 Chard, Somerset
This handsome market town astride the busy A30 claims to be the birthplace of flight. To find out why, visit the Chard Museum in High Street. Besides flight, you can find out more about blacksmiths, early funerals, historic costumes and even artificial limbs – they were invented here.

i The Guildhall

Captain Hardy, Nelson's flag captain on the *Victory*, was a pupil at the old grammar school.

▶ *From Crewkerne on the A356, signposted Dorchester/ Bridport, turn right on to the A3066 for Beaminster.*

5 Beaminster, Dorset
'The forgotten county' and 'the hidden valley' are two of the epithets ascribed to the scenery

here for a thousand years now, and this is still Europe's biggest netmaking centre. The unusual width of the streets allowed for rope-walks, where the flax strands were laid out to be twisted into shape. In South Street, look out for St Mary's Church with its hamstone tower and 13th-century knight's tomb.

i 47 South Street

▶ *Leave Bridport heading for West Bay, then turn on to the B3157 for 8 miles (13km) to Abbotsbury.*

7 Abbotsbury, Dorset
Abbotsbury shelters in a valley between high chalk downs and the shingle coast of Chesil Bank, that sweeps round to the 'Isle' of Portland. A long main street of thatched limestone cottages heralds your approach to the village centre, clustered round the 15th-century church and the Ilchester Arms public house. From opposite here a narrow, unsignposted road leads high up over Black Down Hill to the Hardy Monument, an obelisk commemorating Vice-Admiral Hardy. St Catherine's Chapel, built for seamen in the 15th century, looks down from its grassy knoll near by, and near the church are the remains of an 11th-century Benedictine abbey. The one surviving feature is a fine thatched tithe barn, the largest in England.

▶ *Leave Chard on the A30 for Crewkerne (8miles/13km).*

The countryside around Beaminster

FOR CHILDREN

The Wildlife Park at Cricket St Thomas is set in a deep, wooded valley just off the A30 between Chard and Crewkerne. It was here that the park is home to a great variety of animals and birds – from wild deer to penguins, elephants and parrots. There are plenty of leisure park features, including a scenic railway and an adventure playground.

---

around Beaminster. This town, in the Brit Valley, is virtually unspoilt. Three fires in 200 years once rendered the town 'the pityfullest spectacle that Man can behold' but the mellow honey-coloured hamstone houses testify to the healing power of time. Most streets offer a view of the fine pinnacled tower of the golden church, built in 1503. The Tudor manor house at Parnham, near Beaminster, which was home to John Makepeace's furniture workshops, is now closed to the public.

▶ *Continue south on the A3066 to Bridport.*

6 Bridport, Dorset
In olden times, the term 'Bridport dagger' used to strike fear into the heart of many a criminal, for that was the nickname for the hangman's noose. Ropes and nets have been made

4 Crewkerne, Somerset
Crewkerne is an ancient market town whose wealth was founded on minting coins, and in later centuries on flax-weaving and sail-making. It was here that HMS *Victory*'s sails were made, and more recently the sails for several contenders for the Americas Cup yacht race.

BACK TO NATURE

The Fleet is a large brackish lagoon which lies behind the shelter of Chesil Beach. Towards the western end, the swannery at Abbotsbury is worth visiting, while at the eastern end, the mudflats revealed at low tide support thousands of birds such as waders, gulls and other wildfowl. The shingle flora of Chesil Beach is worth studying, and in the heart of nearby Weymouth lies Radipole Lake, an RSPB reserve.

The Giant of Cerne Abbas

▶ *Leave Abbotsbury uphill on an unclassified road to Martinstown, then turn left and on to the B3159, then left again for Dorchester.*

8 Dorchester, Dorset

The county town of Dorset is in the heart of Thomas Hardy country and is still the busy market town portrayed in *The Mayor of Casterbridge*. Hardy's statue stands near the top of High West Street. Founded as *Durnovaria* by the Romans in AD 70, Dorchester has many fine Georgian buildings. Judge Jeffreys was sent here by King James to punish rebels after the Battle of Sedgemoor in 1685. At Old Crown Court, six local farm-workers were sentenced in 1834 to be transported to Australia for forming a trades union: they became known as the Tolpuddle Martyrs. There are numerous sites of interest, including the floor of a Roman town house and Maumbury Rings, a Roman amphitheatre. The town boasts three museums: the Dinosaur

Museum; the Military Museum, which is the unlikely location for Hitler's desk; and the Dorset County Museum.

ℹ *Unit 11, Antelope Walk*

FOR HISTORY BUFFS

Maiden Castle, 2 miles (3km) southwest of Dorchester, is the finest prehistoric hill-fort in Britain. The massive oval earth-works can be seen for miles around. Three huge ditches were dug by Iron-Age men to protect some 5,000 inhabitants. Archaeological excavations have revealed a history stretching back to the Stone Age, and among the finds have been the skeletons of 34 people.

▶ *From Dorchester head north on the A352 for Cerne Abbas.*

9 Cerne Abbas, Dorset

Before entering Cerne Abbas, as you pass through Godmanstone,

look out for the smallest pub in England, the Smith's Arms, just 20 by 10 feet (6 by 3m). Cerne Abbas itself is a charming village and its main source of interest is not difficult to spot. Cut into the steep chalk hillside behind the village, the Cerne Giant, a well-endowed figure 180 foot (55m) high, is a fertility symbol dating from Roman times.

▶ *Continue north on the A352 for Sherborne.*

10 Sherborne, Dorset

Sherborne claims, with some justification, to be one of the most beautiful towns in England. Set in a gentle valley among wooded hills, it has a charming stone-built centre. Two kings of Wessex were buried in Sherborne's Saxon abbey, the mother cathedral of the Southwest until 1075. Sherborne Old Castle dates from the 12th century, and Sherborne New Castle was built by Sir

Walter Raleigh in the 1590s. It was here that Sir Walter was 'extinguished' by a servant who first saw him smoking tobacco he brought from the New World.

To the south of Sherborne is a ridge between Leweston and Lillington. This is a watershed, with rain in Leweston running to the English Channel at Christchurch and Lillington's rain finding the Bristol Channel at Burnham.

[i] *3 Tilton Court, Digby Road*

▶ *Leave Sherborne on the **A30** heading west for Yeovil.*

11 Yeovil, Somerset
Yeovil is a thriving industrial and administrative centre, known for its gloves and helicopters. It suffered disastrous fires in 1499, 1623 and 1640, and during World War II air raids destroyed many of its oldest buildings. One to

Below: the charming hamstone town of Montacute
Right: Wells Cathedral's clock

survive was the 14th-century stone church, impressive for its simplicity and size.

[i] *Heritage and Visitor Centre, Hendford, Yeovil*

▶ *Leave Yeovil on the **A30** and turn right on to the **A3088**, turning left for Montacute.*

12 Montacute, Somerset
This is yet another delightful hamstone village. In a corner of the square is the entrance to its showpiece, Montacute House, a splendid Tudor mansion in formal, landscaped gardens. It was built by Sir Edward Phelips, chief prosecutor of Guy Fawkes in 1605.

Although on a smaller scale than Montacute, nearby Tintinhull House and Garden attracts many visitors each year.

▶ *From Montacute take the **A3088** to Stoke-sub-Hamdon, then the **A303** and right on to the **B3165**. Join the **A372** heading for Westonzoyland.*

13 Westonzoyland, Somerset
Westonzoyland's 100-foot (30m) church tower looks boldly over Sedgemoor, once covered by sea and now a vast expanse of fenland – the largest wetland of its type anywhere in Britain. A map in the church porch will show you how to explore the historical connection, for near here the last battle on English soil was fought. A granite monument on this quiet open land is all that marks the spot for posterity.

▶ *From Westonzoyland continue on the **A372** for 4 miles (6.5km) to Bridgwater.*

Hills & Vales
of West Wessex

From Wiltshire's gentle valleys and downlands to the rugged hills and expansive wetlands of Somerset, the Wessex scenery constantly changes. This tour takes in one of Britain's finest cathedrals, one of Europe's loveliest gardens and the world's most famous prehistoric temple.

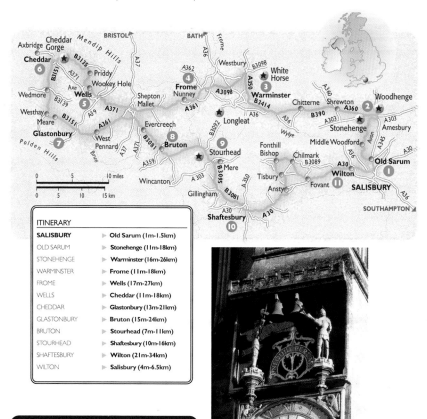

3 DAYS • 137 MILES • 221KM

Built for ceremonies long forgotten, Stonehenge remains a mystery

ℹ️ *Fish Row, Salisbury*

▶ *Leave Salisbury on the **A345** signed Amesbury and in 1 mile (1.6km) reach Old Sarum.*

1 Old Sarum, Wiltshire
Iron-Age men, Romans, Saxons, Danes and Normans in turn chose this windy hilltop for their settlements. Within a huge circular mound are the foundations of the Norman cathedral and castle that once stood here. Bishops Osmund and Roger built the cathedral, but cathedral life wasn't easy, and castle and clergy did not get on. In 1220 the bishop chose a new site in the valley, known today as Salisbury, and materials from the demolished cathedral were then used for Salisbury's new glory.

▶ *Continue on the **A345**, then take the first left on to unclassified roads for the Woodfords. In 5 miles (8km) reach Amesbury and 1 mile (1.6km) further north on the **A345** is Woodhenge. Return to the*

A303 and head west signed Honiton, then right on to the A360 to Stonehenge.

2 Stonehenge and Woodhenge, Wiltshire
A henge is a prehistoric monument, usually of religious significance. Woodhenge, the neolithic precursor of Stonehenge, had six concentric rings of timber posts, surrounded by a ditch. The holes marking the site are now marked by concrete posts.

At Stonehenge huge stones 15 to 20 feet (4.5 to 6m) high have been the subject of enormous speculation. Was it a temple for Romans or Druids? How were 26-ton stones brought here? One thing is certain – the axis is aligned with the midwinter and midsummer sun; perhaps this revered monument is a giant calendar.

▶ *From Stonehenge continue on the **A360**, turning left on to the **B390** just past Shrewton. On reaching the **A36** turn right, then right again after 1 mile (1.6km) on to the **B3414** to Warminster.*

3 Warminster, Wiltshire
Warminster was formerly a wool town and corn market; today it is the home of the Army School of Infantry and the REME (Royal Electrical and Mechanical Engineers) workshops. Four miles (6.5km) to the west is Longleat, seat of the Marquess of Bath and nationally famous as a wildlife park.

ℹ️ *Central Car Park, Warminster*

▶ *Take the **A350** for Westbury. Leave by the **A3098** for 7 miles (11km) to Frome.*

RECOMMENDED WALK

Westbury's White Horse, cut into the chalk escarpment of Salisbury Plain in the 18th century, is said to replace one carved in AD 879 to commemorate King Alfred's victory over the Danes at Ethandun. Climb from the church at Bratton on the B3098, east of Westbury, or drive up to Westbury Hill, turning right from the B3098, just before the cemetery.

---

gral shops, and St John's Church.

Three miles (5km) from Frome, on the A361, is Nunney, with its romantic moated 14th-century castle.

ℹ️ *The Round Tower, Bridge Street*

▶ *Leave Frome to join the **A361** for Shepton Mallet, 11 miles (18km), then by the **A371** to Wells (6 miles/10km).*

SPECIAL TO...

The Royal Bath and West Show is held at the end of May and attracts huge crowds from far and wide to the showground near Shepton Mallet, 11 miles (16km) from Frome.

As well as the agricultural activities, attractions include aerobatics, showjumping and motorcycle displays.

4 **Frome,** Somerset

'Friendly Frome' (say Froom), on the River Frome, is an attractive market town which grew rich on trade in woollen cloth. Its steep narrow streets are scattered with medieval and Tudor buildings. Cheap Street, with its ancient shops and leat gutter is a must, as are the 1726 Blue House, the bridge with its inte-

5 **Wells,** Somerset

Wells is England's smallest city, lying in the shadow of the Mendip Hills, and gets its name from the springs that bubble in to a pool in the bishop's garden. The splendid cathedral was begun in the 12th century and finished in the 15th, and its astronomical clock in the north transept is one of the oldest

cathedral clock-faces in Britain. South of the cathedral is the moated Bishop's Palace, where the swans used to ring the bell by the bridge for food.

St Cuthbert's Parish Church in High Street is the largest in Somerset, with a 122-foot (37m) tower.

ℹ️ *Town Hall, Market Place*

FOR CHILDREN

Stalactites and stalagmites, soaring caverns and bottomless pits are all to be found at Wookey Hole Caves near Wells, first inhabited 50,000 years ago. On the surface, visitors can walk around a mill which still produces watermarked paper from rags, distort themselves in the mirrors of the old fairground and change new pence for old to play original one-arm bandits at the Penny Pier Arcade.

▶ *Leave Wells on an unclassified road to Wookey Hole, and shortly after the Wookey Hole Caves fork right for Priddy, then left on the **B3135** for Cheddar (5 miles/8km).*

Elizabethan Longleat House, seat of the Marquess of Bath

BACK TO NATURE

Ebbor Gorge, on the route between Wookey Hole and Priddy, is thought by many to be the loveliest and most unspoilt Mendip gorge.

6 Cheddar, Somerset

The rugged grandeur of the Cheddar Gorge unfolds slowly and magically as you descend a meandering road. Cliffs tower to a height of 450 feet (137m) here, and the 'Beware of falling rocks' sign is no idle warning. Climb the 274 steps of Jacob's Ladder at the south end for the best views, or rest in the Garden of Fragrance, especially created for the blind. At the bottom of the gorge, Gough's and Cox's Caves offer a chance to go subterranean in search of the lost River Yeo.

Cheddar would not be Cheddar without its cheese, but the product outgrew the place and has largely gone elsewhere. A 1990 replica of a 1920s factory shows how it used to be made.

i The Gorge

FOR HISTORY BUFFS

Axbridge, near Cheddar, is a fine example of a close-knit, winding medieval town. The jewel is King John's Hunting Lodge, at the corner of High Street and The Square. This handsome three-storeyed building has nothing to do with either King John or with hunting, but has been exquisitely restored by the National Trust, and now houses the Axbridge Museum, open on summer afternoons.

▶ *Leave Cheddar on the B3151 for Glastonbury (12 miles/19km).*

7 Glastonbury, Somerset

Said to be the 'cradle of English Christianity', Glastonbury is a town steeped in Christian and Arthurian legends. The focal point is the ruined abbey, which may have originated in the 1st century, but was sacked at the Dissolution in 1539. Joseph of Arimathea is reputed to have come here as a missionary in AD 63, and a thorn in the Abbot's kitchen is said to derive from his wooden staff, which turned into a thorn bush. The chapel on the Tor dates from AD 179. Through the ages, writers have speculated that this is the site of Avalon, King Arthur's final resting place. The chalice which Christ used at the Last Supper is said to be beneath the Chalice Spring on the Tor. Of particular note in the town are the Abbey Barn, now housing the Somerset Rural Life Museum, the fine 14th-century George and Pilgrims Hotel, and The Tribunal, once a courthouse and now a museum.

i The Tribunal, 9 High Street

▶ *Leave Glastonbury on the A361 and in 7 miles (12km)*

turn left on to the **A37**, then right on to the **A371** sign-posted Castle Cary. Shortly, fork left on to the **B3081** for Bruton, (4 miles/6.5km).

8 Bruton, Somerset

Bruton, on the River Brue, has a charm of its own. Be sure to explore The Bartons, narrow alleys leading down to the river, which is crossed by an unusual packhorse bridge. St Mary's Church, with its twin towers, is particularly fine, and prominent in the town is King's School, established in the 16th century. The tall building on the hill as you leave is the Bruton Dovecote, formerly belonging to the abbey which once existed here.

▶ *Leave Bruton by the B3081, signposted Wincanton. In Redlynch turn left at the*

Nature tamed: the classical order and opulence of Stourhead

crossroads and in 3 miles (5km) right, and shortly right again to join the B3092 to Stourhead (½mile/1km).

9 Stourhead, Wiltshire

Henry Hoare, an eminent banker, decided to landscape his Palladian Wiltshire home, Stourhead, in the grand manner. He began in 1740 by damming springs of the Stour to create a sweeping lake with wooded islands. This is one of the finest gardens in the world, now in the care of the National Trust. An unmistakable landmark on the border of the Stourhead estate is Alfred's Tower, a triangular brick structure 160 feet (49m) high, built in 1772. It marks the spot where King Alfred rallied his troops to fight the Danes in AD 879.

▶ *Leave Stourhead on the B3092 for Mere (2 miles/3km). Take the B3095, then turn left on to the B3092 to Gillingham (2½ miles/4km), then Shaftesbury (3 miles/5km) via the B3081.*

10 Shaftesbury, Dorset

Perched on a hill 700 feet (213m) above sea-level, the pretty town of Shaftesbury commands marvellous views across Dorset's Blackmoor Vale. The local history museum near St Peter's Church contains the Byzant, a strange ornamental relic, formerly carried by townsfolk in a ceremony confirming their rights to draw water from wells at the foot of the hill.

i 8 Bell Street

▶ *Leave Shaftesbury on the A30 signposted Salisbury. In 6 miles (10km) turn left for Ansty and Tisbury. Continue north, then turn right on the B3089 at Fonthill Bishop. In 2 miles (3km) turn at Chilmark to Fovant (3 miles/5km). Go left on the A30 to Wilton.*

11 Wilton, Wiltshire

In Saxon times, Wilton was capital of Wessex. Thousands now flock here each year to visit Wilton House, built in the 1540s and remodelled by Inigo Jones

Shaftesbury's most famous street, cobbled Gold Hill

in the 17th century. The Double Cube Room, now restored, is especially ornate. There is a world-famous collection of paintings by Rubens, Van Dyck and Tintoretto, among others.

▶ *Leave Wilton by the A36 for Salisbury (4 miles/6.5km).*

SCENIC ROUTES

On the B3151 south of Cheddar, it is worth stopping as you approach Wedmore to look back over Sedgemoor, one of England's few wetlands, stretching away to the marvellous backdrop of the Mendip limestone ridge.
As you ascend the steep hill to enter Shaftesbury, look back over the rich farmland of Dorset's lovely Blackmoor Vale, with the wooded ridge of Stourhead and Alfred's Tower beyond.

THE SOUTH & SOUTHEAST

Despite being well populated, the five counties of Surrey, Sussex, Kent, Hampshire and Dorset have retained large areas of rich farmland, commons and heaths and forested areas. Perhaps the most famous area is the New Forest in Hampshire, much of which is heathland; 'forest' was originally a term for hunting ground.

Architectural styles are especially distinctive in the Weald of Sussex and Kent, where tile-hung houses can be seen in many villages, as well as thatched houses and oasthouses — though most of these are now residences, having ceased production of beer from locally grown hops. Further west is Hardy Country: many of Dorset's attractive towns and villages can be related to the writings of Thomas Hardy and his views of life in the 18th century.

The scenery varies from gentle, undulating landscapes to steep escarpments on the edges of the North and South Downs and dramatic coastal cliffs, notably at Beachy Head, where the South Downs reach the sea. At the foot of the white cliffs of Dover, where the North Downs reach the coast, the Channel Tunnel dives beneath the sea on its way to France.

Seaside resorts such as Bournemouth and Folkestone attract large numbers of visitors, especially in the summer months and at weekends, although many of the beaches are not very sandy in the more easterly part of the region.

Religion plays an important part in the life of this region, where Winchester and Canterbury are at opposite ends of the Pilgrim's Way. Fine cathedrals can be seen in both these towns, and a great many impressive churches are hidden away in small villages. These were often financed from agricultural profits and competition was fierce, with villages trying to outdo their neighbours with bigger or better churches. Near the chalk hills, many of these churches are built of this soft rock, but are faced with a layer of resistant flint.

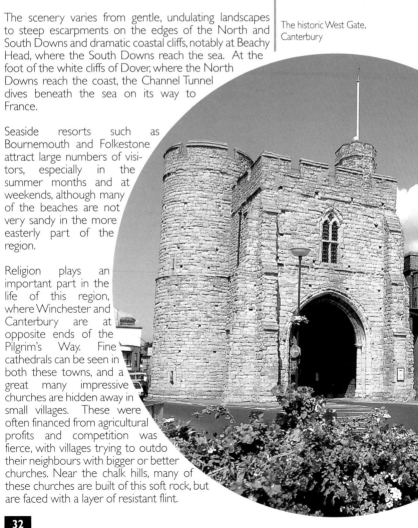

The historic West Gate, Canterbury

New Alresford's ancient fulling mill on the River Itchen

Royal Tunbridge Wells

This spa town has been a fashionable market and trading centre for many years; even in the 17th century, the Pantiles was an established shopping centre. The town first developed as a spa when its chalybeate spring was discovered in 1606; it can still be seen, in Bath Square. The surrounding countryside consists of miles of common, on which stand the spectacular High Rocks.

Canterbury

Canterbury's cathedral dominates the landscape for miles around, but there is much more to see in this ancient city, often thought of as the birthplace of English Christianity. A walk round the streets is a walk through history, and a visit to the Museum of Canterbury is a good way to start a tour. The city walls, St Martin's church, the ruins of St Augustine's Abbey, the Royal Museum and the Old Weavers' House are among the buildings you must not miss. There are also modern entertainments, including two theatres and an excellent pedestrianised shopping area.

Winchester

There is so much to see in this City of Kings that it is worth taking a guided walking or driving tour. Winchester is a place of history and legend. The Round Table in the castle's Great Hall is actually a medieval creation which celebrates the King Arthur legend. From here you can walk past the old Butter Cross in the centre of town and make a diversion to the fine cathedral – before taking a look at the statue of King Alfred, which recalls Winchester's past status as his kingdom's capital.

Bournemouth

This town developed along with the Victorian enthusiasm for the seaside, when a few rich families built villas on what used to be a fairly desolate heath. An attractive beach stretches for miles along the coast, and windsurfing, swimming and boating are popular. There are beautiful gardens to visit with subtropical vegetation which thrives in the mild climate. Quiet, wooded walks can be taken in the steep valleys called chines, which slope down from the cliff tops to the shore.

A Journey
Across the Weald

Over undulating

3 DAYS • 122 MILES • 197KM

sandstone hills, through the orchards of the 'Garden of England', and the once vast Forest of Anderida, this is an area of delightful villages, superb castles and immaculate gardens. Church spires and towers and tile-hung Wealden houses all add to its beauty, as the buildings and countryside compete with each other to provide the most delightful views.

ITINERARY

ROYAL TUNBRIDGE WELLS	▶ Penshurst (7m-11km)
PENSHURST	▶ Hever (6m-10km)
HEVER	▶ Limpsfield (10m-16km)
LIMPSFIELD	▶ Sevenoaks (9m-14km)
SEVENOAKS	▶ Ightham (6m-10km)
IGHTHAM	▶ Mereworth (6m-10km)
MEREWORTH	▶ Lamberhurst (14m-23km)
LAMBERHURST	▶ Cranbrook (10m-16km)
CRANBROOK	▶ Tenterden (11m-18km)
TENTERDEN	▶ Northiam (8m-13km)
NORTHIAM	▶ Bodiam (5m-8km)
BODIAM	▶ Burwash (10m-16km)
BURWASH	▶ Rotherfield (13m-21km)
ROTHERFIELD	▶ Royal Tunbridge Wells (7m-11km)

▶ *Leave Tunbridge Wells on the A264, then take the B2188 north to Penshurst.*

❶ Penshurst, Kent

Penshurst is a small village with stone houses and a magnificent church, but the main attraction is 14th-century Penshurst Place, one of the outstanding stately homes of Britain, set in superb Tudor gardens. The famous chestnut-beamed Great Hall dominates the manor with its medieval splendour, and its scale and grandeur are almost beyond belief. It also houses a fascinating toy museum. The Elizabethan poet, Sir Philip Sidney, was born here in 1554, and the Sidney family still lives in the manor. The family became Earls of Leicester, and the village has the original Leicester Square – named after a favourite of Elizabeth I. The Church of St Michael the Archangel dates from the 13th century and contains impressive memorials to the Sidney family.

▶ *Take the road past the church and follow the B2176, B2027 and unclassified roads for 6 miles (10km) to Hever.*

❷ Hever, Kent

Hever is best known for its associations with Anne Boleyn, Henry VIII's second wife. The village inn is called King Henry VIII, and the fine church has a memorial to Sir Thomas Bullen, Anne's father, who is buried here. Hever Castle was the family home, and it was here that Henry VIII courted her. This fine, moated manor house was acquired by William Waldorf Astor in 1903, who did much work restoring it. He created the modern lake and superb Tudor-style gardens, including a spectacular Italian Garden, and built a mock-Tudor village behind the house. The house itself contains a superb collection of furniture and paintings, and the Tudor Long Gallery

features a fascinating exhibition of scenes from the life and times of Anne Boleyn.

Just east of Hever is Chiddingstone. The entire village is owned by the National Trust, including Chiddingstone Castle, a late 18th-century Gothic manor house. The main street is lined with beautifully preserved half-timbered 16th- and 17th-century houses. The Chiding Stone, after which the village is named, is a piece of local sandstone where nagging wives were publicly chided by the village population.

Three miles (5km) west of Hever is Edenbridge. The 16th-century Crown Hotel is noteworthy. The 13th-century church here has a massive tower which is crowned with a spire of a later date.

Two miles (3km) west of Edenbridge, at Haxted, is a late 16th-century watermill, which, though now a restaurant, can still be visited.

▶ *From Haxted Mill take unclassified roads north to Limpsfield.*

The gardens at Penshurst Place
Left: Bust at Hever Castle

❸ Limpsfield, Surrey

This small town nestles at the foot of the North Downs in wooded countryside. The composer Frederick Delius is buried among the yews in the churchyard here.

A little further is the village of Westerham. General Wolfe, who beat the French in Quebec in 1759, was born here. His boyhood home, 17th-century Quebec House, is near the green. Near by is Squerryes Court, a William and Mary manor house built in 1681 and owned by the Warde family for over 250 years. Wolfe received his commission here, and a room is set aside for Wolfe memorabilia. The house also contains fine paintings, tapestries and furniture, and the magnificent garden has lakes, flowers and shrubs. There is a statue of Wolfe in the High Street, and on the tiny green one of Sir Winston Churchill, who lived at Chartwell, just south of town, from 1924 until his death. The house is filled with reminders of the great statesman, from his hats and uniforms to gifts presented by Stalin and Roosevelt. There are paintings of Churchill and also many works by Churchill himself. An exhibition gives visitors an insight into his life during his years at Chartwell, and his studio is arranged with easel at the ready.

Chartwell was Winston Churchill's country home until his death

RECOMMENDED WALKS

Many excellent walks can be found near Titsey, to the north of Limpsfield, southwards towards Edenbridge along the Vanguard Way, and east and west along the North Downs Way, which follows much of the old Pilgrim's Way from Winchester to Canterbury, giving fine views of southern England.

▶ Follow the **A25** to Sevenoaks.

4 Sevenoaks, Kent
The traditional seven fine oaks which gave the town its name were reduced to only one in the great storm of October 1987, but new trees have been planted. Sevenoaks is notable for Knole, which dates from 1456 and is the largest private house in England. Thomas Sackville, the 1st Earl of Dorset, was granted the house by Elizabeth I. Set in a wide rolling deer park, it contains an important collection of 17th-century furniture, fine staircases and fireplaces, two state beds of James II and galleries hung with original tapestries. Beer has been brewed in the area for centuries, and you can also sample one of the wines from an increasing number of local vineyards.

i Buckhurst Lane

▶ Leave Sevenoaks on the **A225**, and rejoin the **A25** to Ightham.

5 Ightham, Kent
Visiting Ightham is like stepping back in time. Ightham Mote is an unspoilt, medieval, moated manor house surrounded by beautiful Wealden scenery. Undisturbed by time, the great hall, chapel and crypt have survived in fine condition. There are many fine old half-timbered medieval buildings in the village, including an oast house and the Old Coaching Inn. The Church of St Peter is mainly 14th- and 15th-century and contains some splendid stained glass and several brasses and sculptures.

▶ Continue east on the **A25**, which joins and becomes the **A20**. Turn south on to the **B2016** to the turning east for Mereworth.

6 Mereworth, Kent
This is the heart of the 'Garden of England'. The unusual church was rebuilt in 18th-century neo-classical style, like nearby Mereworth Castle, and has a remarkable large steeple. The castle, built in the early 18th century as a copy of the Villa La Rotunda near Vicenza, in Italy, has the appearance of an ancient temple. The present village was built by Lord Westmoreland, who destroyed the original in order to use the site for the extravagant and exotic castle.

On the road to Lamberhurst you will pass the Hop Farm at the Kentish Oast Village at Paddock Wood. Set in 400 acres of unspoilt Kent countryside, this once-working hop farm is one of Kent's most popular tourist attractions. The farm has the finest collection of Victorian oast houses in the world, now turned into craftsmen's work-shops and a hop museum, recapturing the life of hop farmers in the past. Among other attractions are shire horses, farm animals and pets corner, wartime tanks and military vehicles, a nine-hole crazy golf course, a bouncy castle, a children's craft centre, and a programme of special events running throughout the year.

▶ From Mereworth return to the **B2016** via the **A26**. Continue south on the **B2016, A228, B2160** and **A21** for 14 miles (23km) to Lamberhurst.

7 Lamberhurst, Kent
This village was the centre of the Wealden iron industry and at one time produced railings for St Paul's Cathedral in London.

Bayham Abbey, 2 miles (3km) west of the village, is said to be the most impressive group of monastic remains in Kent, with church, monastery and a former gatehouse all well preserved. Set in the wooded Teise Valley, the ruins date back to the 13th century.

The beautiful gardens at Scotney were carefully planned in the 19th century around the remains of the old, moated Scotney Castle. There is something to see at every time of year, with spring flowers followed by gorgeous rhododendrons, azaleas and a mass of roses, and then superb autumn colours. Open-air opera performances are given in mid-July.

South of Goudhurst is Bedgebury Pinetum, an attractive place to visit at any time of the year. It is set in a big park surrounding a Louis XIV-style mansion. Rhododendrons and azaleas are specialities, but there are numerous varieties of fungi and conifers. The mansion is now a girls' school, but most of the park is open. The Pinetum contains a nationally important collection of pine trees – several of the plants came originally from Kew Gardens, but the Forestry Commission now manages these woodlands. Bird-watchers come to Bedgebury, especially during the winter months, to see interesting species such as hawfinch, crossbill and firecrest.

▶ *Continue southeast on the A21, taking the unclassified road on the left after 1½ miles (2km), through Kilndown to the A262 and Goudhurst. About 1½ miles (2km) after Goudhurst, turn right on to the B2085, then left to Cranbrook on meeting the A229.*

8 Cranbrook, Kent

Cranbrook is a pleasant town with many 18th-century buildings. In the centre is Union Mill, the finest working smock windmill in England. Often called the 'Capital of the Weald', Cranbrook was built from the profits of the wool trade in the 15th century. The fine medieval church, 'the Cathedral of the Weald', has a porch built in 1291, and the local museum recaptures much of the history of the area.

The beautiful gardens at Sissinghurst contain many intimate and romantic areas

Three miles (5km) from the town is Sissinghurst Castle. The popular and colourful gardens were created in the 1930s by Vita Sackville-West and her husband, Sir Harold Nicolson. Derelict buildings and wild vegetation were transformed into this beautiful series of gardens with orchards, herbs and the famous 'white garden' where only white or grey flowers grow. Visitors can look at the quaint tower room where Vita wrote her novels.

i *Vestry Hall, Stone Street, Cranbrook*

▶ *Continue on the A262, then the A28 to Tenterden.*

A stretch of the line along the Kent and East Sussex Railway at Tenterden

9 Tenterden, Kent

Described as the 'Jewel of the Weald', the centre of this Wealden market town is dominated by the marble tower of St Mildred's Church. It is worth the climb up the tower because of the fine views across the Weald and, on a clear day, as far as France. The high street has shops and houses, many with original Georgian fronts. William Caxton, the father of English printing, is believed to have been born in Tenterden, and at the western edge of the town is the William Caxton Inn. Pub signs are often quite revealing about the past, and near the church is the Woolpack Inn, a reminder that much of the town's wealth came from sheep during the 15th and 16th centuries.

Woollen cloth was traded overseas, using Small Hythe as a port. It is difficult to visualise this countryside location, now far removed from the sea, as a thriving port and shipbuilding centre.

Dame Ellen Terry lived in Smallhythe Place, an early 16th-century timbered harbour master's house, from 1899 until she died in 1928, and the house is open to visitors during the

summer months. Spots Farm, at Small Hythe, has 20 acres (8 hectares) of vineyards you can walk through, as well as an amazing herb garden containing over 500 varieties, possibly the largest collection in the UK.

> ⓘ *Town Hall, High Street*

> ▶ *Follow the **A28** for 8 miles (13km) to Northiam.*

10 Northiam, East Sussex

The gnarled old oak tree on the village green achieved fame when Elizabeth I dined beneath it in 1573, while on her way to Rye. She is said to have taken her shoes off during the occasion and left them to the villagers when she continued her journey.

Great Dixter, half a mile (1km) away, is a large manor house dating back to the 15th century with a half-timbered and plastered front. The house was enlarged and restored by Sir Edward Lutyens in 1910. Its gardens are specially noted for their clematis.

> ▶ *Return towards the main road, taking the narrow road, first on the right, and follow country lanes to Bodiam.*

11 Bodiam, East Sussex

Bodiam Castle is a magnificent moated fortress, built in the 1380s to stop French raiders coming up the Rother Valley. The castle survived the French, who did not attack, but could not survive Cromwell's armies, who destroyed it. The outside walls are still intact, but it is now an empty shell. Life in a medieval castle is shown on a video, and there are 'Activity Days', when school children can dress up in medieval costumes for living history lessons.

Five miles (8km) southwest of Bodiam is Robertsbridge. Its half-timbered and weather-boarded cottages, a feature of the area, line the High Street, and it is the home of Gray-Nicolls, makers of cricket bats since 1875.

A mile (1.6km) east, a no-through-road leads to the ruins

of a Cistercian abbey, which was founded in 1176.

▶ *Follow the unclassified road past the station to Etchingham, then the **A265** to Burwash.*

12 Burwash, East Sussex

Burwash is an outstandingly attractive village of 16th- and 17th-century houses. Inside St Bartholomew's Church is a cast-iron grave slab which is thought to be the oldest in the country.

Seventeenth-century Bateman's, half-a-mile (1km) away, was the home of Rudyard Kipling from 1902 until 1936, providing the inspiration for much of his work. His study has been kept as it was during his lifetime, and the enormous 10-foot (3m) long desk has a few untidy pieces left standing on it. Much of the neighbourhood is featured in his novel *Puck of Pook's Hill.*

Upstream there is a watermill which has been restored to

working order, and near by is the water-driven turbine Kipling had installed in 1902 to provide his house with electricity.

▶ *Take the **A265**, turning right on to the **A267** past Heathfield. Turn left on to unclassified roads shortly after Five Ashes and follow signs to Rotherfield.*

13 Rotherfield, East Sussex

On the edge of the Ashdown Forest, Rotherfield sits in the heart of beautiful countryside. It is a delightful place to stop off and walk about. There is a fine church dedicated to St Denys, which contains 13th-century wall-paintings including Doom, and St Michael weighing souls, and in the east window is some splendid stained glass by Edward Burne-Jones and William Morris.

▶ *Return via unclassified roads to the **A26**. Turn right and return to Tunbridge Wells.*

FOR HISTORY BUFFS

The 'Heart of Kent' was formerly a vast forest, and the abundance of oak in medieval times gave rise to the characteristic timber-framed and half-timbered houses of the area. The houses often included a central hall and projecting upper storeys.

SCENIC ROUTES

The roads leading into Mereworth, Lamberhurst, Scotney and Bodiam are particularly memorable. The combination of villages, old Wealden buildings, hills, valleys and woods create a picturesque landscape. Villages such as Ightham are very photogenic, as are the North Downs.

Bodiam Castle's moat could not protect it from Cromwell's army

From Cathedral to Cliffs

2/3 DAYS • 107 MILES • 174KM

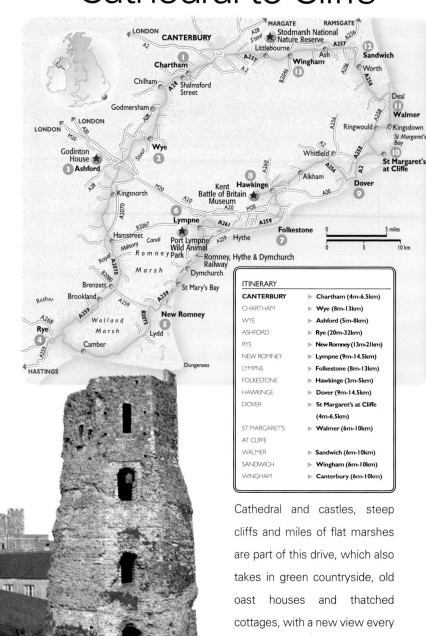

ITINERARY

CANTERBURY	▶ Chartham (4m-6.5km)
CHARTHAM	▶ Wye (8m-13km)
WYE	▶ Ashford (5m-8km)
ASHFORD	▶ Rye (20m-32km)
RYE	▶ New Romney (13m-21km)
NEW ROMNEY	▶ Lympne (9m-14.5km)
LYMPNE	▶ Folkestone (8m-13km)
FOLKESTONE	▶ Hawkinge (3m-5km)
HAWKINGE	▶ Dover (9m-14.5km)
DOVER	▶ St Margaret's at Cliffe (4m-6.5km)
ST MARGARET'S AT CLIFFE	▶ Walmer (6m-10km)
WALMER	▶ Sandwich (6m-10km)
SANDWICH	▶ Wingham (6m-10km)
WINGHAM	▶ Canterbury (6m-10km)

Cathedral and castles, steep cliffs and miles of flat marshes are part of this drive, which also takes in green countryside, old oast houses and thatched cottages, with a new view every few minutes.

i The Buttermarket, Canterbury

BACK TO NATURE

Stodmarsh National Nature Reserve lies a few miles to the east of Canterbury. Vast reed-beds and areas of open water attract huge numbers of wild-fowl. Reed warblers, Cetti's warblers and bearded tits can be found in the winter, some-times in the company of short-eared owls.

▶ *Take the **A28** to Chartham.*

1 Chartham, Kent

The valley of the Great Stour, with gravel pits and small lakes, is noted for fishing and bird life, and Chartham is a well-known angling centre. St Mary's Church dates from the 13th century and has one of the oldest sets of bells in the country. There is a beautiful garden centre near Chartham.

Further along is Chilham, where the village square is set at the gateway to Chilham Castle, built for Henry II in 1174. The castle is not open to the public, although on rare occasions events are held in the grounds. The village has quaint pubs and antiques shops. The church has a stone-and-flint tower, and the largely unspoilt houses around the square are in Tudor and Jacobean style.

▶ *From Chilham return to the **A28**, travel south for 2 miles (3km) then turn off on to unclassified roads to Wye.*

2 Wye, Kent

This village is the location of the famous Agriculture School of London University, housed in a college first set up in the mid-15th century by John Kempe, a native of the town, who became Archbishop of Canterbury. The town is also the location of 18th-century Olantigh Hall, with gardens occasionally open to the public.

Picturesque timbered Chilham
Left: Dover Castle and Pharos

▶ *Return to the **A28** for 5 miles (8km) to Ashford.*

3 Ashford, Kent

This old market centre for Romney Marsh and the Weald of Kent is now a thriving shopping and touring centre. Medieval, Tudor and Georgian houses still survive and the 14th- and 15th-century parish church retains much of its old character.

Godinton House, northwest of town, was built in the 17th century. The rooms are full of Chippendale and Sheraton furniture, and there is fine topiary work in the garden.

i 18 The Churchyard

▶ *Follow an unclassified road to the **A2070**, then the **A259** across Romney Marsh to Rye.*

4 Rye, East Sussex

Rye is one of the Cinque Ports, a group of maritime towns

which were originally responsible for providing ships and men to guard against invasion. At one time Rye was almost encircled by the sea, but the harbour silted up in the 16th century and eventually the water receded. In the winter, when mists roll in across the countryside, Romney Marsh can be sinister and mysterious – a fitting background to the haunting tales of the infamous parson and smuggler Dr Syn.

i Heritage Centre, Rye

▶ Head back on the **A259** to East Guldeford, then take an unclassified road through Camber to Lydd to join the **B2075** to New Romney.

5 New Romney, Kent
Another ancient Cinque Port, now inland from the sea, New Romney was destroyed in 1287 by a violent storm which changed the course of the River Rother. The Romney, Hythe and Dymchurch narrow gauge railway opened in 1927, with locomotives and carriages which are one-third full size. Toys and models can be seen at New Romney station.

Getting up steam on the Romney, Hythe and Dymchurch Railway

▶ Take the **A259** again, then unclassified roads for 9 miles (14.5km) to Lympne, then via the **B2067** to the **A261** which leads eastwards to Hythe.

6 Lympne, Kent
The 11th-century castle at Lympne (pronounced *Lim*) stands on top of a cliff which was once a coastline. Below the castle (not open to the public) extensive remains of a Roman fort can be seen.

Just outside town is Port Lympne Wild Animal Park, set in 300 acres (121 hectares) of gardens surrounding a mansion. East of Lympne is Hythe,

another Cinque Port which is now a popular seaside resort and the terminus for the Romney, Hythe and Dymchurch Railway. The town has several historic buildings and summer boating along the old Royal Military Canal.

i Lydd, New Romney

▶ Follow the **A259** from Hythe to Folkestone.

7 Folkestone, Kent
The harbour of this resort handles cross-Channel ferries, and still has a fishing fleet and a fish market. The Museum and Art Gallery in Grace Hill has displays on the town's maritime history. Spade House was the former home of the author H G Wells. The Leas, a wide grassy promenade along the cliff top, has fine views and provides an excellent walk through wooded slopes down to the beach. Here the Metropole Galleries (see panel below), established in the 1960s, offer a year-round programme of high-quality exhibitions.

i 103 Sandgate Road

▶ Head inland along the **A260** as far as Hawkinge.

8 Hawkinge, Kent
Set in the heart of the Downland west of Hawkinge is the Kent Battle of Britain Museum, which conjures up visions of World War II. It houses the largest collection of fragments of British and German aircraft involved in the fighting.

▶ Take unclassified roads eastwards from Hawkinge, eventually running south on to the
A256 for Dover.

9 Dover, Kent

Dover, famous for its White
Cliffs, was the chief Cinque
Port. It was known to the
Romans as *Dubris*, and the
Painted House, discovered in
1970, dates from about AD 200.
Among the paintings are several
references to the theme of
Bacchus, the god of wine. More
recent is the Old Town Gaol,
which has been restored and
now houses the visitor information centre. On Snargate Street
you can see the Grand Shaft, a
140-foot (43m) staircase cut into
the white cliffs, built in

Napoleonic times as a short cut
to the town for troops stationed
on the Western Heights. The
views across to France can be
best seen from Dover Castle,
which overlooks the town. The
Pharos, a Roman lighthouse,
stands within its walls near the
fine Saxon Church of St Mary de
Castro.

i Old Town Gaol, Biggin Street

▶ Take the **A258**, then an
unclassified road to St
Margaret's at Cliffe.

10 St Margaret's at Cliffe, Kent

The flint-faced church in the
upper part of this village is
typical of chalkland buildings.

St Margaret's Bay is a popular start
for cross-Channel swimmers

Massive chalk cliffs dominate
the scene, and sheltered beneath
them is the Pines Garden,
created in the 1970s with trees,
shrubs, a lake and waterfall, and
a statue of Sir Winston
Churchill.

Three miles (5km) further is
Ringwould, which has another
fine church, with an attractive
17th-century tower. Bronze-Age
barrows can be seen at nearby
Free Down, and at Kingsdown
there is a lot of flint, both on the
buildings and on the shore.

▶ Rejoin the **A258**, then take an
unclassified road from
Ringwould to Walmer.

Sandwich is one of the oldest
Cinque ports
Opposite: Winchester's Round Table

11 Walmer, Kent

Henry VIII built the castle here,
along with over 20 other forts to
defend the coast of southeast
England. This fine coastal
fortress, shaped like a Tudor
rose, has been transformed into
an elegant stately home with
beautiful gardens, and is the official residence of the Lord
Warden of the Cinque Ports.
Lord Wellington was Warden
from 1829 to 1852, and his
famous boots are on display.

Further on, Deal Castle, also
built by Henry VIII, is in the
shape of a six-petalled flower,
and tells the full story of the
Tudor castles in the exhibition
room. The Time Ball Tower,
which used to give time signals
to shipping is a unique four-
storey museum of time and
maritime communication on the
sea front. The museum in
St George's Road has a collection
of old photographs, model sailing ships and maps.

i *Landmark Centre, Deal*

RECOMMENDED WALKS

The North Downs Way can
provide a long walk; there are
clearly marked trails from
Dover to Deal along the coast,
or along an inland route. The
route from Deal to Sandwich
on the coast or inland will provide fabulous views.

▶ *Take the* **A258** *to Sandwich.*

12 Sandwich, Kent

The oldest of the Cinque Ports,
Sandwich is separated from the
sea by 2 miles (3km) of sand
dunes. Its white windmill dates
from about 1760, and now
houses the White Mill Rural
Heritage Centre with domestic
and farming exhibits. Sandwich
golf course, between the town
and Sandwich Bay, is a world-
class championship course.

i *The Guildhall, Market Square*

▶ *Follow the* **A257** *taking a
detour through the village of
Ash to Wingham.*

13 Wingham, Kent

This picturesque village
contains a magnificent church
with a green spire, caused by
oxidisation. The Wildlife Park
has cockatoos, macaws, owls and
waterfowl, all with plenty of
flying space, as well as rare farm
animals and pets. Valuable
research work takes place here
to help endangered species, and
to overcome man's destruction
of natural habitats. A little
further out of town is the village
of Littlebourne. Fruit and hops
are grown around here, and
there is an ancient thatched barn
near the flint-faced church.

▶ *Continue along the* **A257** *to
Canterbury (6 miles/10km).*

SCENIC ROUTES

Romney Marsh and the Downs
are a delight, and the inland
countryside, with fields,
orchards and crops, is very
attractive. Along the coast
there are dramatic cliffs and
sea views between Folkestone,
Dover and Sandwich.

SPECIAL TO...

The original Cinque Ports
were Hastings, Romney, Hythe,
Dover and Sandwich, with Rye
and Winchelsea. They were
given charters by Edward I in
1278 and were really trading
and fishing ports which
worked together to defend
the coast and fight sea battles.
In return they were granted
royal charters and privileges.

The Downs &
Valleys of Hampshire

The Hampshire Downs provide a gentle interlude between harsh sandy heaths near London and the valleys of the Southwest. From Winchester this tour takes you through lush valleys to panoramic views of where battle fleets throughout history set sail.

1/2 DAYS • 99 MILES • 159KM

ITINERARY		
WINCHESTER	▶	**Stockbridge (9m-14.5km)**
STOCKBRIDGE	▶	**Middle Wallop (6m-10km)**
MIDDLE WALLOP	▶	**Mottisfont (12m-19km)**
MOTTISFONT	▶	**Romsey (4m-6.5km)**
ROMSEY	▶	**Marwell (11m-18km)**
MARWELL	▶	**Bishop's Waltham (4m-6km)**
BISHOP'S WALTHAM	▶	**Portsdown Hill (10m-16km)**
PORTSDOWN HILL	▶	**Hambledon (10m-16km)**
HAMBLEDON	▶	**Queen Elizabeth Country Park (7m-11km)**
QUEEN ELIZABETH COUNTRY PARK	▶	**New Alresford (18m-29km)**
NEW ALRESFORD	▶	**Winchester (8m-13km)**

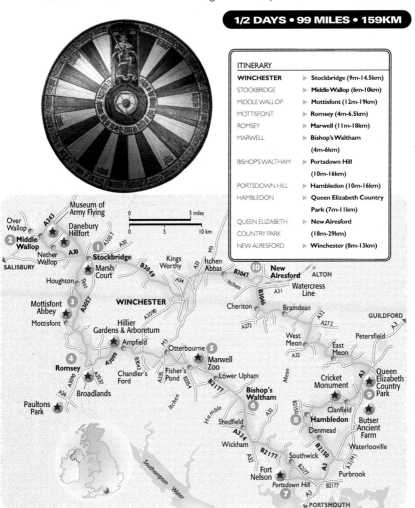

Statue of King Alfred, who made Winchester his capital

Eyes' Cunningham led his nightfighters into battle, the airfield is now the home of the Army Air Corps, and pilots train here in attack, reconnaissance and transport. Inside the modern Museum of Army Flying are many aircraft and ancient balloons, the world's first helicopter, a Tiger Moth and airworthy Sopwiths from World War I, as well as cockpits to clamber into, videos and displays.

▶ *From Middle Wallop take the road through Nether Wallop to join the* **A30** *heading back towards Stockbridge. Just before Stockbridge turn right and follow the unclassified road through Houghton to Mottisfont, a total distance of 12 miles (19km).*

3 Mottisfont Abbey, Hampshire

You will find no abbey here, but there is an elegant National Trust property in tree-lined grounds by the River Test; the original priory was converted after the Dissolution. Of special note is Rex Whistler's blue drawing room, with its visual tricks. Gardeners will appreciate the fine old roses here, and it is worth seeking out the 'font', a tamed spring of clear water. If this gives you a thirst, have lunch or tea at the village post office, where you can sit outside under the spreading walnut tree.

This is the heartland of the trout fishing for which the Test is world-famous, and the area is

i The Guildhall, The Broadway, Winchester

▶ *Leave Winchester on the* **B3049** *heading west for 9 miles (14.5km) to Stockbridge.*

1 Stockbridge, Hampshire

A curious 'one-horse' town unique in Hampshire, Stockbridge has a straight main street backed by water-meadows. Before the railways, Welsh cattlemen stopped here with their herds on the way to the great fairs at Farnham and Maidstone. On the north side of High Street, beyond the distinctive porch of the Grosvenor Hotel, is a charming Edwardian garage, a relic of the days of running boards and red flags. Stockbridge has several good antiques shops, and exceptional crafts and fishing shops.

Outside the town to the east, Stockbridge Down, above your road of entry, is a downland nature reserve and is home to many rare flowers and butterflies. Marsh Court, on the back road to King's Somborne, was designed by Lutyens and is partly built of chalk blocks.

RECOMMENDED WALKS

Houghton, on the route south of Stockbridge, is a pretty village on the Test, where the river is at its clearest and most beguiling. Two of Hampshire's major footpaths intersect here. The Clarendon Way, which runs between Salisbury and Winchester, meets rolling downland and lovely woods to east and west; and the Test Way, stretching 50 miles (80km) from the downs to Southampton Water, follows the old 'sprat-and-winkle' railway line along the valley between bursting hedgerows and rippling water.

▶ *Leave Stockbridge by the* **A30**, *then turn right signed Danebury Hillfort and in 2½ miles (4km) turn left on to the* **A343** *for Middle Wallop.*

2 Middle Wallop, Hampshire

The Wallops, Over, Middle and Nether, take their name from the brook which links these three pretty villages. Built as a wartime RAF base, where 'Cat's

The 12th-century church is all that remains of Romsey Abbey

jealously guarded, with barbed-wire fences protecting anglers' huts and benches by private manicured paths.

▶ *Return to the **A3057** and drive for 3 miles (5km) to Romsey.*

4 Romsey, Hampshire
Years ago, travellers here were greeted at every turn by notices reading 'You're in the Strong Country'. Strong's brewery is no more: the waft of hops last drifted here in 1981, and the malthouse you see ahead has other uses, but lots of good things survive in this lively little place.

Its greatest treasure is the 12th-century abbey, a fine unspoiled Norman church, which only escaped the ravages of the Dissolution when the townspeople bought it for £100. Buried within is Earl Mountbatten of Burma, who lived at Broadlands. This imposing 18th-century mansion gives on to Capability Brown lawns sweeping down to the Test. Another former owner, Lord Palmerston, still keeps an eye on Romsey from his perch in Market Square. Traffic is poorly managed here, so it is worth parking at Broadlands and walking into town. Children should enjoy the Rapids leisure pool, with its giant flume and swirling water; and if you visit in November, go to Saddler's Mill, where Test Valley salmon perform gymnastic feats to reach their spawning grounds upstream.

i 13 Church Street

The Museum of Army Flying, Middle Wallop

*Leave Romsey on the **A3090** heading east. Shortly after Ampfield, turn right at the Potters Heron signed Chandlers Ford. Cross the **B3043** and drive along Hocombe Road. At a T-junction turn left over the flyover towards Otterbourne. On entering the village turn right on to an unclassified road, cross the River Itchen and the **A335** (dogleg right and left) and proceed along Church Lane, turning at its end on to the **B3354**. Turn left on to the **B2177**, then left for Marwell.*

FOR CHILDREN

Paultons Park, off the M27 at Ower near Romsey, is a family leisure park offering a wealth of entertainment and activity for children. Set in 140 acres (56 hectares) of beautiful parkland, Paultons grows every year as features are added; it is now the second-largest attraction in the South. A giant adventure playground, an astra glide, bumper boats, pirate ship, flying saucer, train rides and a pets' corner are just a few of the experiences to be had, along with a trip to Wind in the Willows.

5 Marwell Zoo, Hampshire

Set in the 100-acre (40-hectare) park of a Tudor hall, this is one of the biggest zoos in Britain. The approach here is modern, and the animals enjoy considerable freedom. Marwell's biggest claim to fame is the work done here for animal conservation – rescuing threatened species, breeding from them and returning them to the wild. You might bump into a scimitar-horned oryx or perhaps a Przewalski's horse, both snatched from imminent extinction. Children will particularly enjoy patting pot-bellied pigs in their own farmyard! Also recommended are Marwell's Wonderful Railway and the licensed Treetops restaurant.

i Marwell Zoo Park, Colden Common

*Return to the **B2177** and continue to Bishop's Waltham.*

6 Bishop's Waltham, Hampshire

As you approach, tall flint ruins on the right give a clue as to how the town got its name. For 400 years, Bishops of Winchester lived here in a splendid palace, built in 1135, and all but destroyed by Cromwell's troops. Little remains except the walls of the great hall, but the site is open to the public. In the town centre, shops and houses span eight centuries of architecture, many hiding salvaged palace beams. Look out for the Bishop's Mitre in the Square, last remnant of the Market Hall. The town's history is charted in the small museum in Brook Street.

Four miles (6km) to the south of Bishop's Waltham, on the A334, is the elegant Georgian town of Wickham, birthplace of William of Wykeham, founder of Winchester College and Chancellor of England. As you leave on Bridge Street, watch for the Chesapeake Mill, built in 1820 from the timbers of a captured American Man o' War, the *Chesapeake*.

Peaceful Southwick, further on, is where Eisenhower made his 1944 headquarters at Southwick House. In the village he and Montgomery met world leaders and planned the world's greatest seaborne invasion.

▶ *From Southwick take the Porchester road to Portsdown Hill.*

❼ Portsdown Hill,
Hampshire
The view from Portsdown's chalk heights is one of the finest in Britain. Ahead is Portsmouth and its spreading harbour, home of the Royal Navy, and beyond is the Isle of Wight. In between lies Spithead, where naval fleet reviews take place and, further west, the Solent, now a yachtsman's paradise. Portchester's 3rd-century Roman castle, Nelson's flagship, Victoria's beloved Osborne House and the homes of Charles Dickens and Lord Tennyson are all within sight of Portsdown.

For a fascinating look at history, trek down the tunnels in one of 'Palmerston's follies'.

These were giant forts built by the Prime Minister in the 1850s to guard the Solent against the French. Fort Nelson is open to the public.

▶ *From Portsdown Hill take the A3 heading northwards, and at Waterlooville turn on to the B2150 through Denmead to Hambledon.*

❽ Hambledon, Hampshire
The cause of Hambledon's worldwide fame lies 2 miles (3km) from its pretty Georgian centre on the Clanfield road. In front of the Bat and Ball pub, a granite monument stands near a thatched hut and beautifully mown sward of grass.

For sporting people the world over, this is a shrine, for it was here on Broadhalfpenny Down that Hambledon got its title 'the cradle of cricket'. It was in Sussex that shepherds first played the game, but here rules were established and skills honed. Richard Nyren, the landlord of the Bat and Ball in 1760, was the manager of the village team which, back in 1777, played All England and won – and his victuals were equally good. Players, we are told, 'struck dismay into a round

of beef' and his punch was 'such that would have made a cat speak'!

▶ *Leave Hambledon on an unclassified road, passing through Clanfield, then follow Petersfield signs to join the A3. In a mile (1.6km) turn off for Queen Elizabeth Country Park.*

The Bat and Ball at Hambledon is full of cricketing memorabilia

❾ Queen Elizabeth Country Park, Hampshire
Set in a deep valley, with steep downland on either side, this is the ideal place to leave the car and stretch your legs. On one side, dense woodland stretches upward; on the other, smooth grassland, speckled with sheep, climbs impressively to the viewpoint on Butser Hill.

Butser Ancient Farm is a reconstruction of real Iron-Age farm remains. Here, visitors can walk freely round the huts and pens, finding out for themselves in a unique and graphic way what life was like in the prehistoric age. The Park Centre, with café and shop, organises a host of activities – pony trekking, grass skiing and guided walks are

The Iron-Age reconstructed at Butser Ancient Farm
Right: Swan Green, Lyndhurst

daily occurrences, and there are annual 'specials', among them sheep events and in July, the Hampshire Country Park Show.

i *Queen Elizabeth Country Park, Gravel Hill, Horndean*

▶ *Rejoin the **A3** towards Petersfield, turning left via unclassified roads to East Meon and West Meon. Turn right on to the **A32**, then left at traffic lights on to the **A272** signposted Bramdean. In 4 miles (6km) go right (**B3046**) through Cheriton to New Alresford.*

10 **New Alresford,** Hampshire Alresford (pronounced Orlsford) is a town rich in history. Built in the 13th century by the Bishops of Winchester as a wool centre, it annually played host to 200,000 sheep, from medieval times to as recently as 1972. The best way to sample its charm is to descend picturesque Broad Street, turning left into Ladywell Lane to the ancient mill on the River Alre, where woollen cloth was fulled – that is, cleaned and

thickened – returning to the town centre via The Dean.

Alresford's main attraction is its elegance, and everywhere there are small clues to the town's chequered history. For instance, the steep pitch of the tiled roofs hint at previous thatching. The town was ravaged by a series of fires between the early 15th century and 1689, which spread quickly along the thatch, but the prac-

tice continued despite an edict from Winchester banning it.

▶ *Leave Alresford on the **B3046** then turn left on to the **B3047**. In 6 miles (10km) cross the **A33** at Kings Worthy and return to Winchester.*

1/2 DAYS • 105 MILES • 169KM

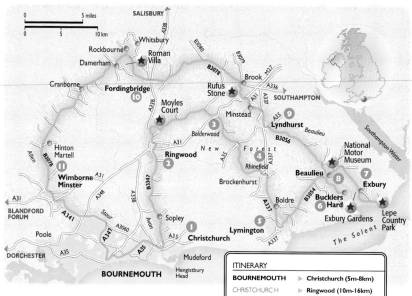

Ancient Hunting Ground of Kings

A combination of seashore, downland and forest should satisfy the appetite of those who like their terrain varied but not too rugged. On the way are picturesque towns and villages reflecting 1,500 years of history, peaceful trout streams flowing south to the sea and, at the heart of the tour, the New Forest, an ancient hunting ground of kings.

Native ponies in the New Forest

i *Westover Road, Bournemouth*

▶ *Leave Bournemouth on the A35 and head east for 5 miles (8km) to Christchurch.*

❶ Christchurch, Dorset
Formerly Twineham, this town was one of Alfred the Great's walled strongholds against the Danes, between the Rivers Avon and Stour. The walls have long gone, and dominating the busy centre now is the fine 12th-century priory church, the reason for the town's change of name. Legend has it that a beam, cut too short, was lengthened and positioned overnight by a mystery workman, thought to have been Christ. Within easy reach are the museum, art gallery and ancient Place Mill on the Quay.

i *49 High Street*

FOR CHILDREN

Try a spot of crab fishing at Mudeford, near Christchurch. You will need some simple equipment – a line or string – and a hook is optional: you can tie the bait on instead. The shops on the quayside should have all the necessities. Station yourself by the rails near the shops and have a go.

RECOMMENDED WALKS

One different option from the many forest walks on the tour is to sample the seaside breezes at Mudeford. Take the little ferry across the mouth of the harbour, and walk along the beach to Hengistbury, which rises steadily to over 120 feet (36m) – a gentle round trip of 2 to 3 miles (3 to 5km).

▶ *Take the B3347 to Ringwood.*

❷ Ringwood, Hampshire
Upstream on the Avon lies this unassuming bustling market town. The trout fishing is good

through open heaths and lovely woods to high parts of the Forest, past the spot where naturalist Eric Ashby makes his fascinating films of the badgers, foxes and other creatures that thrive here. If you want to walk you are spoiled for choice: forest tracks with shafting sunlight to your right, high sandy ridges with panoramic views and open heathland to your left.

i The Furlong

▶ *Leave Ringwood by the A338 signed Salisbury, then turn right in 2 miles (3km) on to an unclassified road and continue east for about 5 miles (8km) before going under the A31 for Bolderwood.*

❸ Bolderwood, Hampshire
Here, in the heart of the New Forest, the Forestry Commission has created three waymarked walks of different lengths among the trees, which range from native oak and beech to foreign wellingtonia. A leaflet helps you identify them as you walk. There are many deer in the New Forest, but normally only the silent, the patient or the fortunate see them – except at the Bolderwood Deer Sanctuary, where a sighting is guaranteed; bring your binoculars. Near by is a memorial along the pines dedicated to Canadian fliers serving at Stony Cross who were killed in the war.

The ponies which wander in parts of the Forest are not wild, but belong to Commoners, people living in the Forest with rights to graze animals (and to an annual ration of free cordwood for their fires). Look out for the brand mark of the owner; every autumn the ponies are rounded up and rebranded, and surplus ponies are sold at the Beaulieu Road sales. Feeding the ponies is illegal.

You might like to stop at the Knightswood Oak, reputedly the oldest in the Forest (600 years old) and 21 feet (7m) round. In the snake pit at Holidays Hill (on the A35, just east of your

crossing point), the less squeamish can get a close-up look at the native vipers and adders.

▶ *From Bolderwood follow an unclassified road southeast across the A35 to Rhinefield.*

❹ Rhinefield, Hampshire
Towering above you are some of the tallest conifers in Britain – Douglas firs, redwoods and spruces – planted in 1859 as an approach to Rhinefield hunting lodge, now demolished. Behind the drive, on either side, are attractive mixed woodlands of oaks, beeches and pines, through which runs the 1½-mile (2km) Tall Trees nature trail.

Rhinefield House, nearby, is a hotel housed in a bizarre Victorian creation that is half-castle, half-house. You can have a meal or afternoon tea here.

Brockenhurst is a lively and prosperous village, popular as a centre for New Forest camping and touring. Within the shadow of the Norman/Early English church lie the bones of Brusher Mills, New Forest character and killer of snakes.

▶ *From Brockenhurst turn right on to the A337 for Lymington.*

❺ Lymington, Hampshire
Signs of Lymington's early prosperity as a salt town, spa and seaport can still be seen in the charming houses which line the quay and the wide High Street climbing the hill. The town enjoys a different sort of maritime wealth these days as a popular yachting centre. The Isle of Wight car ferry snakes down the Lymington River through serried masts of luxury yachts. Two buildings of particular note here are Pressgang Cottage, by the quay; and Georgian St Thomas's Church at the top of High street, unusual for its cupola.

i New Street

▶ *Leave Lymington by the B3054 signed Beaulieu and in 6 miles (10km), just before*

here, and the town has many attractive Georgian and Queen Anne houses, with a splendid Early English parish church near the bypass. Near by, on the A31, is the Avon Forest Park, with many acres of contrasting meadow, heath and moorland. From Ringwood you can take in the New Forest, which spreads east and north. A narrow road between old gravel pits, converted into reservoirs, brings your first taste of the Forest at Moyles Court. The manor house, now a school, was the home of Alice Lisle, who sheltered the rebellious Duke of Monmouth's men, and was sentenced to death by Judge Jeffreys. The route winds

Beaulieu, turn right for Bucklers Hard.

Exbury Gardens are famous for their rhododendrons and azaleas

6 Bucklers Hard,
Hampshire
When you leave your car on the edge of Bucklers Hard, prepare to step back in time. Little has changed here since 1800, when this was one of Britain's ship-building centres. Three of the ships which fought under Nelson at Trafalgar were built here. Twin rows of shipbuilders' cottages, carefully preserved, slope down to the water, where the slipways were. Some are open for the public to view, and a Maritime Museum tells the story of this unique place.

▶ *From Bucklers Hard turn right for Exbury.*

7 Exbury, Hampshire
The name of de Rothschild is synonymous with wealth, and at Exbury House, home of the banking family, no expense was spared to create the magnificent 200-acre (81-hectare) woodland garden, which is open to the public. Crowning glories here are the displays of rhododendrons and azaleas, best seen in late spring.

Beside the waters of the Solent, Lepe Country Park offers a chance to picnic or walk along the shore, with lovely views across to the Isle of Wight. To the east is the Spithead shore near Portsmouth; ahead, Cowes and Osborne, Queen Victoria's final home; and to the west, Yarmouth, Hurst Castle and the open sea. Half a mile (1km) of crumbling concrete marks the point where D-Day's Mulberry Harbour was made. Evenings can be particularly lovely here, and big ships describe wide arcs as they follow the deep water out to sea.

▶ *Return to Beaulieu.*

8 Beaulieu, Hampshire
Charming Beaulieu, with its pond and river, is the setting for a world-famous museum. The National Motor Museum stands in the grounds of 13th-century Beaulieu Abbey, home of the Montagus, which retains much beauty despite the destruction wrought after the Dissolution. A monorail winds through the 3rd Baron Montagu's modern show-case for over 250 vintage cars

Beaulieu – home of Lord Montagu and his National Motor Museum

and motorcycles. The collection includes record breakers *Bluebird* and *Thrust 2*, and there are many other attractions in the grounds.

i John Montagu Building

▶ *Take the B3056 to Lyndhurst.*

9 Lyndhurst, Hampshire
Open roads through rolling gorse heathlands bring you to Lyndhurst, the 'capital' of the New Forest, a busy tourist town in the summer. Alice Hargreaves (née Liddell), the original Alice of Lewis Carroll's *Alice in Wonderland*, is buried in Lyndhurst churchyard. At Queen's House the Verderers, guardians since Norman times of Commoners' rights, hold their

bi-monthly ancient court on Mondays. They employ agisters to patrol the forest daily, often on horseback, to supervise and control animals grazing on the 90,000 acres (36,423 hectares). Forest ponies have their tails cut specially to indicate their own agister. The New Forest Museum offers an insight into the fascinating history and tradi-tions of the popular area.

i New Forest Museum and Visitor Centre

▶ *Leave Lyndhurst on the A337 signposted Cadnam. In 2 miles (3km) turn left through Minstead, then left, immedi-ately left and immediately right to cross the A31 to Brook, then keep left on the B3078 for Fordingbridge.*

10 Fordingbridge, Hampshire
The town of Fordingbridge, on the River Avon, had a quiet time in the 1970s and '80s, but is now coming to life again, with new shops opening and industries arriving. Stand on the old bridge and look for trout or pike. On this spot, during the time of William the Conqueror, a guard was posted to arrest New Forest deer poachers on their only escape route to the west. The fine medieval parish church stands on the Alderholt road.

▶ *Leave Fordingbridge heading northwest and follow unclassi-fied roads to Rockbourne. Turn southwest through Damerham and Cranborne, and on to Wimborne Minster.*

11 Wimborne Minster, Dorset
On the way to Wimborne Minster, you pass through Rockbourne, with its pretty Tudor and Georgian cottages by a stream. To the south of the village is the excavated site of a Roman villa, open to the public. Wimborne Minster itself, though medieval in its street pattern, is no sorry relic of a bygone age. It has a Town Trail which explores its rich heritage of fine medieval and Georgian buildings – details obtainable from the Information Bureau. Central to it all is the Minster, of Saxon origin and curiously chequered in grey and brown stone. After all the history, you might want to browse through the hundreds of stalls at Wimborne's huge week-end market, or visit the model town on King Street.

i 29 High Street

▶ *Leave by the B3078 crossing the A31 and immediately bear left via Canford Magna to join the A341 and the A347 to Bournemouth.*

FOR HISTORY BUFFS

King William II (Rufus or red-haired), son of the Conqueror, fully deserved the fate which met him while out hunting in the New Forest in August 1100. An arrow, supposedly fired by a companion, missed the stag and mortally wounded him. But questions remain. Was it an accident? Was it Sir Walter Tirel who fired the arrow, and then fled to France? Or was it the mysterious Purkes, who took the body to Winchester? You can visit the site of the King's death, marked by the Rufus Stone in a glade just off the A31 near Minstead.

WALES & THE MARCHES

Wales is a small country of great beauty. Few parts of the world can contain as much varied scenery in such a restricted area. North Wales has the nation's highest peaks, in the Snowdon area, but there are dramatic mountain ranges in central and southern Wales, too. The Brecon Beacons, which are a dividing line between the south and the rural midlands, form one of the Welsh National Parks, the others being Snowdonia and the old county of Pembrokeshire. Here, in the narrow strip of land around the coastline, is the Pembroke Coast National Park, which winds its way round inlets and coves, cliffs and beaches, and is marked by a long-distance footpath. Even in the industrial parts of Wales, especially in the south where the coal valleys are world famous, there is fine hill scenery just a few miles from the old mining towns. Wales is also a land of railways and castles. There are a few main-line railways along the north and south coasts and a scenic cross-country route to Aberystwyth, but there are several small, privately or voluntarily operated lines, such as at Ffestiniog, Bala or Llanberis.

Caernarfon Castle, begun during Edward I's conquest of Wales

Wales has a long history of rebellion and conflict, and centuries of struggle against English rule have left a legacy of imposing fortresses. Caernarfon is probably the outstanding example, built to mark Edward I's conquest of the north. Penrhyn, near Bangor, is really a stately home, providing an ornate illustration of the wealth generated by the North Wales slate industries – for a few, at least.

The Welsh coastline has several popular resorts with sandy beaches, but for quieter attractions venture inland, where the wild landscape is sparsely populated. Wales is a walkers' paradise, and wherever you are you will find walks of all distances to suit all tastes. You should leave the car whenever possible, to enable you to appreciate the landscape to the full.

Chepstow

This is a border town which has grown up at a crossing point of the River Wye and is now located conveniently close to the M4. There was an Iron Age as well as a Roman settlement near here, but the town was really created by the Normans. They began to build the castle in 1067, and it still dominates the town from its site over the River Wye. The museum opposite the castle describes the history of the town throughout the ages, and St Mary's parish church is worth a visit.

Tenby

Described as 'the Jewel in the Crown of the Welsh Riviera', Tenby's narrow streets and tiny shops are huddled within medieval town walls. This is one of Britain's finest historic towns, containing over 300 buildings of special architectural or historic interest. The picturesque harbour has long been a hub of activity, and there are regular sailings to Caldy Island. Fine sandy beaches and excellent walking provide an abundance of holiday entertainment for young and old.

Aberystwyth

Aberystwyth, the largest town and principal shopping centre of mid Wales, is set in the middle of glorious Cardigan Bay, into which flow the rivers Ystwyth and Rheidol. The ruined castle, built by Edward I, overlooks the small harbour in the Rheidol Estuary, and on a hill above the town is the modern campus of the University College of Wales, which includes the National Library of Wales, housing early Welsh manuscripts. The narrow-gauge Vale of Rheidol Railway line runs to the deep gorge of Devil's Bridge, and at the northern end of the beach and promenade the longest electric cliff railway in Britain climbs to the top of Constitution Hill.

Barmouth

Situated where the mountains meet the sea, this is one of the most picturesque resorts on Cardigan Bay. It has a fine golden beach and a small harbour busy with pleasure craft and fishing boats. Visit the Royal National Lifeboat Institution Museum and two other buildings which re-create the history of this area: Tŷ Crwn, the old lock-up for drunken seamen, and Tŷ Gwyn y Bermo, a restored 15th-century building. After exploring the town you could walk alongside the estuary to take in the lovely coastal scenery all around.

Bangor

This ancient town, surrounded by water and high mountains in an area of great natural

Beddgelert is a beautiful wooded village set deep in the heart of the Snowdonia National Park

beauty, is a long-established religious centre: the present cathedral was built on the site of a monastery founded in AD 525 – earlier than the cathedral in Canterbury. The northern college of the University of Wales is based here, on a high ridge overlooking the city. Bangor sits on the Menai Strait, and you can see the island of Anglesey from its restored pier, or cross the Strait on Telford's Menai Bridge or the later Britannia Bridge. The Gwynedd Museum and Art Gallery traces life in Wales from prehistoric times; and on the outskirts of town is the magnificent Penrhyn Castle.

2/3 DAYS • 172 MILES • 277.5KM

Castles on the
Welsh Marches

This route passes through the Wye and Usk Valleys. The castles built along the Welsh borders are testaments to a turbulent age, when this was an area of constant fighting between the Normans and the Welsh.

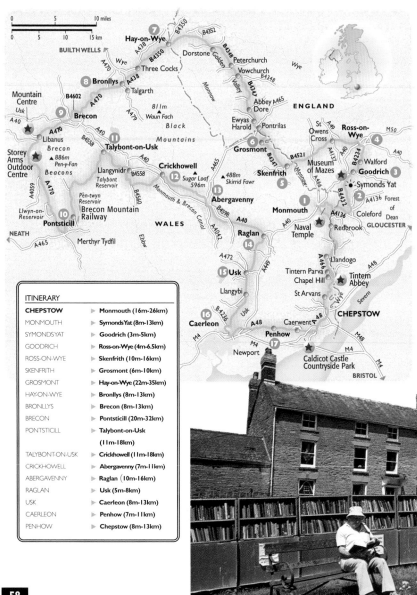

ITINERARY	
CHEPSTOW	▶ **Monmouth (16m-26km)**
MONMOUTH	▶ **Symonds Yat (8m-13km)**
SYMONDS YAT	▶ **Goodrich (3m-5km)**
GOODRICH	▶ **Ross-on-Wye (4m-6.5km)**
ROSS-ON-WYE	▶ **Skenfrith (10m-16km)**
SKENFRITH	▶ **Grosmont (6m-10km)**
GROSMONT	▶ **Hay-on-Wye (22m-35km)**
HAY-ON-WYE	▶ **Bronllys (8m-13km)**
BRONLLYS	▶ **Brecon (8m-13km)**
BRECON	▶ **Pontsticill (20m-32km)**
PONTSTICILL	▶ **Talybont-on-Usk**
	(11m-18km)
TALYBONT-ON-USK	▶ **Crickhowell (11m-18km)**
CRICKHOWELL	▶ **Abergavenny (7m-11km)**
ABERGAVENNY	▶ **Raglan (10m-16km)**
RAGLAN	▶ **Usk (5m-8km)**
USK	▶ **Caerleon (8m-13km)**
CAERLEON	▶ **Penhow (7m-11km)**
PENHOW	▶ **Chepstow (8m-13km)**

ⓘ *The Castle Car Park, Chepstow*

▶ *Drive north on the A466 to Monmouth.*

❶ Monmouth,
Monmouthshire

Monmouth was an old Roman settlement, but its main growth came after 1066, and in 1673 the 1st Duke of Beaufort built Great Castle House on the site of the old Norman castle. Near Agincourt Square, dominated by the 18th-century Shire Hall, is a statue of C S Rolls, of Rolls Royce fame, whose family lived near here. East of town is Kymin Hill, where the Naval Temple commemorates British admirals. The walk up to it from the town follows the line of Offa's Dyke Long Distance Footpath.

ⓘ *Shire Hall, Agincourt Square*

FOR HISTORY BUFFS

Tintern Abbey, just off the road to Monmouth in the Wye Valley, was a Cistercian foundation in 1131 which survived until the Dissolution of the Monasteries by Henry VIII. The abbey church has survived almost intact, and the ruins of many monastic buildings can still be seen.

▶ *Take the A4136, then turn left on to the B4228 just past Staunton. Bear left on to the B4432 after a further ½ mile (1km) to Symonds Yat.*

The River Wye, from Symonds Yat
Left: Hay Cinema bookshop

❷ Symonds Yat,
Herefordshire

The scenery of the Wye Valley is among the finest in Britain and Symonds Yat is a particularly impressive beauty spot, above the deep gorge. The river flows for 4 miles (6km) in a large meander before returning to within 400 yards (365m) of the same point. An AA viewpoint on the summit at 473 feet (144m) affords magnificent views.

▶ *Continue north via an unclassified road, turning right on to the B4227 to Goodrich.*

❸ Goodrich, Herefordshire

Imposing Goodrich Castle is a red sandstone ruin which Cromwell lost to the Royalists

FOR CHILDREN

As you enter the Jubilee Maze at the Museum of Mazes in Symonds Yat, you will be met by a maze man, wearing Victorian boating costume. There are 12 routes to the centre, where the Temple of Diana awaits you. Evening illuminations create a labyrinth of eerie shadows. The museum tells the history of mazes, and of magic spells and witchcraft.

during the Civil War, but then battered with a mortar which fired 200lb (90kg) shots. This dramatically situated castle had a moat which was excavated from solid rock, and you can still look down the 168-foot (51km) well in the courtyard.

▶ *Cross the River Wye and take the B4234 to Ross-on-Wye.*

4 Ross-on-Wye,
Herefordshire
The splendid 208-foot (63m) spire of St Mary's Church rises high above the roofs of this attractive town. Interesting old streets spread out from the market-place, with its 17th-century red sandstone Market Hall. Notable features include several ancient alms houses and 16th-century Wilton Bridge.

ℹ️ *Swan House, Edde Cross Street*

▶ *Leave on the A49, then the B4521 Abergavenny road to Skenfrith.*

5 Skenfrith, Monmouthshire
Skenfrith Castle was built as one of a group of three castles, along with Grosmont and White, to guard the Marches against Welsh uprisings. Its remains include a

central keep enclosed by a four-sided curtain wall and a moat. A small stone village clusters round the castle, with a quaint little 13th-century church and a mill with a working water-wheel.

▶ *Continue along the B4521, then turn north on to the B4347 to Grosmont.*

6 Grosmont,
Monmouthshire
Set on a hillside by the River Monnow, Grosmont is the site of another Norman fortress, taken and re-taken several times during the Welsh uprisings of the 13th to 15th centuries. The castle ruins can be reached by footpath from the town. Grosmont's 13th-century parish church is noted for its huge but crude effigy of an armoured knight. At Abbey Dore, further along the road, the abbey remains include a vast, atmospheric church, tucked away in the Golden Valley.

▶ *Follow the B4347, then the B4348 through the Golden Valley and on to Hay-on-Wye.*

7 Hay-on-Wye, Powys
Hay stands high above the southern bank of the River Wye.

Hay Castle was built by the Marcher Lord William de Braose

Folk hero Owain Glyndŵr destroyed its castle during the 15th century, but the keep, parts of the walls and a gateway remain. The town's cinema has become the biggest second-hand book shop in the world; in fact the whole town seems to be taken up with second-hand books. Thousands flock to the annual Hay-on-Wye literary festival.

▶ *Head southwest for 8 miles (13km) along the B4350 and A438 to Bronllys.*

8 Bronllys, Powys
From Bronllys there are clear views of the Brecon Beacons ahead and the Black Mountains, which dominate the scenery to the left. The 12th-century church, now rebuilt, has a very odd detached tower, and a stone-built Malt House is still in excellent condition and contains its original equipment. Bronllys Castle is half a mile (1km) along the A479.

▶ *From Bronllys take the A438, the A470 and the B4602 to Brecon.*

9 Brecon, Powys

Brecon is a pure delight, encircled by hills at the meeting point of the Rivers Usk and Honddu. The cathedral, originally the church of a Benedictine priory, dates mainly from the 13th and 14th centuries, and Brecon Castle is now in the grounds of the Castle Hotel. The County Hall houses the Brecknock Museum, with its wealth of local history, and the South Wales Borderers Army Museum has relics ranging from the Zulu War in 1879 to World War II and later. East of town is the terminus of the Monmouth and Brecon Canal, and to the south is the Brecon Beacons National Park. The Mountain Centre, off the A470, west of the little village of Libanus, is an ideal starting point for exploring the Park.

i *Cattle Market Car Park*

SPECIAL TO...

Brecon's Brecknock Museum has a superb display of Welsh lovespoons, traditional gifts of betrothal which were carved out of single pieces of wood. From the 17th to the 19th centuries the lovespoon developed into complex and intricate works of art, with keys, bells and other motifs worked into the design.

▶ *Continue southwards along the A470 then take unclassified roads northwards to Pontsticill.*

RECOMMENDED WALKS

A good starting point for walking on the Brecon Beacons is at Storey Arms on the A470, which is at 1,425 feet (427m) above sea-level and gives the shortest route to Pen y Fan, the highest point in the Beacons. Take an OS map, food supplies and weatherproof clothes, even in fine weather. It should not be attempted in poor weather or visibility.

---

10 Pontsticill, Mid Glamorgan

Walking and boating are major attractions in this area; or you could have a journey on the steam train of the Brecon Mountain Railway, which runs for 4 miles (6km) up the valley.

▶ *Take unclassified roads to Talybont-on-Usk.*

11 Talybont-on-Usk, Powys

This delightful little village is now a tourist centre, especially for walkers and outdoor activities; there is an Outdoor Pursuits Centre in the old railway station. The 18th-century Monmouth and Brecon Canal, which passes through the village, was built to carry coal and iron ore. Closed in 1962, it was reopened by volunteers in 1970 for pleasure craft.

▶ *Follow the B4558 to Llangynidr, then the B4560 and an unclassified road to Crickhowell.*

12 Crickhowell, Powys

The name of this little market town is derived from the Iron-Age fort Crug Hywel (Howell's Cairn). The town grew up around Alisby's Castle, which was captured and destroyed in 1403 by Owain Glyndŵr, and is now a picturesque ruin. The River Usk is crossed by an old bridge, dating from the 17th century, which appears to have 13 arches on one side but only 12 on the other – the result of 19th-century alterations.

i *Beaufort Chambers, Beaufort Street*

▶ *Take the A40 to Abergavenny.*

13 Abergavenny, Monmouthshire

Abergavenny, known as the 'Gateway to the Vale of Usk', is overlooked by the Sugar Loaf mountain, 1,955 feet (596m) high, and Ysgyryd (Skirrid) Fawr, 1,595 feet (488m). Its ruined castle was founded in 1090. Impressive buildings in the town include the stone tithe barn, and the red sandstone

Working a lock on the Brecon and Monmouth Canal

Lloyds Bank. St Mary's Church is built on the site of a former Benedictine priory.

i *Swan Meadow, Monmouth Road*

▶ *Continue along the A40 to Raglan.*

14 Raglan, Monmouthshire

One of Britain's finest ruins is 15th-century Raglan Castle which was actually built as a fortified manor. The keep is outside the main castle and Parliamentary troops overcame the Royalists here during the Civil War, by approaching from the opposite side. The castle houses an exhibition on the history of Raglan.

▶ *Follow an unclassified road south to Usk.*

15 Usk, Monmouthshire

Usk is a small market town on the site of an ancient Roman settlement, *Burrium*. Visit the church to see the remarkable restored Tudor rood screen; and, at the other end of the town, the Usk Rural Life Museum, in an old stone malt barn, which is

Raglan Castle was the last to fall to Cromwell in the Civil War
Right: Dylan Thomas's writing shed, Laugharne

crammed with exhibits about life in the area. Usk Castle is privately owned but you can visit the ruins of the Priory next to the church.

▶ *Cross the river and continue along unclassified roads for 8 miles (13km) to Caerleon.*

16 Caerleon, Gwent
One of the four permanent Roman legions in Britain was based here, and parts of the Roman city of *Isca* are displayed in an excellent exhibition room. The major find has been the amphitheatre outside the city

walls. This oval earth mound seated 5,000 people, and is the only fully excavated amphitheatre in Britain. The National Roman Legion Museum has relics from the barracks.

▶ *Take the B4236, then an unclassified road to join the A48 for Penhow.*

17 Penhow, Gwent
The oldest inhabited castle in Wales is Penhow Castle, which is perched on a hillside above the main road. Now privately owned, it is closed to the public but is an excellent example of the smaller type of fortified manor house.

Three miles (5km) further is Caerwent, on the site of Venta Silurium, the only walled Roman

civilian town in Wales. Remnants of the wall and mosaic pavements can still be seen. Caldicot Castle Countryside Park, 2 miles (3km) away, surrounds the 12th-century castle.

▶ *Continue straight along the A48 to Chepstow.*

BACK TO NATURE

The Forest of Dean is an excellent area for the bird-watcher. Woodpeckers, tits and nuthatches can be seen, and pied flycatchers are often spotted at the RSPB's Nagshead reserve, where nest boxes encourage the species.

The Pembroke
Coast National
Park

2 DAYS • 137 MILES • 220.5KM

The county of Pembrokeshire has a magnificent heritage coastline. The inland scenery, though less dramatic, is enhanced by
pretty villages and several fine castles.

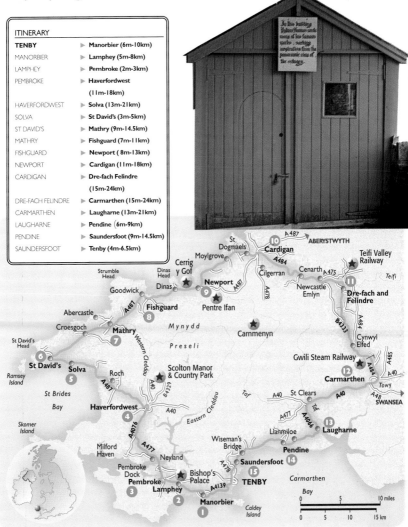

ℹ️ *The Croft, Tenby*

▶ *Leave Tenby on the **A4139** and then turn left on to the **B4585** to Manorbier.*

1 Manorbier, Pembrokeshire
The medieval traveller and scholar, Gerald of Wales (Giraldus Cambrensis), was born here in 1147 and described it as the 'pleasantest spot in Wales'. There is a castle dating from Gerald's time, which gives an impressive view out to sea from the ramparts. The sandy beach has rocky pools, and is a perfect playground for the children.

▶ *Return to the **A4139** for 5 miles (8km) to Lamphey.*

2 Lamphey, Pembrokeshire
The romantic ruins of a 13th-century Bishop's Palace lie to the northeast of Lamphey. The Palace, with its ornate parapets, fishponds and notable 16th-

Tenby Harbour overlooks two bays

century chapel, was built as a country retreat for the Bishops of St David's.

▶ *Continue along the **A4139** to Pembroke.*

3 Pembroke, Pembrokeshire
This ancient town was built around the great 12th- to 13th-century fortress of Pembroke Castle, the largest castle in the area, and the birthplace of Henry Tudor. It still has its fine round keep, and beneath the castle is a huge natural cavern known as The Wogan. There is an interpretative centre with a Pembroke Yeomanry exhibition.

Near by Pembroke Dock produced nearly 300 ships, including some of the most powerful in Queen Victoria's navy and four famous Royal Yachts. The dockyard closed suddenly in 1926, with disastrous consequences for the local workforce.

ℹ️ *Visitor Centre, Commons Road*

▶ *Take the **A477**, then join the **A4076** to Haverfordwest – 11 miles (18km).*

4 Haverfordwest, Pembrokeshire
The 12th-century castle on the hill high above the town is now a ruin. There is more history next door at Castle House, location of the Town Museum. The town is cut in two by the River Cleddau.

ℹ️ *Old Bridge*

FOR CHILDREN

Scolton Manor, 4 miles (6km) northeast of Haverfordwest, is set in magnificent grounds where there is plenty to keep children occupied: nature trails, guided walks, an adventure playground and play area, exhibitions and, in the summer months, a vintage car rally and model aircraft show.

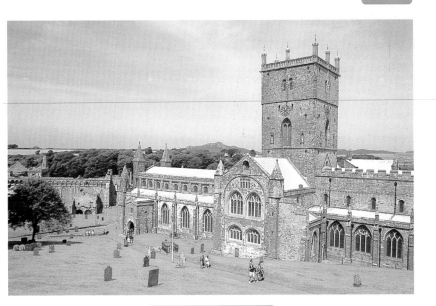

St David lies buried in the town which bears his name

▶ *Head northwest along the A487 to Solva.*

5 Solva, Pembrokeshire
Solva's old port still has warehouses and a restored lime kiln, and is a favourite sailing spot. Some of its cottages and merchants' houses have been converted to quality craft shops. Visit Middle Mill, a woollen mill specialising in carpets, tapestry and floor rugs; it is one of only two remaining woollen mills in Pembrokeshire – in 1900 there were 26.

▶ *Keep on along the A487 for 3 miles (5km) to St David's.*

6 St David's,
Pembrokeshire
The city of St David's – the smallest in Britain – was founded on the site of an early Christian community, and is dominated by the cathedral and the graceful, medieval walled Bishop's Palace. Sea-based activities include whale and dolphin watching. The Queen visited St David's in 1995 to confer city status upon it.

BACK TO NATURE

St David's Head has some superb coastal scenery and a wonderful display of coastal heathland flowers. Look for ling, bell heather and dwarf gorse growing alongside thrift and sea campion. For the best views of seabirds, visit Stackpole, or better still Skomer Island, a few miles off the coast and reached by ferry from Martin's Haven. Puffins, razorbills, kittiwakes, lesser black-backed gulls and choughs all put on a fine display.

SPECIAL TO...

A boat trip around Pembrokeshire's offshore islands with the Thousand Islands Expeditions at St David's takes you on a 50-mile (80km) voyage past the highest sea cliffs in Wales, the longest sea caves and the largest grey seal colony, on Ramsey Island. The boat speeds over strong tidal currents in the narrows between the islands, including the notorious Bitches of Ramsey Sound, with its 20mph (32kph) tidal current.

[i] *NP Visitor Centre, The Grove*

RECOMMENDED WALKS

Walk from St David's cathedral to the coast at Whitesand Bay. If you wish to add 2 miles (3km) and double the length of this walk, go north and do a round tour of St David's Head.

▶ *Turn northeastwards, still on the A487 to Mathry.*

7 Mathry, Pembrokeshire
This little village overlooks the Western Cleddau source stream. Mountain bikes can be hired for rides into the Preseli Hills, from where 33 dolerite stones were transported to Stonehenge. Northwest of Mathry is Abercastle, where there is a burial chamber with a 16-foot (5m) capstone resting on three of its original seven supports.

▶ *Continue along the A487 to Fishguard.*

8 Fishguard, Pembrokeshire
Fishguard has two parts. Upper Fishguard stands back from the sea, and from it the road falls

steeply to Lower Fishguard, a quaint and largely unspoilt town. There are many ancient links with boating here. The July Fishguard Music Festival is another attraction.

For a windblown and bracing day, take a return trip on the ferry to Rosslare, across the Irish Sea. Tregwynt Woollen Mill, at St Nicholas, is a working mill open to the public, which produces traditional Welsh weaves.

[i] *The Library, High Street*

▶ *Head east to Newport, still travelling on the **A487**.*

9 Newport, Pembrokeshire
Just outside the town is the Pembrokeshire Candle Centre, where you can see handmade candles being produced, and the Mini Museum, next door, has displays on the history of candle making. The remains of Newport's 12th-century castle can still be seen.

One and a half miles (2.5km) west of town is Cerrig y Gof, a group of burial chambers forming a circle. Pentre Ifan Cromlech lies 2 miles (3km) southeast of Newport.

▶ *Turn left along unclassified roads through Moylgrove and St Dogmaels, then take the **B4546** to Cardigan.*

The Ship Inn, Fishguard

10 Cardigan, Ceredigion
St Dogmaels Abbey, just outside Cardigan, was founded in 1115, and the ruins include large fragments of the north and west walls standing almost to their original height. One of Cardigan's most striking architectural features is the ancient bridge, which spans the River Teifi, but little now remains of Cardigan Castle, where the first National Eisteddfod took place in 1176. The magnificent towers of Cilgerran Castle, best reached from along the A484, overlook the gorge of the Teifi just upstream from the town. Watch out for the coracle demonstrations in the Welsh Wildlife Centre, and there is a coracle centre and mill at Cenarth, a few miles along the A484.

[i] *Theatr Mwldan, Bath House Road*

▶ *Follow the **A484**, then turn right along an unclassified road to Dre-fach and Felindre.*

11 Dre-fach and Felindre, Carmarthenshire
Just before the turning to Dre-fach and Felindre, a left turn leads to the Teifi Valley Railway at Henllan, where tiny engines pull the trains along a narrow-gauge railway. The Teifi valley has long been a woollen producing area, and the Museum of the Welsh Woollen Industry is in the village. There are still a few

small mills in the area where you can see the cloth being made. The original mill building has an exhibition showing the processes involved in cloth-making, and there are spinning and weaving demonstrations.

▶ *Continue south along unclassified roads to join the **B4333**, then the **A484** to Carmarthen.*

12 Carmarthen, Carmarthenshire
Carmarthen is believed to be the oldest town in Wales, and the birthplace of Merlin. Remains of Roman occupation include an amphitheatre site. The Gwili Steam Railway at Bronwydd opened in 1860, but closed in 1973 when the milk traffic was transferred to road tankers. It was reopened in 1978 and now operates for 1.6 miles (2.5km) from Bronwydd Arms to Llwyfan Cerrig, following the course of the River Gwili. A nature trail has been developed

at Llwyfan Cerrig and there is also a children's activity area.

i 113 Lammas Street

▶ *Go west along the A40, turning left at St Clears to join the A4066 for Laugharne.*

🔞 Laugharne,
Carmarthenshire

Laugharne had a strong influence on Dylan Thomas, and the town hall, clock tower and many of the people became part of *Under Milk Wood.* Thomas moved into the Boathouse with his family in 1949 and along the path to it is 'The Shack', which became his workshop. The Boathouse is now a museum, Dylan Thomas is buried in the local churchyard and there is a festival of his work every third year in July. The castle by the sea was built in the 12th century, but the present building is mainly Tudor.

▶ *Follow the A4066 to Pendine.*

🔞 Pendine, Carmarthenshire

Pendine is best noted for its golden sand, on which Sir Malcolm Campbell and others made land speed record attempts. Amy Johnson took off from here in 1933 for the start of her epic transatlantic flight. Nowadays the beach is used for bathing and fishing, and there are beautiful cliff walks near by.

▶ *Take the B4314, then unclassi-fied roads to Saundersfoot.*

🔞 Saundersfoot,
Pembrokeshire

This 19th-century fishing port and coal port has become a family holiday centre with three sandy beaches, rock pools and a

---

SCENIC ROUTES

There are superb views of the coastline on the route from Pendine to Saundersfoot.

Gwili Steam Railway, Bronwydd Arms Station

sheltered harbour. Boats are available for fishing and pleasure trips. The village is in a sheltered valley, and there are good walks along the coast.

i The Barbecue, Harbour Car Park

▶ *Drive south along the B4316, then the A478 back to Tenby.*

FOR HISTORY BUFFS

Ancient settlements were numerous in the Preseli Hills and elsewhere in southwest Wales; among the important Bronze-Age relics are those at Carnmenyn. An ancient route known as the Great West Road passes a pile of rocks called Mynachlog Ddu, the bluestone believed to have been used at Stonehenge.

Land of Rivers
& Mountains

From the sandy beach of Borth and the muddy estuary of the Dyfi, this drive takes you through the man-made scenery of Llyn Clywedog – a striking contrast with the wild hills all around. There are rivers and water-falls, wooded valleys and wide rolling hills.

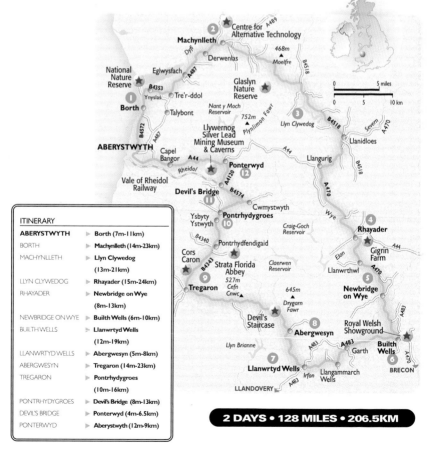

ITINERARY		
ABERYSTWYTH	►	**Borth** (7m–11km)
BORTH	►	**Machynlleth** (14m–23km)
MACHYNLLETH	►	**Llyn Clywedog** (13m–21km)
LLYN CLYWEDOG	►	**Rhayader** (15m–24km)
RHAYADER	►	**Newbridge on Wye** (8m–13km)
NEWBRIDGE ON WYE	►	**Builth Wells** (6m–10km)
BUILTH WELLS	►	**Llanwrtyd Wells** (12m–19km)
LLANWRTYD WELLS	►	**Abergwesyn** (5m–8km)
ABERGWESYN	►	**Tregaron** (14m–23km)
TREGARON	►	**Pontrhydygroes** (10m–16km)
PONTRHYDYGROES	►	**Devil's Bridge** (8m–13km)
DEVIL'S BRIDGE	►	**Ponterwyd** (4m–6.5km)
PONTERWYD	►	**Aberystwyth** (12m–9km)

2 DAYS • 128 MILES • 206.5KM

Rock-hopping at Aberystwyth
Left: carving, Strata Florida Abbey

ⓘ *Terrace Road, Aberystwyth*

▶ *Follow the coast northwards for 6 miles (10km) along the A487 and B4572 to Borth.*

❶ Borth, Ceredigion
Three miles (5km) of sand can be found just to the north of this small village, which consists mainly of one street of cottages. The National Nature Reserve at Ynyslas (see panel) has remark-able dunes, a submerged forest and varied birdlife. When you look out to sea you may see bottlenose dolphins, regular visitors to Cardigan Bay.

▶ *Head inland along the B4353, then turn left on to the A487 at Tre'r-ddol and follow it through to Machynlleth.*

SPECIAL TO...

Ynyslas is the area of sand dunes to the north of Borth which blocks off much of the Dyfi estuary from the sea. Behind the dunes is an expanse of reclaimed marsh; this area is now a major nature reserve. Ferries used to run across the estuary to Aberdyfi, and remains of a refuge tower can still be seen, where passengers could wait if they became stranded by the incoming tide.

❷ Machynlleth, Powys
On the way to Machynlleth, visit the village of Furnace. The large barn-like building beside the A487 gives Furnace its unusual name. This is an historic metal smelting site, dating from the 17th century when silver refin-ing took place here. The water-

---

wheel has been restored and you can see the magnificent waterfall that once supplied its power.

Machynlleth itself is the chief market town of the Dyfi Valley and gained fame in the 15th century as the seat of Owain Glyndŵr's short-lived Welsh parliament. The Owain Glyndŵr Centre houses an exhibition of his campaigns. The Centre for Alternative Technology, to the north of the town, is a fascinating place to visit. Here you can see a Green Community at work, using windmills, solar panels and water-driven machinery. There is an ecological maze to explore, a children's play area and a restaurant.

ⓘ *Royal House, Penrallt Street*

BACK TO NATURE

The Glaslyn Nature Reserve, off the road between Machynlleth and Llanidloes, contains heather moorland and blanket bog, together with small areas of scree, crag, rough grass and narrow river valley. Breeding birds include pipits, wheatears, ring ouzel and red grouse, and red kites, peregrines and merlins are sometimes seen.

▶ *Leave on the A489, then take the unclassified road south-eastwards to join the B4518 and on to Llyn Clywedog.*

❸ Llyn Clywedog, Powys
This impressive reservoir, built between 1964 and 1968, has the highest concrete dam of its kind in Britain – 237 feet (72m) high – and holds up to 11,000 million gallons (50,000 million litres) of water behind it. From the dam there are excellent views of the surrounding hill country. For walkers, the Glyndŵr's Way and other waymarked walks follow the Clywedog valley.

Four miles (6km) further is Llanidloes. This is the first town on the River Severn, and there are several interesting buildings along its tree-lined streets. The most famous is the 16th-century half-timbered Old Market Hall, with its open ground floor – one of the last of its kind in Wales.

i 54 Longbridge Street

▷ *Drive southwards along the A470 from Llanidloes for 15 miles (24km) to Rhayader.*

RECOMMENDED WALKS

Llanidloes is a marvellous centre for walking with Owain Glyndŵr's Way and the Cross Wales Walk both passing through the town. Shorter walks include Allt Goch, which takes less than an hour and gives excellent views over the town and the Severn valley.

4 Rhayader, Powys

This small market town on the River Wye is an ideal centre for visiting the 'Lakeland of Wales'. The lakes are the reservoirs of the Elan valley, which provide Birmingham with its water supply. Pony trekking and

Newbridge on Wye

angling are particularly popular here. Although Rhayader is now a peaceful little town, it has had its share of excitment in the past. The 19th-century Rebecca riots, protesting against toll gate impositions, centred around the town, and the castle was destroyed during the Civil War. At the Welsh Royal Crystal Glass Factory you can watch the art of glass-blowing, and there are numerous craft shops and a pottery. Gigrin Farm, half a mile (1km) to the south, offers a farm trail of nearly 2 miles (3km) in beautiful surroundings, and there are pets and a children's playground.

i Leisure Centre, North Street

BACK TO NATURE

The Elan Valley Visitor Centre, near Rhayader, organises guided walks for bird-watchers. Golden plover, ring ouzel and dunlin nest near by, and there are red grouse and a few merlins up on the moors. Dippers, grey wagtails and a flashing blue kingfisher may be seen on the streams, and the rare red kite floats around overhead.

▷ *Follow the A470 to Newbridge on Wye.*

5 Newbridge on Wye, Powys

The 'new' bridge of the town's name was built in 1910 to replace an old wooden structure. The church was founded in the late 19th century by the Venables family, who own Llysdinam Hall. There is a Field Study Centre in the Hall's grounds belonging to the University of Wales' Institute of Science and Technology.

▷ *Continue southwards on the A470 to Builth Wells.*

6 Builth Wells, Powys

Builth Wells was one of a string of Welsh spa towns which drew crowds of health-seeking Victorians, but it was an important centre long before that. The castle was built in Norman times by James de San George, who was also responsible for Harlech, Caernarfon, Beaumaris and Conwy castles. The Wyeside Arts Centre provides a fine selection of entertainment throughout the summer with films, exhibitions and theatre. Just outside town, in the village of Llanelwedd, is the Royal

Welsh Showground, which hosts the Royal Welsh Agricultural Show in July.

ℹ️ *Groe Car Park*

▶ *Take the **A483**, then turn left along unclassified roads at Garth to Llanwrtyd Wells.*

7 Llanwrtyd Wells, Powys
The smallest town in Britain, Llanwrtyd Wells is on the River Irfon. Traces of its Victorian grandeur recall the town's heyday, when travellers flocked here to sample its sulphur water – and traces of its odour remain along the river. The Abergwesyn Pass, which leads over the mountain from Llanwrtyd, has some of Wales' finest scenery.

▶ *Drive northwards into the hills along an unclassified road to Abergwesyn, 5 miles (8km).*

8 Abergwesyn, Powys
The road that crosses the mountains from Abergwesyn to Tregaron is one of Britain's most spectacular routes. It was originally a drovers' route, along which cattle were taken to the markets of the Midlands and London in the 18th and 19th centuries. The views around the Devil's Staircase, a steep and tortuous zigzag section of the road, are particularly impressive.

▶ *Take the mountain road to Tregaron.*

9 Tregaron, Ceredigion
Tregaron is a small, Welsh-speaking community, famous as the birthplace of outlaw Twm Sion Catti, and of Henry Richard, the 'Apostle of Peace' who founded the Peace Union, forerunner of the League of Nations.

Cors Caron, the Red Bog

At the foot of steep hills, and at the southern end of a great expanse of bog, Tregaron is a popular pony trekking centre.

The often bleak and misty marshland, Cors Caron, was formerly a lake fed by the River Teifi, and is now a National Nature Reserve, with restricted public access. At the Kite Centre there is a small museum of local history, and information on the rare Red Kite.

▶ *Follow the **B4343** for 10 miles (16km) to Pontrhydygroes and the **B4574** to Cwmystwyth, 4 miles (6km) further.*

10 Pontrhydygroes, Ceredigion
The village of Pontrhydygroes grew around the lead-mining industry and is now a quiet

Devil's Bridge straddles the lovely Mynach Gorge

Vale of Rheidol Railway climbs 680 feet (207m) in the 12 miles (19km) from Aberystwyth along a lovely scenic route to terminate at Devil's Bridge Station.

▶ Take the **A4120** northwards to Ponterwyd.

12 Ponterwyd, Ceredigion
This small cluster of houses round a craggy gorge featured in the writings of 19th-century traveller George Borrow, whose book *Wild Wales* relates his stay at the village inn, now the Borrow Arms. A mile (1.6km) west of the village is the Llywernog Silver Lead Mining Museum and Caverns and there are fine views stretching to Cardigan Bay from Nant-yr-Arian Visitor Centre, further along the road.

community set among wooded hills. The surrounding area was part of the Hafod estate in the 18th century, where Thomas Johnes began the task of afforesting the land. Further along, Cwmystwyth is another old mining settlement; the mines here were once worked by the Romans and the monks of Strata Florida Abbey.

▶ Head northwest along the **B4574** for another 4 miles (6km) to Devil's Bridge.

11 Devil's Bridge, Ceredigion
The River Mynach meets the River Rheidol here to create spectacular falls over 300 feet (91m) high. Three bridges were built across the chasm, one above the other, and Devil's Bridge is the earliest one, probably the 12th-century work of the monks from nearby Strata Florida Abbey. The higher bridges date from 1753 and the early 20th century. Ninety-one steep steps, called Jacob's Ladder, lead down to the river. The narrow-gauge

---

FOR HISTORY BUFFS

On the road from Tregaron to Pontrhydygroes you will pass the ruins of the Cistercian Strata Florida Abbey, founded in 1164. It was here, in 1238, that Llywelyn the Great gathered all the Welsh princes to swear allegiance to his son Dafydd. The abbey fell into disrepair after the Dissolution, but the magnificent Norman arch still remains.

FOR CHILDREN

Gold, silver, lead and copper were mined from the rocks of the Cambrian Mountains in former centuries, and many of the relics of those days can still be seen. The Llywernog Silver Lead Mining Museum and Caverns near Ponterwyd has many old machines, some of which have been restored to make a fascinating working museum. You can try your hand at panning for gold and working the hand pumps, and visit the underground drift mine, with its floodlit cavern.

▶ Head west along the **A44** back to Aberystwyth.

SCENIC ROUTES

Just before descending into Borth there are fine views of the sandy coast with the estuary and hills beyond. There are magnificent hill views all around Clywedog; as well as on the minor roads near Abergwesyn and the B4574 near Cwmystwyth.

Water, Water
Everywhere

Follow the magnificent coastline with its glorious sandy beaches before turning inland and heading into the hills. Tumbling rivers and large lakes are constant companions from Trawsfynydd as far as Corris, and man-made features include dams and a huge nuclear power station.

2 DAYS • 150 MILES • 244KM

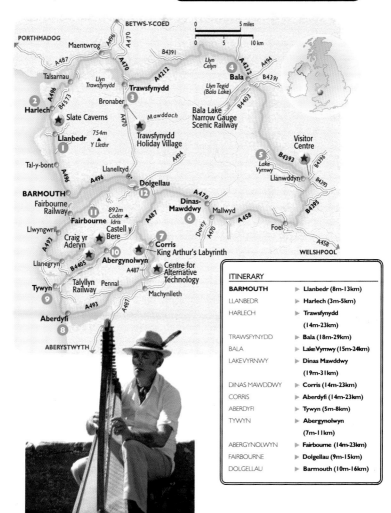

ITINERARY	
BARMOUTH	▶ Llanbedr (8m-13km)
LLANBEDR	▶ Harlech (3m-5km)
HARLECH	▶ **Trawsfynydd**
	(14m-23km)
TRAWSFYNYDD	▶ Bala (18m-29km)
BALA	▶ Lake Vyrnwy (15m-24km)
LAKE VYRNWY	▶ Dinas Mawddwy
	(19m-31km)
DINAS MAWDDWY	▶ Corris (14m-23km)
CORRIS	▶ Aberdyfi (14m-23km)
ABERDYFI	▶ Tywyn (5m-8km)
TYWYN	▶ Abergynolwyn
	(7m-11km)
ABERGYNOLWYN	▶ Fairbourne (14m-23km)
FAIRBOURNE	▶ Dolgellau (9m-15km)
DOLGELLAU	▶ Barmouth (10m-16km)

Magnificent Harlech Castle

i The Station, Barmouth

▶ *From Barmouth follow the A496 north to Llanbedr.*

❶ Llanbedr, Gwynedd
At Llanfair, just to the north of Llanbedr on the A496, are the exciting slate caverns, where you can walk through the old workings and see the enormous Cathedral cavern, but be sure to wear warm clothing, as the temperature inside is normally 10°C (50°F) or below.

▶ *Continue along the A496 to Harlech.*

❷ Harlech, Gwynedd
Harlech Castle is one of the most magnificently sited of Welsh castles, looking out over Cardigan Bay. It was built in the

13th century by Edward I to subdue the Welsh but was captured by Owain Glyndŵr in 1404. Harlech's theatre presents a varied programme throughout the year.

i Llys y Graig

▶ *Keep on along the A496, then turn off right on to the A487 for 2 miles (3km) before joining the A470 for Trawsfynydd.*

❸ Trawsfynydd, Gwynedd
The lake here is a man-made reservoir which provided cooling water for the decommissioned nuclear power station. Nature trails have been created around the lake, and there is excellent fishing. To the south, along the A470, is the Trawsfynydd Holiday Village, an ideal centre for hiking and mountain biking.

▶ *Drive into the hills along the A4212 to Bala.*

❹ Bala, Gwynedd
Situated at the top of Llyn Tegid (Bala Lake), the largest natural lake in Wales, Bala has become a great water sports centre. Sailing, windsurfing, fishing and canoeing all take place on the River Tryweryn. The other big lake near by is Llyn Celyn, a man-made reservoir, which supplies Liverpool

with some of its water and is a popular trout-fishing lake. The Bala Lake Narrow Gauge Scenic Railway runs 4½ miles (7km) to Llanuwchllyn through splendid scenery. Bala was the home of the Methodist cause and has retained much of its Welsh character and culture.

i Penllyn, Pensarn Road

▶ *Leave Bala on the B4391, then follow the unclassified road southwards over the hills and on to the B4393 to Lake Vyrnwy.*

5 Lake Vyrnwy, Powys
This vast reservoir was created in the late 19th century to supply Liverpool with water; the village of Llanwddyn was levelled to make way for it and rebuilt on higher ground. The lake and the surrounding woodlands are now a reserve of the RSPB. There is a small visitor centre, and nature trails and hides are provided to enable you to view the wildlife in the area, which includes red squirrels, polecats and badgers.

▶ *Continue along the B4393, then turn right on to a minor road to join the B4395. Turn right again on to the A458 through Mallwyd, then head north on the A470 to Dinas Mawddwy.*

6 Dinas Mawddwy, Gwynedd
This little village is an ideal base for outdoor holidays in the area. Meirion Mill Shop, an outlet for clothing and other crafts, is based at the old woollen mill. Pottery and slate goods are available as well as woollens, and the old railway line is a good place for a stroll.

▶ *Continue along the A470 and then left on the A487 for 14 miles (23km) to Corris.*

7 Corris, Gwynedd
Corris is an old slate mining village with a new centre for traditional industries, where

tourists can watch craftsmen at work. There is also a Railway Museum and, to the south, at the disused Llwyngwern Quarry, is the Centre for Alternative Technology (see page 69).

i Craft Centre

▶ *Drive southwards along the unclassified road on the eastern side of the river through Esgairgeiliog. Turn right on to the B4404, join the A487 for a short distance, then turn right on the A493 to Aberdyfi.*

8 Aberdyfi, Gwynedd
Sailing boats have now replaced the cargo ships that once traded at this harbour on the sheltered Dyfi Estuary. There is a fine sandy beach along the coast, and you can take a ferry trip across to Ynyslas, with its vast expanse of sand dunes and marshland. The

Dinas Mawddwy is an ideal base for exploring the area

town achieved fame in the song *The Bells of Aberdyfi*; ghostly church bells are said to ring from an ancient town which was completely flooded by the sea.

i The Wharf Gardens

▶ *Drive north along the A493 for 5 miles (8km) to Tywyn.*

9 Tywyn, Gwynedd
There are miles of golden sandy beaches at this popular seaside resort which is excellent for surfing and sailing. St Cadfan's Church dates back to Norman times and houses St Cadfan's Stone, a 7-foot (2m) monument some 1300 years old. The inscriptions on it are thought to be the oldest known writing in Welsh. Tywyn is famous for the

Dolgellau is situated in an area of outstanding scenery
Right: the Ffestiniog Railway

Talyllyn Railway, which runs inland for 7 miles (11km).

ℹ️ High Street

SPECIAL TO...

The Talyllyn Railway, which runs inland from Tywyn to Nant Gwernol, was built in 1865 to handle slate traffic. This was the first railway in the world to be taken over by a voluntary preservation society, and it is now operated as a tourist attraction.

▶ *Leave Tywyn on the A493, but turn inland along the B4405 to Abergynolwyn.*

🔟 Abergynolwyn, Gwynedd

Two miles (3km) west of Abergynolwyn, along an unclassified road, is the romantic ruin of Castell y Bere, built by Llywelyn the Great in the 13th century. Further still is Craig yr Aderyn (Bird Rock), thought to be the only inland nesting place of cormorants in Britain, but also the home for choughs, kestrels and feral goats.

▶ *Take an unclassified road heading westwards through Llanegryn back to the coast, then the A493 to Fairbourne.*

🔟🔟 Fairbourne, Gwynedd

Fairbourne is a popular holiday base with a sandy beach and miles of safe swimming, where windsurfing is a great attraction. So, too, is the Fairbourne Railway which was built in the 1890s as a horse-drawn tramway. It was later converted to steam and now runs 1½ miles (2.5km) from Fairbourne to the end of the peninsula. The main line Cambrian coast railway also runs through here.

▶ *Rejoin and continue along the A493 to Dolgellau.*

🔟🔟 Dolgellau, Gwynedd

Dolgellau has always been a major route centre and is still an important regional capital and market centre. Tourism has replaced its main industry, flannel-weaving, and all that remains of this former occupation are the ruins of the fulling mills on the banks of the River Aran. Every July the town hosts a folk and rock festival based around Eldon Square. Walking is popular, and there are strenuous walks up to the summit of Cader Idris, as well as gentle strolls. A delightful route near by is the Torrent Walk, from Brithdir to the falls of the Afon Clywedog.

ℹ️ Tŷ Meirion, Eldon Square

▶ *Join the A470 to Llanelltyd, then turn left on to the A496 back to Barmouth.*

FOR HISTORY BUFFS

Dolgellau is built on the site of an ancient settlement among green hills. Three Roman roads met here, and it remained an important centre for the Welsh people throughout the Middle Ages. The Welsh leader Owain Glyndŵr signed his alliance with Charles VI, the King of France, here.

Quarries, Castles & Railways

From Bangor make a brief visit to the island of Anglesey before heading down the coast to Caernarfon and then inland to Snowdonia. The hills are scarred with quarries in places, but still create an overpoweringly beautiful backdrop.

2 DAYS • 113 MILES • 182KM

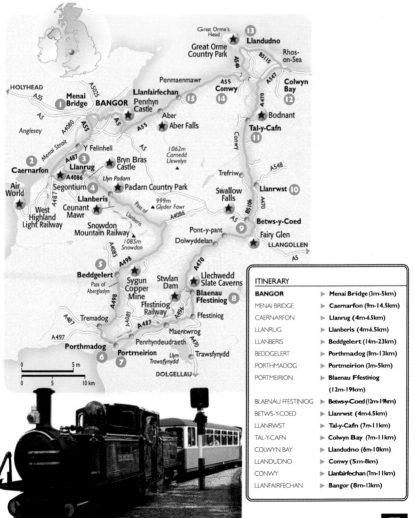

ITINERARY		
BANGOR	▶	**Menai Bridge** (3m-5km)
MENAI BRIDGE	▶	**Caernarfon** (9m-14.5km)
CAERNARFON	▶	**Llanrug** (4m-6.5km)
LLANRUG	▶	**Llanberis** (4m-6.5km)
LLANBERIS	▶	**Beddgelert** (14m-23km)
BEDDGELERT	▶	**Porthmadog** (8m-13km)
PORTHMADOG	▶	**Portmeirion** (3m-5km)
PORTMEIRION	▶	**Blaenau Ffestiniog** (12m-19km)
BLAENAU FFESTINIOG	▶	**Betws-y-Coed** (12m-19km)
BETWS-Y-COED	▶	**Llanrwst** (4m-6.5km)
LLANRWST	▶	**Tal-y-Cafn** (7m-11km)
TAL-Y-CAFN	▶	**Colwyn Bay** (7m-11km)
COLWYN BAY	▶	**Llandudno** (6m-10km)
LLANDUDNO	▶	**Conwy** (5m-8km)
CONWY	▶	**Llanfairfechan** (7m-11km)
LLANFAIRFECHAN	▶	**Bangor** (8m-13km)

ⓘ *Town Hall, Bangor*

▶ *Drive along the **A5122** for 3 miles (5km) to Menai Bridge.*

❶ Menai Bridge, Gwynedd
Menai Bridge takes its name from the suspension bridge built by Telford between 1819 and 1826 high above the Menai Strait. Nowadays, traffic on the busy A5 uses Stephenson's Britannia Bridge, whose original tubular structure was rebuilt after a fire in 1970, with a road deck above the railway.

From a lay-by on the A545 beyond Menai Bridge, there are superb views of both bridges, with the mountains of Snowdonia beyond. In Menai Bridge itself is the Oriel Tegfryn Gallery, which features the work of contemporary Welsh artists.

▶ *Follow the **A4080** to the **A5**, recross the Menai Strait on the Britannia Bridge, then on to the **A487** to Caernarfon.*

❷ Caernarfon, Gwynedd
The airport south of Caenarfon is a great all-weather attraction. It used to be an RAF camp during World War II, and is now a hands-on museum, where you

Thomas Telford's graceful suspension bridge over the Menai Strait

can climb into exhibits, touch the controls and use a flight simulator. You can also have a flight over Caernarfon Castle or round Snowdon. In 1969, Prince Charles was invested in the castle, following a tradition set by Edward I, whose first-born son was presented to the people as the Prince of Wales. Inside the castle you can see the investiture robes, and an explanation of the history of the castle and surrounding area, as well as the Museum of the Royal Welch Fusiliers.

Just outside the town, at Segontium, are the remains of a fine Roman fort which served as an important outpost of the Empire for three centuries.

ⓘ *Oriel Pendeitsh, Castle Street*

▶ *Take the **A4086** eastwards and turn on to an unclassified road to Llanrug.*

❸ Llanrug, Gwynedd
The lived-in castle at Bryn Bras, to the south of Llanrug, has spacious lawns, tranquil woodland walks and excellent mountain views. This neo-Norman building on the fringe of Snowdonia was built in the 1830s on the site of an earlier castle, and the majestic gardens are worth visiting in their own right.

▶ *Return to and continue along the **A4086** to Llanberis.*

❹ Llanberis, Gwynedd
At Llanberis you can take a 40-minute trip in a narrow-gauge train along the shores of Llyn Padarn, in the Padarn Country Park. The famed modern pump storage hydro scheme is close by at Dinorwic.

Dolbadarn Castle is in the town, and less than a mile (1.6km) from the High Street is Ceunant Mawr, one of the most impressive waterfalls in Wales. The most popular footpath up Snowdon starts here, as does the Snowdon Mountain Railway, the only public rack-and-pinion railway, which climbs 3,000 feet (915m) to the summit in less than 5 miles (8km). Each train can take a maximum of 59 passengers and will normally not run with fewer than 25. Services depend on demand and weather conditions, which can be very harsh at the top of Snowdon, even when Llanberis is pleasant and sunny. The views can be superb.

ⓘ *41b High Street*

▶ *Leave on the **A4086**, then turn right on to the **A498** for 14 miles (23km) to Beddgelert.*

RECOMMENDED WALKS

From Llanberis, walk around the eastern end of Llyn Padarn at the foot of the Dinorwic quarries, then along the northern side of the lake. Visit the National Slate Museum and pass through the woods and via the tramway bridge, before going round the western end of the lake and back into Llanberis.

5 Beddgelert, Gwynedd
The grave of Gelert is one of the saddest memorials you are likely to see. According to legend, which may actually be a 19th-century invention, Gelert was a faithful wolfhound killed by Prince Llywelyn, who thought it had killed his son, when in fact the dog had saved him from a wolf. Just outside this small town is the award-winning Sygun Copper Mine, where you can explore the tunnels of a 19th-century mine which was once one of the world's major copper producers. A guided tour will take you past veins of ore containing gold, silver and other metals. From Beddgelert the drive takes you through the picturesque Pass of Aberglaslyn.

i *Canolfan Hebog*

▶ *Follow the A498 southwards to Porthmadog.*

6 Porthmadog, Gwynedd
Porthmadog was the creation of William Alexander Madocks, who hoped to benefit from the tourist traffic to Ireland; in fact, the town made its money from slate. The Ffestiniog Railway, which runs through magnificent scenery to Blaenau Ffestiniog, once carried the slate here to be shipped abroad, and is now a major tourist attraction. It uses horseshoe bends and a complete spiral at one point to gain height. Porthmadog also has the little Welsh Highland Railway, where you have the chance to climb on the locomotives.

Italian-style Portmeirion

i *High Street*

▶ *Drive along the A487 before turning right on to an unclassified road to Portmeirion.*

7 Portmeirion, Gwynedd
This Italianate garden village, surrounded by woods and beaches, was created by the Welsh architect Sir Clough Williams-Ellis. Portmeirion was used as the setting for the 1960s cult television series *The Prisoner*, and now produces a distinctive range of colourful pottery.

FOR CHILDREN

Padarn Country Park is open all year round and has picnic spots, boats for hire, a slate museum and a deserted village. You can ride on the narrow-gauge railway running along the shore of Llyn Padarn and walk along the nature trail or the archaeological trail, by the lakeside or in the woodlands.

▶ *Return to and take the A487 eastwards, turning left on to the A496 at Maentwrog. Shortly turn right on to the B4391, which joins the A470 at Ffestiniog. Turn left on to the A470 and continue to Blaenau Ffestiniog.*

8 Blaenau Ffestiniog, Gwynedd
Blaenau Ffestiniog depended for its livelihood on the slate quarries, until demand for slate fell away. Now visitors can get first-hand experience of the slate miners' working conditions at the Llechwedd Slate Caverns, where the Deep Mine tour will take you down on Britain's steepest passenger incline. The Miners' Tramway is a guided rail tour of an 1846 route, through a chain of enormous caverns first opened to the public in 1972. A modern industry is established at Tan-y-grisiau, where hydro-electricity is produced in a pumped storage scheme. Drive

Set on a rock above the town, Conwy Castle is an imposing sight

Jones in 1636, and the Gwydir Chapel contains the coffin of Llywelyn, Prince of Wales. Take a tour around the Trefriw Wells Roman Spa, where the water has been used as an aid to healthy living since Roman times, and is said to ease rheumatism and nervous tension. At the Trefriw Woollen Mills, you can see bedspreads and tweeds being manufactured, using electricity generated from the River Crafnant.

FOR HISTORY BUFFS

Trefriw has been known for its spa water since the 1st century, when Roman soldiers tunnelled into the Allt Coch mountains to reach the source. The water is rich in chalybeate; at the Victorian Pump House you can enjoy a sample of the water, which is said to help eliminate fatigue, nervous tension, stress, lumbago and anaemia.

▶ *Continue along the **A470** to Tal-y-Cafn.*

⓫ Tal-y-Cafn, Gwynedd
The 80-acre (32-hectare) garden at Bodnant is claimed to be one of the finest gardens in the world. Now owned by the National Trust, it is located in the beautiful Conwy Valley, with views out to the Snowdon mountains. Throughout the year visitors can find much of interest, with native and exotic trees and flowers, and there is a nursery where plants are propagated.

▶ *Keep going along the **A470** and then the **A547** to Colwyn Bay.*

⓬ Colwyn Bay, Clwyd
Colwyn Bay is a lively seaside town, which grew in the late 19th century as a result of the arrival of the railway, and the pier, promenade and many hotels and shops date from this period. The town is famous for its parks and gardens. The Welsh Mountain Zoo has chim-

up the mountain road to the Stwlan Dam for the remarkable view along the Vale of Ffestiniog. The Ffestiniog Railway runs through 13½ (22km) scenic miles to Porthmadog, and the more energetic can join a mountain bike trail from Trawsfynydd Holiday Village.

▶ *Unit 3, High Street*

▶ *Continue along the **A470** to Betws-y-Coed.*

❾ Betws-y-Coed, Gwynedd
Betws-y-Coed is a popular inland resort set among forested land and magnificent mountains. The River Conwy is met by three tributaries here, and there are numerous bridges, waterfalls, and river pools with walks and

play areas for children. Upstream are the Swallow Falls, one of the most famous of all tourist attractions in North Wales, and downstream is Fairy Glen, a much photographed and painted beauty spot. Back in the centre of the small town, there are many interesting shops and a craft centre. The 14th-century Church of St Mary has a Norman font and an effigy of the great-nephew of Llywelyn the Great. There is a Motor Museum here.

▶ *Royal Oak Stables*

▶ *Leave Betws-y-Coed on the **A5**, shortly turning right on to the **B5106** and follow it north for 4 miles (6.5km) to Llanrwst.*

❿ Llanrwst, Gwynedd
This historic market town is set in a delightful landscape of hills, forests, rivers and lakes. The bridge was designed by Inigo

The impressive Aber Falls

panzees, birds of prey, a sea lion display and jungle adventure land. Its garden setting enjoys a panoramic view over the North Wales coast and the mountains of Snowdonia to the south.

ℹ️ *Prince's Drive*

▶ *Follow the **B5115** coast road for 6 miles (10km) to Llandudno.*

13 **Llandudno,** Gwynedd

St Tudno gave his name to the town in the 5th century, and a church still stands on the site of his cell. The town is the largest holiday resort in Wales, with two excellent sandy beaches situated between the headlands of Great Orme and Little Orme. The Great Orme Summit Complex can be reached on the Great Orme Tramway, which has been taking passengers up to the top of the 679-foot (207m) summit since 1902. The energetic can enjoy the artificial ski slope and the 2,300-foot (700m) toboggan run, and there are fun rides for the children. Llandudno retains some of its Victorian elegance while catering for modern visitors. Lewis Carroll was a visitor, and Alice Liddell, for whom he wrote *Alice in Wonderland*, stayed here. A White Rabbit statue recalls Carroll's connections with the town, and there is an Alice exhibition in The Rabbit Hole, on Trinity Square.

ℹ️ *Mostyn Street*

▶ *Drive south along the **A546** for 5 miles (8km) to Conwy.*

14 **Conwy,** Gwynedd

Conwy's castle dominates the town, and inside it is a model of the castle and town as they were in the 14th century. This ancient city still has its complete medieval walls, and you can take a pleasant stroll along the ramparts. There are three remarkable bridges crossing the river, including the Conwy Suspension Bridge, designed and built by Thomas Telford in 1826 and renovated in 1990. The smallest house in Britain, a mere 6 feet (2m) wide and 10 feet (3m) high, stands on the quay.

There is a Butterfly Jungle in Bodlondeb Park, where exotic varieties fly freely around in a natural environment.

ℹ️ *Conwy Castle Visitor Centre*

▶ *Head west along the **A55** to Penmaenmawr and further along to Llanfairfechan.*

15 **Llanfairfechan,** Gwynedd

Penmaenmawr has one of the finest beaches in North Wales, stretching between two granite headlands, and this is a fun holiday centre for the children. Further along, at Llanfairfechan, there is a sandy beach and beautiful inland scenery.

There are excellent walks near by, notably up to the Aber Falls, 3 miles (5km) west of the town. The village of Aber was once the location of the palace of the Welsh king, Llywelyn the Great.

▶ *Keep on along the **A55** before turning right on to the **A5122**, passing Penrhyn Castle on the return to Bangor.*

CENTRAL ENGLAND & EAST ANGLIA

This large area of England stretches from the Welsh Borders to the North Sea, and covers a great variety of scenery: volcanic peaks in Shropshire; the steep scarp of the Cotswolds; the lowlands of East Anglia, and the flat Fens near King's Lynn.

The Fens and East Anglia are rich agricultural lands, growing potatoes, sugar beet and flowers and large expanses of prairie-like wheat fields. Further west, in the cattle country of Shropshire and Gloucestershire, the climate is wetter and the countryside takes on a patchwork appearance – in marked contrast to the open landscapes of Norfolk, Suffolk and Lincolnshire. On the higher lands of the Cotswolds, a golden, mellow stone is used to build walls and houses, giving a gentle beauty to farmland, villages and towns. Grand mansions such as Blenheim Palace and imposing churches have been built out of the Cotswold limestone, as have some of the Oxford colleges. Fine churches are characteristic of this area and are generally the result of wealth earned from the sale of wool.

The Cambridge colleges include some of the most impressive buildings in England, but perhaps the most dramatic sight on this flat landscape is Ely cathedral, which can be seen from many miles away. Other striking landmarks on the fenlands are the windmills, which were once vitally important means of pumping away surplus water.

Timber-framed house, Saffron Walden

From Lincoln the landscape changes as the tour moves into Robin Hood country, where a considerable expanse of forest has survived. There are also areas of forest to be seen on the Shrewsbury tour which follows the trail of industrial development, visiting Ironbridge, the birthplace of the 'industrial revolution'. After tracing the achievements of industry you can celebrate a literary genius at Stratford, on the Gloucester tour, where visitors from all over the world make their pilgrimage to the birthplace of William Shakespeare.

Lincoln

Lincoln's fine triple-towered cathedral dominates the city and the surrounding country-side, from its site on a lime-stone ridge overlooking the River Witham. Fascinating old buildings can be seen in the cathedral close, including the old tithe barn and the Bishop's Palace, and the 11th-century castle sits high on the city's steep hill. Don't miss the Museum of Lincolnshire Life, and The Collection, the county's new museum of art and archaeology.

King's Lynn

This historic port and market town grew up in the 'Lin', a marshy area alongside the River Ouse along which ships travelled, bringing wealth into the town. Warehouses and merchants' houses can be seen today, but particularly notable features include the amalgam of buildings forming the Guildhall; the 1683 Custom House, standing alone along-side the quay; and the 12th-century St Margaret's Church.

Ipswich

There has been a settlement here since the Stone Age, but the port's real development started with Anglo-Saxon settlers in the 7th century. Cardinal Wolsey was born here in 1475. Industry has contributed much to the growth of this important regional and shopping centre, and there are some fine old buildings, such as the 16th-century Ancient House and the Custom House. The Ipswich Museum and the Town Hall Galleries are both worth a visit.

Oxford

Oxford is a captivating place. Its ancient university build-ings in their mellow stone have a tranquil dignity, despite being within walking distance of the busy shopping centre. Magdalen, built in the 15th century, is a particularly

King's College Chapel, Cambridge

beautiful college. The 17th-century Ashmolean is Britain's oldest museum and the Bodleian Library, begun in 1598, contains over 5 million books. There are countless other collections and muse-ums and a walk through the streets or along the Cherwell or Thames will convey the city's unique charm.

Gloucester

The Romans built the forti-fied port of Glevum here to aid their attack on Wales; a small part of the wall sur-vives, and there are many more relics to be seen in the City Museum. Gloucester's cathedral is one of the finest in the world, with a massive nave and 14th- to early 15th-century cloisters. The port has

declined in recent years, but be sure to visit the National Waterways Museum in the Llanthony Warehouse.

Shrewsbury

Shrewsbury, on the River Severn, is bordered by park-land and crossed by many bridges. The red sandstone castle guards a narrow strip of land leading into the original town, where there are many fascinating buildings includ-ing Rawley's Mansion and the Lion Coaching Inn, as well as a good selection of modern shops. The famous Shrewsbury School, where Charles Darwin was a pupil, looks down on the town and the river.

Through Fen,
Forest &
Farmland

2 DAYS • 122 MILES • 197KM This is a tour through history and legend, visiting the land of Robin Hood, one of England's most famous folk heroes. It crosses the edge of the fenland region of Britain, taking in the great ducal estates of Nottinghamshire – Clumber Park, Thoresby Hall and Welbeck Abbey – as well as the ancient woodlands of Sherwood Forest.

ITINERARY	
LINCOLN	▶ **Bardney** (10m-16km)
BARDNEY	▶ **Woodhall Spa** (9m-14.5km)
WOODHALL SPA	▶ **Heckington** (16m-26km)
HECKINGTON	▶ **Sleaford** (5m-8km)
SLEAFORD	▶ **Leadenham** (9m-14.5km)
LEADENHAM	▶ **Newark-on-Trent** (10m-16km)
NEWARK-ON-TRENT	▶ **Southwell** (8m-13km)
SOUTHWELL	▶ **Edwinstowe** (16m-26km)
EDWINSTOWE	▶ **North Leverton** (18m-29km)
NORTH LEVERTON	▶ **Dunham Bridge** (7m-11km)
DUNHAM BRIDGE	▶ **Lincoln** (14m-23km)

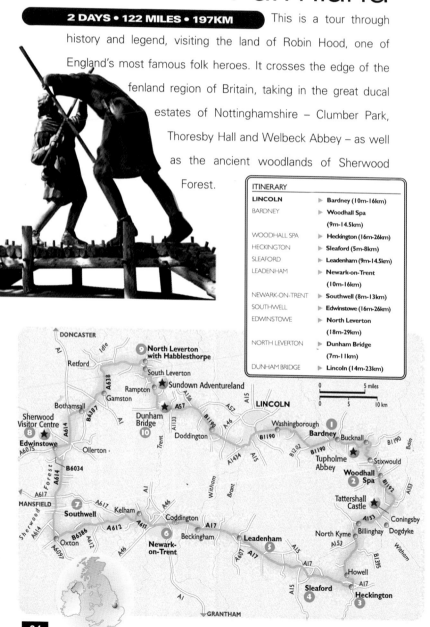

One of the Spitfires housed in the old RAF station at Coningsby

[i] *9 Castle Hill; 21 Cornhill, Lincoln*

▶ *From Lincoln take the B1190 east to Bardney.*

1 Bardney, Lincolnshire

A small fen town on the River Witham, Bardney is dominated by its sugar beet factory, which was opened in 1927. The town's appearance is more practical than beautiful, but some fine examples of Georgian buildings can be seen among the Victorian houses. Bardney Abbey, dating from the 7th century, was destroyed by Vikings and refounded in 1087. Ethelred the Unready built Tupholme Abbey, 2 miles (3km) beyond the river bridge, and restoration work is being carried out here.

BACK TO NATURE

Chamber's Wood, near Bardney, is a Forestry Commission oak woodland which is particularly good for the bird-watcher, especially in the spring when everything is singing. Look for several species of tits as well as chaffinches, woodpeckers, nuthatches and treecreepers. Interesting flowers include giant bellflowers and lilies of the valley.

▶ *Continue along the B1190, then just after Bucknall turn south on to unclassified roads to Woodhall Spa.*

2 Woodhall Spa,
Lincolnshire

This inland watering place was once famous for its natural springs and has a pump room built in the 19th century. Today it is best known for its championship golf-course. The 60-foot (18m) Tower on the Moor is thought to have been erected by the builders of Tattershall Castle, further south, whose fine keep is a relic of the castle built in 1440 by Ralph Cromwell, one of the richest men in the kingdom. He also built a magnificent collegiate church, in which perpetual prayers for his soul were to be said. There are excellent views from the castle looking across the low countryside as far as Lincoln and Boston. The only working fen steam engine in the country is at nearby Dogdyke Pumping Station.

[i] *Iddesleigh Road, Woodhall Spa*

▶ *From Tattershall take the A153, the B1395 at North Kyme, and in a short distance turn right on to an unclassified road, crossing the A17 into Heckington.*

3 Heckington, Lincolnshire

The flat, open and exposed landscape round Heckington is an ideal location for a windmill, and there has been one on the same site since 1830. The Friends of Heckington Windmill have fully restored the present mill, which is the only eight-sailed windmill still working in the country, and was used for drainage as well as grinding corn. One of the several pubs in the village, the Nag's Head, claims that Dick Turpin, the infamous highwayman, once stayed there. The magnificent decorated cruciform church dates from the 14th century.

▶ *Follow the B1394, then the A17 to Sleaford, entering the town on the B1394.*

4 Sleaford, Lincolnshire

Sleaford is a small town set on the River Slea and the partly navigable Sleaford Canal. St Denys' Church, which dominates the town, has a 144-foot (44m) solid stone spire, one of the oldest in the country, and its window tracery is exceptionally fine. The Black Bull Inn's sign dates from 1689 and illustrates

The keep of Tattershall Castle
Opposite: Robin Hood and Little John, Sherwood Visitor Centre

the old sport of bull-baiting, which continued in these parts until 1807. The large mounds beside Castle Causeway are all that remains of the 12th-century castle, where King John was taken ill with a fatal fever on the night after losing the crown jewels while crossing the Wash.

The National Centre for Craft and Design, called the Hub, in Carre Street, is the second largest in the country.

i Money's Yard, Carre Street

the Roman Fosse Way and the Great North Road intersect near by, and the River Trent has been canalised here. The cobble-stoned market-place, the scene of Prime Minister William Gladstone's first major political speech, still survives, and you cannot miss the massive 252-foot (77m) spire of St Mary Magdalen, which is 30 feet (9m) higher than the total length of the church.

i The Gilstrap Centre, Castlegate

▶ Take the **A15** north to rejoin the **A17** and continue to Leadenham.

5 Leadenham, Lincolnshire
This little village grew up along the line of limestone hills called Lincoln Cliff, which stretches from near Humberside as far south as Grantham. It is worth visiting just for the lovely church spire, but there are many attractive stone houses and the Old Hall is built entirely of golden-coloured stone.

▶ Follow the **A17** to Newark-on-Trent via the village of Coddington.

6 Newark-on-Trent,
Nottinghamshire
The sign on the edge of the town reads 'Historic Newark-on-Trent', and this is certainly a treasure house of history. The ruined 12th-century castle is where King John died in 1216, and is opposite the Ossington, a Victorian flight of fancy.

Travellers have been passing through the town for centuries:

▶ Take the **A617** and the **A612** west to Southwell.

7 Southwell,
Nottinghamshire
Visitors to this market town are taken by surprise as the spires of the magnificent Minster suddenly come into view above the rolling countryside. This 12th- and 13th-century building, with a Romanesque nave and transept, is the mother church of Nottinghamshire and replaced an earlier Saxon church. Charles I spent his last few hours of freedom at the Saracen's Head Inn, just along the road, and another famous visitor, the poet Lord Byron, often stayed at Burgage Manor near by – Byron wrote the well-known epitaph for the local carrier, John Adams, who died of drunkenness:

John Adams lies here, of the parish of Southwell,
A carrier who carried his can to his mouth well.

He carried too much, and he carried so fast,
He could carry no more – and so was carried at last.

▶ Take the **B6386** to Oxton, then the **A6097** north which becomes the **A614**, and finally turn left on to the **B6034** to Edwinstowe.

8 Edwinstowe,
Nottinghamshire

Edwinstowe is an old colliery village, and it was at St Mary's Church that Maid Marian is said to have married Robin Hood. The massive and ancient Major Oak, named after Major Rooke, a local 18th-century antiquary, is claimed to be the oldest tree in the forest. Near by is the Sherwood Visitor Centre, where there are walks, nature trails, exhibitions and amusements. Sherwood Forest Village, just down the road, is a holiday complex with indoor facilities.

i Sherwood Heath, Ollerton Roundabout

▷ *Return via the A6075 to the A614 heading north then turn right on to unclassified roads passing Bothamsall, then along the B6387 crossing the A1 to the A638 to Retford. Take unclassified roads east from Retford to North Leverton.*

9 North Leverton,
Nottinghamshire

Dutch-style houses give this village a flavour of Holland, which fits in well with the flat, fenland landscape. A windmill, three storeys high and still in working order, stands above the plain, but is dwarfed by the vast cooling towers of the power station to the north along the Trent valley. Further south is the village of Rampton, surrounded by rich farmland criss-crossed with drainage ditches, used to reclaim the area from marshland.

FOR CHILDREN

Sundown Adventureland is a children's theme park on the road from North Leverton to Rampton. Its many attractions include a pirate ship, Noah's ark, a miniature farm with pets and farm animals, and there are secret passages to explore in a Tudor village.

Lincoln's majestic cathedral soars above the rooftops of the town

▷ *Continue south along unclassified roads then join the A57 to Dunham Bridge.*

10 Dunham Bridge,
Nottinghamshire

Prepare to pay when you cross the River Trent, as a toll is levied here – a rare occurrence on British roads. The A57 out of Dunham runs alongside a major drainage ditch which dates from Roman times. Further along, Doddington brings you back into Lincolnshire. The landscape round here has been drained and cultivated for hundreds of years, and this delightful village has a fine Elizabethan hall as its focal point, with impressive ceramics. A medieval scold's bridle is among many other curiosities.

▷ *Return to Lincoln on the B1190.*

Fen, Farm
& Coast

Through flat fields and across the fenland, you are drawn to the magnificence of Ely's cathedral, then on to the undulating ground of rural Norfolk. The farming landscape continues to the coast, before ending with lavender and a royal residence.

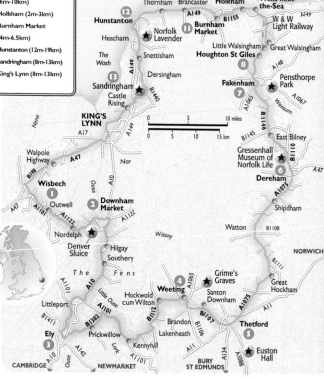

BURNHAM MARKET

2 DAYS • 151 MILES • 243KM

Above: Thetford Forest gives way to natural woodland

tance under Hereward the Wake. Ely also has a parish church, St Mary's, and the vicarage was the home of Oliver Cromwell for 11 years. Nine hundred-year-old Ely Cathedral's greatest glory is its unique octagon, designed by Alan de Walsingham after the earlier tower collapsed in 1322.

i *Oliver Cromwell's House, 29 St Mary's Street*

▶ *Leave Ely on the B1382 through Prickwillow, then take the A1101 to Kennyhill, turning left on to an unclassified road to Lakenheath. Pick up the B1112 as far as Hockwold cum Wilton, and finally another unclassified road to Weeting.*

4 Weeting, Norfolk

Weeting is a good centre for exploring Breckland, a region of heathland that straddles the Suffolk and Norfolk border. Grime's Graves are found here and Thetford Forest Park is at Santon Downham. There are deer and red squirrels in the forest, and a rich variety of trees. Weeting Heath is the place to see the classic Breckland bird, the stone curlew.

FOR HISTORY BUFFS

Grime's Graves, named after the Anglo-Saxon god Grim, are situated on a patch of common land in Breckland. These grassy hollows are about 4,000 years old, and this is the largest known group of flint mines in Britain. You can climb down one on an iron ladder to see where the miners worked with wooden tools or deer antlers.

▶ *Follow an unclassified road and the A1065 to Brandon, then the B1107 to Thetford.*

5 Thetford, Norfolk

Formerly the capital of the region, Thetford is a cathedral city and contained as many as five monasteries. Some of the oldest fragments are the

---

i *The Custom House, Purfleet Quay, King's Lynn*

▶ *Take the A47 to Wisbech, entering via the B198.*

1 Wisbech, Cambridgeshire

Wisbech is at the centre of a rich flower- and fruit-growing area. It was once only 4 miles (6km) from the sea, but due to land reclamation is now 11 miles (17km) inland. The Wisbech and Fenland Museum illustrates local history.

Near by is the Aviation Museum, containing an interesting but rather morbid exhibition of aircraft equipment recovered from crashes in the area. The church has two naves, and a Braille Plan for blind visitors in the garden. The Brinks, two rows of houses along the River Nene, are among the finest examples of Georgian architecture in England, and Peckover House contains fine panelling and furniture; in its garden is the ginkgo, or maidenhair tree – the tallest in the land until a storm took away the top.

---

i *2–3 Bridge Street*

▶ *Follow the A1101, then the A1122 to Downham Market.*

2 Downham Market, Norfolk

There has been a settlement in this area since Roman times. Denver Sluice, 2 miles (3km) away, is where the River Great Ouse and the Old and New Bedford Rivers are regulated in order to prevent flooding. The most interesting building in the town is the Church of St Edmund, with its Early English tower.

▶ *Leave Downham Market eastwards to join the A10 then turn south and follow to Ely.*

3 Ely, Cambridgeshire

Ely ('Eel Island') refers to the staple diet of the Saxons who once lived here. The Fens cathedral city is still a small market centre with ancient buildings and medieval gateways but has a busy quayside. It was founded as a religious community in the 7th century, and during the Norman Invasion was the centre of Anglo-Saxon resis-

A lone windmill stands sentinel in the Fens

remains of the 12th-century Cluniac priory, Castle Hill, the site of Iron-Age earthworks, and a Norman castle mound. You should find time to visit Euston Hall, the 18th-century home of the Duke and Duchess of Grafton, which has some fine paintings by Stubbs, Van Dyck and Lely. The 15th-century timber-framed Ancient House Museum has beautifully carved beamed ceilings and exhibits on local history.

▶ *Leave Thetford on the A1075 heading north to Dereham.*

6 Dereham, Norfolk
St Withburga founded a nunnery here in the 7th century, and St Withburga's Well is in the churchyard of St Nicholas's Church. The town has some fine Georgian buildings, and Bishop Bonner's Cottage has attractive pargeting.

At Gressenhall, on the road north to Fakenham, is the Museum of Norfolk Life, including a farm, which has rare breeds of sheep, cattle, pigs and poultry, and an interesting museum of farming.

▶ *Continue north on the B1110, then take the B1146 to Fakenham.*

7 Fakenham, Norfolk
Fakenham is a delightful small market town which dates from Saxon times. Its parish church has a commanding 15th-century tower, and the two old coaching inns in the Market Place have traces of earlier architecture behind their Georgian façades. The fascinating Gas Museum, which is open on occasional days throughout the summer, explains how gas was made and contains the only complete gasworks in England.

Just a mile (1.6km) away is the Pensthorpe Park, which houses a large selection of birds, and aims to protect waterfowl and wetland habitats.

▶ *Cross the A148 and follow an unclassified road to Houghton St Giles.*

8 Houghton St Giles, Norfolk
The attractive village of Houghton St Giles has old links with Walsingham, including a

❾ Wells-next-the-Sea, Norfolk

The Wells and Walsingham Light Railway runs through 4 miles (6.5km) of countryside to the famous pilgrimage villages of Walsingham, and is the longest 10¼-inch (26cm) narrow-gauge steam railway in the world.

The town of Wells still has many of its 18th- and 19th-century houses, set in a network of alleys and yards near the small quay, which first started trading in wool over 600 years ago.

i Staithe Street

BACK TO NATURE

East of Wells-next-the-Sea, much of the coastline is owned by the National Trust, and there are several miles of nature reserves.

The sand and shingle spit of Blakeney Point can be reached by foot from Cley, or by boat from Blakeney or Morston Quay. Common and sandwich terns nest on the spit, together with waders such as ringed plover and oystercatcher, and several species of duck.

The Norfolk Wildlife Trust reserve at Cley has hides overlooking pools and reedbeds. Bitterns, spoonbills, bearded tits and grey herons are regularly seen and a wide range of waders can be found during migration times.

▶ Follow the **A149** west for 2 miles (3km) to Holkham.

❿ Holkham, Norfolk
In a beautiful deer park with a lake landscaped by Capability Brown, is the 18th-century mansion of Holkham Hall, just south of the village of Holkham. Its art collection includes work by Rubens, Van Dyck and Gainsborough and there is an amazing marble hall. In the Bygones Collection, over 4,000 items have been assembled from kitchens, dairies and cars.

▶ Continue further along the **A149**, then left on to the **B1155** to Burnham Market.

⓫ Burnham Market, Norfolk
Burnham Market is the main village in a group of seven Burnhams, clustered closely together, and has a handsome, wide village green surrounded by elegant 18th-century houses. The Burnhams were made famous by Horatio Nelson, who probably learned to sail on the muddy creeks of the coast before being sent away to sea at the age of 12. He was born in 1758 at Burnham Thorpe, where his father was the rector, and the lectern in the church is made from timbers from his ship, the *Victory*.

▶ Return to the **A149** for 12 miles (19km) to Hunstanton.

⓬ Hunstanton, Norfolk
Hunstanton developed as a seaside resort in the 19th century, and is famous for its red-and-white striped chalk cliffs and excellent beaches. At the Sea Life Centre fish, seals

Bishop Bonner's Cottage at Dereham

small chapel on the old Walsingham Way, known as the Slipper Chapel because pilgrims would remove their shoes before completing their journey barefoot to Little Walsingham, which has been a Christian shrine since 1061. The Anglican Shrine and the Roman Catholic Shrine are at either end of the Holy Mile, and a ruined abbey stands amid pleasant gardens.

Great Walsingham, just a few minutes along the unclassified road from Little Walsingham, is well known for its textile centre, where you can watch the screen-printing process.

▶ Return to the unclassified road from Great Walsingham and continue on this road to Wells-next-the-Sea.

TOUR
16 Fen, Farm & Coast

FOR CHILDREN

Hunstanton is an ideal place for children, with its sandy beach, rock pools and endless entertainment; and the Oasis all-weather leisure centre offers swirl pools, a toddlers' pool and a variety of indoor sports.

SPECIAL TO...

Hunstanton cliffs were laid down on the bed of the sea between 135 and 70 million years ago, in the Cretaceous period. Different colours mark the layers of rock. The carstone is reddish or brown, and is often used locally as a building stone; and most of the chalk is white. It is in the chalk that fossils are found: bivalves similar to those found on the beach today, as well as brachiopods, belemnites and ammonites.

Queen Victoria for the Prince of Wales in 1862. The grounds contain the parish Church of St Mary Magdalene, a museum, nature trails and a playground.

A former royal residence can be seen at Castle Rising, where the splendid Norman castle was built in the 12th century for the Earls of Sussex but later belonged to the Earls of Norfolk. The shell of the Great Hall is still impressive.

▶ Take the B1439 back to rejoin the A149, then an unclassified road back to King's Lynn.

SCENIC ROUTES

Driving anywhere near Ely, the tower of the cathedral will draw you towards it like a magnet.
Near Thetford, dark forests dominate the scene, but there are still a few patches of open heathland.

The seaside resort of Hunstanton
Opposite: fine house in Lavenham

and crabs are all around as you walk through varied marine settings. England's only lavender farm, Norfolk Lavender, is just south of town, at Heacham. A national collection of lavender plants is assembled here, and there is a herb garden with over 50 varieties of culinary and decorative plants.

[i] Town Hall, The Green

▶ Head south on the A149, then the B1440 from Dersingham to Sandringham, and further south to Castle Rising.

RECOMMENDED WALKS

Both the Norfolk Coastal Path and the Peddar's Way can be walked from Hunstanton, the first along the coast and the other through the heart of rural west Norfolk. Wherever you are on this tour of west Norfolk you will find a selection of gentle walks along rivers, across heathland, in the forests or along the coast.

13 Sandringham, Norfolk
The royal estate of Sandringham covers 20,000 acres (8,094 hectares) and was bought by

East Anglia's
Churches & Colleges

Thatch, stone and brick are major features of the villages in this rural area, but dominating the countryside are the churches and their spires. This gentle landscape, covered with colourful fields of rape in spring and wheat in summer, provided the inspiration for Constable's paintings and Brooke's poetry.

2 DAYS • 143 MILES • 230.5KM

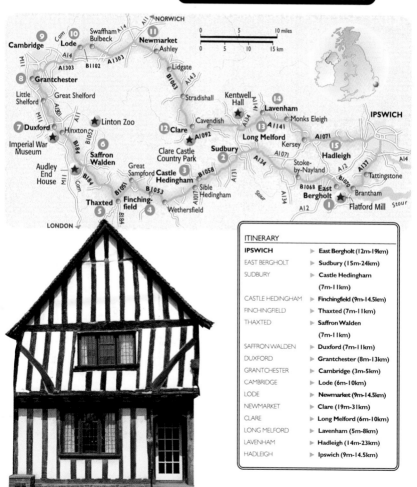

ITINERARY

ℹ️ *St Stephen's Church, St Stephen's Lane, Ipswich*

▶ *Take the A137 from Ipswich, then right on to the B1070 shortly after Brantham and finally an unclassified road via Flatford to East Bergholt.*

❶ East Bergholt, Suffolk

The artist John Constable was born here in 1776 and said of the area: 'These scenes made me a painter'. Clustered round the 15th-century Church of St Mary, with its unfinished tower and remarkable bell house, are Elizabethan cottages set in beautiful gardens. Flatford Mill is now used as a Field Study Centre. Willy Lott's Cottage, an early 18th-century mill-house which appears in Constable's *The Hay Wain*, still stands beside the mill stream.

Thaxted's 15th-century timbered guild house

SPECIAL TO...

Dedham, near East Bergholt, is proud of its connections with the landscape artist John Constable, who went to school here. The beautiful scenery of Dedham Vale is at the heart the area now known as Constable Country.

There is an Art and Craft Centre on three floors of a converted congregational church, and prints, paintings and various crafts are on display and for sale. There is also a toy museum.

RECOMMENDED WALKS

From Flatford Mill there are several beautiful walks in Constable Country. Try the walk to Dedham Mill, a well-known scene to Constable enthusiasts, and only requiring 2 miles (3km) of easy walking.

▶ *Leave on an unclassified road, and cross the A12 on to the B1068 and A134 to Sudbury.*

❷ Sudbury, Suffolk

Charles Dickens used this ancient cloth and market town on the River Stour as the model for 'Eatanswill' in *The Pickwick Papers*. There is a bronze statue of Thomas Gainsborough, the artist, who was born here in 1727, in an elegant Georgian town house now containing many of his paintings. The town was formerly a river port, and one of the old warehouses has been turned into the Quay Theatre. St Peter's Church has fine painted screen panels and a splendid piece of 15th-century embroidery on velvet, the 'Alderman's Pall'.

ℹ️ *Town Hall, Market Hill*

▶ *Leave Sudbury on the A131, turning right on to the B1058 to Castle Hedingham.*

❸ Castle Hedingham, Essex

The De Vere family, Earls of Oxford, built Hedingham Castle on the hilltop in about 1140, and the banqueting hall with its minstrel gallery still survives. The keep overlooks medieval houses, which cluster round the Norman Church of St Nicholas. There are many reminders of the town's prosperous days in the 15th-century Moot Hall and the elegant Georgian houses of the wealthy wool merchants. Just outside the village is the Colne Valley Railway, where there are restored steam engines and carriages.

▶ *Join the A604 south for a short distance, then take unclassified roads on the right via Wethersfield, then right on to the B1053 to Finchingfield.*

❹ Finchingfield, Essex

Finchingfield's charm has survived in spite of its great popularity. One of its many fine buildings is the gabled and barge-boarded Hill House, set opposite a row of 16th-century cottages and Georgian houses. The Church of St John the Baptist has a Norman tower and Georgian-style bell-cote.

▶ *Continue on the B1053 to Great Sampford, then turn left on to the B1051 to Thaxted.*

❺ Thaxted, Essex

Thaxted's 14th-century, cathedral-like flint church is one of the largest in Essex, with a thin, graceful spire rising 181 feet

(55m). Another tall building, the tower windmill, was built in 1804, and now houses a small rural museum. The 15th-century Guildhall is built of local wood and plaster, on a foundation of flint. Composer Gustav Holst once lived in Thaxted, and Sir John Betjeman wrote of it: 'There are few places in England to equal the beauty, compactness and juxtaposition of medieval and Georgian architecture'.

▶ *Head northwest on the B184 to Saffron Walden.*

6 Saffron Walden, Essex
Saffron Walden's flint church rivals that of Thaxted in magnificence and size; 200 feet (61m) long and nearly as high. Its spire was added in 1831. Wool was a major industry here, but the town also prospered from growing saffron for medicine and dyes. There are delightful old narrow streets to explore, and the museum has exhibitions of furniture, ceramics and toys. Jacobean Audley End House, near by, is in grounds landscaped by Capability Brown. Elizabeth I

stayed here with the poet Sir Philip Sidney, in 1578, and the rooms have been laid out to give a 'lived in' feeling.

i *1 Market Place*

FOR CHILDREN

Linton Zoo, north of Saffron Walden on the B1052, was created by the Simmons family and opened in 1972. This is the Cambridgeshire Wildlife Breeding Centre, which focuses on conservation and education. Set in beautiful gardens, the centre has lions, pumas, snakes, owls, spiders and many other animals, as well as a children's play area.

▶ *Continue on the B184 taking the A1301 at M11 junction and, in a short distance, turn left on to an unclassified road through Hinxton to Duxford.*

7 Duxford, Cambridgeshire
Duxford is a small village with a low, squat church and attractive thatched pub, the John Barleycorn. It is famous for the

Imperial War Museum at Duxford Airfield, a former Battle of Britain fighter station.

▶ *Continue along unclassified roads through Little Shelford to Great Shelford, then left on to the A1301 and finally left on to unclassified roads again to Grantchester.*

8 Grantchester, Cambridgeshire
Grantchester was immortalised in a poem by Rupert Brooke in 1912 about the Old Vicarage, where he lived. The village has a characteristic low church, with a small spire protruding.

▶ *Head north to Cambridge.*

9 Cambridge, Cambridgeshire
Cambridge became famous as a seat of learning when the University was established early in the 13th century, and its elegant colleges and chapels of mellow stone give this beautiful city a stately air. But this is an important market centre and a

Duxford Imperial War Museum

Punting along the River Cam under the Bridge of Sighs

leader in high technology industries, as well as a university city, and there are many fine buildings and riverside parklands. King's College Chapel and the Bridge of Sighs are musts for all visitors, and in summer you can punt along the River Cam, which flows around the city. No visit would be complete without seeing the Fitzwilliam Museum, with its priceless collections of porcelain, antiquities, paintings and armour.

BACK TO NATURE

The Fowlmere RSPB Reserve lies just off the Royston to Cambridge road (A10) near the village of Fowlmere. It comprises an area of reed-bed with open water, and attracts breeding birds including sedge and reed warblers. In the winter, look for water rails, kingfishers and bearded tits.

---

i The Old Library, Wheeler Street

▶ *Take the A1303 east, then turn north on to the B1102 to Lode.*

10 Lode, Cambridgeshire
Lode is famous for the Augustinian priory known as Anglesey Abbey, founded in the 12th century and converted into a house in about 1600. The estate was bought by Huttleston Broughton, who created 100 acres (40 hectares) of gardens. A vast collection of paintings, sculpture and *objets d'art* has been assembled inside amid sumptuous furnishings. Lode Watermill has been restored and grinds corn on the first Sunday of each month.

▶ *From Lode follow the B1102 to Swaffham Bulbeck, then follow an unclassified road to the A1303 to Newmarket.*

11 Newmarket, Suffolk
Newmarket has been the headquarters of horse-racing in Britain since the 17th century,

and the National Stud and many training stables are located on the surrounding heath. Guided tours of the Stud are possible by appointment. The National Horse Racing Museum takes you back to the origins of racing.

The famous Rowley Mile is named after a horse owned by Charles II. The Rutland Arms, a former coaching inn has kept some of its rooms in the style of the 1850s.

i Palace House, Palace Street

▶ *Follow the B1063 for 17 miles (27km) to Clare, then eastwards to Cavendish along the A1092.*

12 Clare, Suffolk
This ancient little market town has excellent examples of pargeting – fine plasterwork – such as those seen on the 15th-century Priest's House or Ancient House, now the local museum. The church, which has a most unusual design, is well worth visiting. Norman Clare Castle was built in 1090

Newmarket: the headquarters of horse-racing in Britain

and stands high on a 100-foot (30m) mound.

At Clare Castle Country Park there is a butterfly garden, and you can take a pleasant walk along the old railway track. Three miles (5km) east is Cavendish, the ancestral village of the Dukes of Devonshire. Its attractions include a delightful 16th-century farmhouse just near the church, and philanthropist Sue Ryder's delicate 16th-century rectory, which contains memorabilia and photographs explaining the origins and some of the aims of her work.

▶ *Continue east on the A1092, then turn south on to the A134 to Long Melford.*

13 Long Melford, Suffolk
Long Melford is another of Suffolk's lovely villages, with fine wool merchants' houses. At the end of the mile-long (1.6km) main street is the Church of the Holy Trinity, one of the finest in the country, exhibiting a superb display of flushwork – ornate decoration in flint. The village green is overlooked by Elizabethan Melford Hall, a turreted Tudor mansion with tall chimneys.

One mile (1.6km) north of the village is Kentwell Hall (National Trust), a moated Elizabethan mansion with a brickpaved mosaic maze in the shape of a Tudor rose.

▶ *Follow unclassified roads northeast for 5 miles (8km) to Lavenham.*

14 Lavenham, Suffolk
Lavenham's remarkable church, the Church of St Peter and St Paul, has a flint tower 140 feet (43m) high, and the Guildhall, an early 16th-century timber-framed building, contains a display of local history. The Swan Inn is a famous hostelry which has been carefully preserved. Some of the black-

and-white buildings have been painted pink to add to the colour of this pretty village.

ℹ️ *Lady Street*

RECOMMENDED WALKS

The route from Lavenham to Long Melford, along a disused railway line, gives a gentle 3-mile (5km) walk between two of Suffolk's most appealing small towns.

FOR HISTORY BUFFS

Many of the local towns and villages were important for wool, but the most famous was probably Lavenham. In the time of Henry VIII it was one of the wealthiest towns in England, and the main source of this wealth was wool, yarn and various kinds of cloth.
The town has not changed much since then: there are still half-timbered houses which lean over the narrow streets. Over 300 of the buildings are listed for architectural or archaeological interest.

▶ *Follow the A1141, turning right to pass through Kersey, then continue on the A1071 to Hadleigh.*

15 Hadleigh, Suffolk
Before reaching Hadleigh, enjoy the rural charm of Kersey, with its old priory, ducks paddling in the ford and picturesque, thatched cottages. In Hadleigh itself, the Guildhall and Deanery tower are listed buildings dating from the 15th century. Interesting marks on the side of the 1813 Corn Exchange show where the brickwork was used by schoolchildren for sharpening their slate pencils as they made their way to school.

▶ *Return to Ipswich on the A1071.*

SCENIC ROUTES

The Dick Turpin Heritage Route passes through Saffron Walden and Thaxted, as well as other attractive villages, historic sites and open countryside. On the approach to Thaxted on the B1051, the church and the windmill add variety to the rural charm of the rich farmland.

Cotswold
Wool & Stone

This is mainly a circuit of Cotswold countryside – a landscape of stone walls surrounding fertile fields and distinctive village architecture. The villages contain many fine churches, but the best known structure is the cross in the centre of Banbury. The family homes of two great men can be seen; one Englishman in Blenheim and one American in Sulgrave.

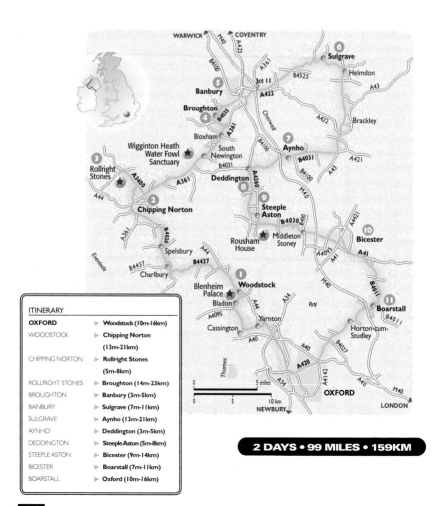

ITINERARY	
OXFORD	▶ **Woodstock (10m-16km)**
WOODSTOCK	▶ **Chipping Norton**
	(13m-21km)
CHIPPING NORTON	▶ **Rollright Stones**
	(5m-8km)
ROLLRIGHT STONES	▶ **Broughton (14m-23km)**
BROUGHTON	▶ **Banbury (3m-5km)**
BANBURY	▶ **Sulgrave (7m-11km)**
SULGRAVE	▶ **Aynho (13m-21km)**
AYNHO	▶ **Deddington (3m-5km)**
DEDDINGTON	▶ **Steeple Aston (5m-8km)**
STEEPLE ASTON	▶ **Bicester (9m-14km)**
BICESTER	▶ **Boarstall (7m-11km)**
BOARSTALL	▶ **Oxford (10m-16km)**

2 DAYS • 99 MILES • 159KM

Bliss Tweed Mill, now flats, near the old wool town of Chipping Norton

i 15 Broad Street, Oxford

▷ *Leave Oxford on the A44 and turn left along an unclassified road towards Cassington. Turn right to Bladon on the A4095, then left on the A44 to Woodstock.*

❶ Woodstock, Oxfordshire
You can stop off in Bladon, to visit the churchyard where Sir Winston Churchill and his wife and parents are buried, before continuing along the road to Blenheim, where he was born. Blenheim Palace was given to the Marlborough family by Queen Anne as a reward for the 1st Duke of Marlborough's victory over the French at Blenheim in 1704.

Just outside the park is the town of Woodstock, with its mellow stone buildings. Kings of England came here for the excellent hunting in the Forest of Wychwood, but modern visitors have gentler interests. A quiet hour can be spent in the Oxfordshire County Museum, in the town centre, where the history of the people and the changing landscape is conveyed in exhibitions ranging from the Stone Age to the present time.

BACK TO NATURE

The grounds of Blenheim Palace, at Woodstock, were landscaped by Capability Brown and comprise rolling, formal parkland and an attractive lake. This harbours breeding dragonflies and is home to Canada geese, mute swans, great crested grebes and kingfishers. In the winter months, look for roaming flocks of siskins, redpolls and long tailed tits in the birch trees.

i Oxfordshire Museum, Park Street

▷ *From Woodstock take the A44 turning left on to the B4437 to Charlbury and then the B4026 to Chipping Norton.*

❷ Chipping Norton, Oxfordshire
Gateway to the Cotswolds and historic market town, this was the market for the sheep farmers of the area, and the wide main street is a relic of those days (the name 'chipping' means market). There are many fine old stone buildings, including the church, market hall, pubs and big houses, but it is the fine wool church which dominates the

town, one of over 40 in the Cotswolds. Paid for by the proceeds from sheep farming, it is mainly 14th- and 15th-century, but much of its stonework has been restored. Another of the town's landmarks is the chimney of Bliss Tweed Mill which is an important reminder of local history.

i The Guildhall

▷ *Take the B4026, then go north along the A3400 for just over a mile (1.6km) and turn left along an unclassified road signed Little Rollright.*

❸ Rollright Stones, Oxfordshire
This Bronze Age circle, which dates from earlier than 1000 BC, was nearly as important as Stonehenge in the neolithic period. Nicknamed the 'King's Men', it measures a full 100 feet (30m) across. Over the road is the King Stone, a monolith, and near by, just along the road, is the group of stones called the Whispering Knights, at the site of a prehistoric burial chamber. The surrounding countryside is

Broughton Castle is a fine example of a gracious Elizabethan Manor

patterned with stone walls of weathered limestone.

▶ *Return to the A3400 and turn south before branching left on to the A361, then turn left in Bloxham along unclassified roads to Broughton.*

FOR CHILDREN

Just before reaching Bloxham, on the road from Rollright to Broughton, you will pass the Wigginton Heath Waterfowl Sanctuary. Conservation is the main aim, with flowers, goats, sheep, lambs and other animals, as well as a bewildering assortment of birds. Various ducks, geese, black swans, owls, doves and peacocks can all be seen at very close quarters. There is also a nature trail and an adventure playground.

---

4 Broughton, Oxfordshire
Broughton Castle is a fortified manor rather than a castle, turned into an Elizabethan house of style by the Fiennes family in about 1600. Surrounded by a great moat lake, it is set in gorgeous parkland, and has a stone church near by. The present owners, Lord and Lady Saye and Sele, are descendants of the family that has lived here for centuries. Celia Fiennes, the 17th-century traveller and diarist, was a member of this family. William de Wykeham, founder of Winchester School and New College, Oxford, acquired the manor and converted the manor house into a castle. The medieval Great Hall is the most impressive room, and suits of armour from the Civil War are on show.

▶ *Drive 3 miles (5km) east along the B4035 to Banbury.*

5 Banbury, Oxfordshire
Banbury is a town of charm and character, with its interesting buildings and narrow medieval streets. Famous for the nursery rhyme 'Ride a cock horse to Banbury Cross', the town is also known for its spice cakes, which have been made here since the 16th century. The unusual church with its round tower replaced an older one demolished in the 18th century. There is still a weekly street market, which has been held regularly for over 800 years, and there used to be a livestock market, too, but nowadays the animals are taken to a permanent site on the edge of town, Europe's largest cattle market.

i Spiceball Park Road

FOR HISTORY BUFFS

Banbury's wool industry was helped by the opening of the Oxford Canal in 1790, connecting the town with the Midland coalfields and markets in London. The narrow boats on the canals used to be pulled by horses which walked along the towpath, and a family would live permanently on the boat.

RECOMMENDED WALKS

Along the Oxford Canal, near Banbury, is the delightful 9-mile (14.5km) Banbury circuit, which takes in the villages of Wroxton with its duckpond, Horley, Hornton, Alkerton, an old Saxon village with ironstone houses, Shennington and Balscott.

▶ Head east along the **A422**. After 2 miles (3km) turn left on to the **B4525**, then to the unclassified road to Sulgrave.

⑥ Sulgrave,
Northamptonshire

The old manor in this attractive stone village was the home of ancestors of George Washington from 1539 to 1659, having been bought by Lawrence Washington, wool merchant and twice Mayor of Northampton. Not to be missed is the family coat of arms with its stars and stripes carved above the entrance porch, and the most treasured possession inside is an original oil painting of George Washington.

▶ Take the unclassified road through Helmdon, heading south to Brackley to join the **A43**, then shortly right on to the **B4031** to Aynho.

⑦ Aynho, Northamptonshire

This limestone village contains apricot trees from which, legend has it, fruit was paid as a toll to the Cartwrights, Lords of the Manor. They lived in the mansion in Aynhoe Park, and there are several memorials to them, including a Victorian marble cross in the church.

▶ From Aynho go west along the **B4031** for 3 miles (5km) to Deddington.

⑧ Deddington, Oxfordshire

Dominating this village, which is built out of the honey-coloured local stone, is the church, with each of its eight pinnacles topped with gilded vanes. Adjacent Castle House was formerly the rectory, and parts of the building date from the 14th century. The area has many links with the days of the Civil War, and Charles I is believed to have slept at the 16th-century Castle Farm near by.

▶ Drive southwards for 5 miles (8km) along the **A4260** and then left on to an unclassified road to Steeple Aston.

⑨ Steeple Aston,
Oxfordshire

Steeple Aston was winner of the Oxfordshire Best Kept Village Award in 1981 and 1983, and is still an eye-catching village. The village inn, Hopcroft's Holt, had associations with Claude Duval, a French highwayman who worked in these parts. Just beyond Steeple Aston is the Jacobean mansion of Rousham House, built by Sir Robert Dormer in 1635 and still owned by the same family. William Kent improved the house in the 18th century by adding the wings and stable block. In the magnificent garden, the complete Kent layout has survived. There is a fine herd of rare Longhorn cattle in the park, and you should be sure not to miss the walled garden.

▶ Another unclassified road leads south on to the **B4030** in turn leading to the **A4095** for the 9 miles (14km) to Bicester.

⑩ Bicester, Oxfordshire

Little can be seen of the Roman town at Alchester, to the south of Bicester, but excavations show that people lived here from about the middle of the 1st century AD until the late Roman period. Bicester's church has elements of a 13th-century building, and there was once a 12th-century priory near by.

▶ Take the **A41** following the line of an old Roman road and then the **B4011** towards Thame before turning sharp right to Boarstall.

⑪ Boarstall, Buckinghamshire

This tiny hamlet is the location of Boarstall Tower, an amazing stone gatehouse which was originally part of a massive fortified house. It dates from the 14th century and is now looked after by the National Trust, who also own Boarstall Duck Decoy. This 18th-century decoy is in 13 acres (5 hectares) of natural old woodland. Attractions include a small exhibition hall, nature trail and bird hide.

▶ Take unclassified roads via Horton-cum-Studley along the edge of Otmoor for the return to Oxford.

The Rural
Heart of England

Across the Severn plain, through | **2 DAYS • 128 MILES • 207.5KM** | a gap in the Malvern Hills and into the Avon valley, this route eventually climbs up on to the hills of the Cotswolds, where stone-built villages have become part of the countryside.

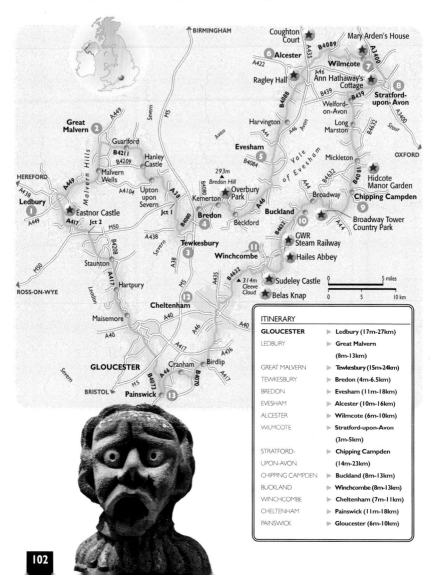

BIRMINGHAM

Coughton Court

Mary Arden's House

6 Alcester

A422
A435
B4089

Wilmcote **7**
A3400

Ragley Hall

A46
Ann Hathaway's Cottage

8
Stratford-upon-Avon
B4439
A3400

B4088
B439
Welford-on-Avon

Great Malvern **2**

A449
Severn
M5

Guarlford
B4211
B4209

Hanley Castle

Harvington
A44
Avon
A46

Long Marston

B4632
Stour

OXFORD

Malvern Wells

Evesham **5**
B4084

Vale of Evesham

Mickleton
B4632
B4081

Hidcote Manor Garden

HEREFORD

A449
Malvern Hills

A4104
Upton upon Severn
A38

293m
Bredon Hill
B4080
Overbury Park

A44
Broadway

Chipping Campden **9**

Ledbury **1**
A438
A417

Eastnor Castle
A449
Jct 2
M50

Jct 1
Kemerton

Bredon **4**
B4080

Beckford

Buckland **10**
B4632
A46

Broadway Tower Country Park

A438

Tewkesbury **3**
Severn
A38

Winchcombe **11**

GWR Steam Railway

Staunton
B4208

A435
B4632

Hailes Abbey

ROSS-ON-WYE
M50

Leadon
A417
Hartpury

Maisemore

Cheltenham **12**
A40

314m
Cleeve Cloud

Sudeley Castle

Belas Knap

0   5 miles
0   5   10 km

A40
A417

A46
B4073

A436

GLOUCESTER
Cranham
Birdlip

B4070
A417

Severn
BRISTOL

Painswick **13**

ITINERARY		
GLOUCESTER	▶	Ledbury (17m-27km)
LEDBURY	▶	**Great Malvern**
		(8m-13km)
GREAT MALVERN	▶	**Tewkesbury (15m-24km)**
TEWKESBURY	▶	**Bredon (4m-6.5km)**
BREDON	▶	**Evesham (11m-18km)**
EVESHAM	▶	**Alcester (10m-16km)**
ALCESTER	▶	**Wilmcote (6m-10km)**
WILMCOTE	▶	**Stratford-upon-Avon**
		(3m-5km)
STRATFORD-UPON-AVON	▶	**Chipping Campden**
		(14m-23km)
CHIPPING CAMPDEN	▶	**Buckland (8m-13km)**
BUCKLAND	▶	**Winchcombe (8m-13km)**
WINCHCOMBE	▶	**Cheltenham (7m-11km)**
CHELTENHAM	▶	**Painswick (11m-18km)**
PAINSWICK	▶	**Gloucester (6m-10km)**

Bredon's medieval tithe barn

ℹ️ *28 Southgate Street*

BACK TO NATURE

The Wildfowl Trust reserve at Slimbridge, southwest of Gloucester off the A38, is known the world over for its impressive collection of wildfowl, at their most spectacular in late winter and early spring when the males are in full breeding plumage.

▶ *Take the A417 for 17 miles (27km) to Ledbury.*

❶ Ledbury, Hereford and Worcester

The unspoilt market town of Ledbury, with its half-timbered buildings, has many literary links: Robert Browning and William Wordsworth used to visit, and John Masefield was born here. Elizabeth Barrett Browning spent her childhood at Hope End, just out of town, and her father lies buried in the north aisle of St Michael's Church. One of the most attractive buildings is the 16th-century Feathers Inn, and Ledbury Park is the house Prince Rupert used as his headquarters during the Civil War. Nineteenth-century Eastnor Castle, with its impressive interior, is surrounded by a beautiful park.

ℹ️ *3 The Homend*

▶ *Follow the A449 through Wynds Gap and Malvern Wells to Great Malvern, 8 miles (13km).*

❷ Great Malvern, Hereford and Worcester

Pure spring water from the Malvern Hills made this a popular spa town in Victorian days. A steep flight of steps by the Mount Pleasant Hotel leads up to St Anne's Well, the source of this water. The town is centred round its greatest treasure, the Priory Church of St Mary and St Michael, which contains exquisite 15th- and 16th-century stained glass and beautiful tiles. Malvern Museum portrays the town through the ages, and there is an elegant Victorian bandstand where bands play on Sunday afternoons in summer.

ℹ️ *21 Church Street*

▶ *Take the B4211 to Upton upon Severn, turning left on to the A4104, and in 1 mile (1.6km) on to the A38 to Tewkesbury.*

❸ Tewkesbury, Gloucestershire

Almost all Tewkesbury's buildings are old timber-framed structures, notably the Bell Inn, and the Royal Hop Pole Inn is mentioned in *The Pickwick Papers* by Charles Dickens. Tewkesbury Abbey is one of the finest Norman abbeys in the country and contains several medieval stained-glass windows.

ℹ️ *Out of the Hat, Church Street*

▶ *Return on the A38 for a short distance, then take the B4080 to Bredon.*

❹ Bredon, Hereford and Worcester

Bredon, alongside the River Avon, at the foot of Bredon Hill, is a picturebook village. Its impressive Norman church has a graceful spire which soars 160 feet (48m) high, and the tithe barn dates from the 14th century. A mile (1.6km) east is the village of Kemerton, with its fine church. Overbury Park, just outside the village, leads to Bredon Hill, which rises to 961 feet (293m). It has a fine Gothic folly on its slopes and the remains of prehistoric and Roman earthworks on its summit.

▶ *Continue along an unclassified road through Kemerton and Beckford, then take the **A46** to Evesham.*

5 **Evesham,** Hereford and Worcester

Evesham is a market town in the heart of the Vale of Evesham, noted for its fruit blossom in spring. A 15th-century half-timbered gateway in the market-place is one of the few remains of Evesham Abbey.

At the centre of town is the 110-foot (33m) high Bell Tower, which was built in 1539. There are two fine churches: 12th-century All Saints' Church and the Church of St Lawrence. A plaque near the river marks the burial spot of Simon de Montfort, the 'father of the English parliament', who led barons in revolt against Henry III and was killed at the Battle of Evesham in 1265.

[i] *The Almonry, Abbey Gate*

▶ *Take the **B4088** and an unclassified road to Alcester.*

6 **Alcester,** Warwickshire

Pronounced 'Olster', this former Roman town contains many old streets and houses, notably Malt

Mill Lane, which is lined with ancient houses. Coughton Court, 2 miles (3km) to the north, is the family home of the Throckmortons, who were implicated in the Gunpowder Plot to blow up Parliament in 1605. The house contains the 'Throckmorton coat', which was made in 1811 to prove that it was possible to take the wool off a sheep and produce a coat from it in one day! Southwest of town is Ragley Hall, a Jacobean mansion whose great hall is decorated with exquisite rococo plaster-work.

▶ *Follow the **B4089**, then unclassified roads east to Wilmcote.*

7 **Wilmcote,** Warwickshire

This sprawling village is best known for the lovely timbered farmhouse which was the home of Mary Arden, Shakespeare's mother. It is now a museum of furniture and the farm buildings contain exhibitions of agricultural implements and country bygones, including man traps

The unpretentious simplicity of Mary Arden's home, Wilmcote

which were used to catch poachers.

▶ *Continue along the unclassified road, then the **A3400** for 3 miles (5km) to Stratford-upon-Avon.*

8 **Stratford-upon-Avon,** Warwickshire

Stratford has retained its role as a market town despite being one of the world's most famous tourist centres. Shakespeare's Birthplace in Henley Street is now a museum and contains exhibits about the poet's life. Stratford is full of interesting places to visit, including the Royal Shakespeare Company Collection. One of the most ornate timbered houses is Harvard House, the former home of the mother of John Harvard, a benefactor of Harvard University in the US. A visit would not be complete without seeing a show at the Royal Shakespeare Theatre beside the River Avon.

[i] *Bridgefoot*

SPECIAL TO...

Shakespeare's Stratford is probably one of the best known towns in England. A tour of selected locations can take you through his life, starting with his birthplace in Henley Street, then on to the 15th-century half-timbered Grammar School in Church Street, which he attended. Most famous of all is Anne Hathaway's cottage, home of the woman he was to marry. New Place, on Chapel Street, was the site of his last home.

▶ *Leave Stratford, going west along the **B439** for 4 miles (6km) before turning south along unclassified roads through Welford-on-Avon and Long Marston to the **B4632**. Turn right and soon left on to the **B4081** to Chipping Campden.*

9 **Chipping Campden,** Gloucestershire

Wool made this town rich, and it retains a wealth of beautiful architecture such as the Jacobean Market Hall in the

Anne Hathaway's House, Shottery, where she lived before her marriage to William Shakespeare

High Street, which was built in 1627 by Sir Baptist Hicks. Other buildings of note are the Woolstaplers' Hall and Grevel House. The Church of St James is one of the most splendid Cotswold churches. Hidcote Manor Garden, to the northeast has six gardens with winter borders, terraces and walks.

▶ *Take the B4081 and the A44 through Broadway, then the B4632 and a minor road to Buckland.*

⑩ **Buckland,**
Gloucestershire

Buckland is a quiet village nestling at the foot of the Cotswolds. The rectory here, is England's oldest and it is the most complete medieval parsonage. Further along the B4632 is the GWR Steam

Railway at Toddington, where you can make a 6-mile (9km) round trip.

Leave the B4632 to visit Hailes Abbey, where the old Cistercian ruins stand alongside the 12th-century parish church. In 1270, a small jar of blood, supposedly that of Christ, was given to the abbey, and brought it much fame as a centre of pilgrimage.

FOR CHILDREN

Broadway Tower Country Park, to the east of Buckland, is an ideal place to spend the day with the family. The late 18th-century mock castle has an observation room and telescope giving views over 13 counties. Other attractions include an educational display of local geology, an adventure playground, and a collection of rare animals.

▶ *Follow the unclassified road to Winchcombe, a distance of 8 miles (13km).*

⑪ **Winchcombe,**
Gloucestershire

This attractive town was once the capital of the Kingdom of Mercia. Its abbey, founded in 797, was destroyed during the Dissolution, but the site has been excavated. The Railway Museum has many relics of the steam age, and the town hall houses the Folk Museum and a Police Museum.

Sudeley Castle, reached through the village, was once the house of Catherine Parr, the last of Henry VIII's wives. The magnificent gardens have been developed and renovated.

Just east of town on the B4632, at the top of the hill at Cleeve Hill, are the remnants of a settlement and earthworks, and much good walking, including the Cotswold Way, a long distance footpath. Cleeve Cloud,

1,031 feet (314m), is one of the highest points in the Cotswolds, and the views from its summit are quite spectacular.

FOR HISTORY BUFFS

From Winchcombe you can drive to within three-quarters of a mile (1km) of the Bronze Age ancient long barrow at Belas Knap on its hilltop site, probably the finest example of a false-entrance longbarrow in the Cotswolds. When it was excavated 36 skeletons were found in 10 separate chambers.

⊡ *Town Hall, High Street*

▶ *Continue along the B4632 to Cheltenham.*

⓬ Cheltenham,
Gloucestershire
Cheltenham started life as a typical Cotswold village, but the discovery of a mineral spring here, in 1718, turned it into a fashionable spa. The Promenade, an elegant, wide street lined with Regency

Below: Hailes Abbey, Winchcombe
Right: Bridgnorth open-air market

houses, has been described as the most beautiful thoroughfare in Britain. The famous Pittville Pump Room, with its colonnade and dome, is a masterpiece of 19th-century Greek revival. Cheltenham has many places worth visiting, such as the Holst Birthplace Museum, which contains rooms with period furnishing. The town is famous for its two schools, the College for Boys and Cheltenham Ladies' College.

⊡ *77 Promenade*

▶ *Take an unclassified road then the A417 south to Birdlip and follow the Stroud road until an unclassified road leads through Cranham and on to the A46 to Painswick.*

⓭ Painswick,
Gloucestershire
Painswick is an old wool town with many buildings of note, but is dominated by 15th-century St Mary's Church and its collection of '99' yew trees. Local tradition says that only 99 will grow at any one time – the Devil always kills off the 100th. Among Painswick's many old houses are Court House, resplendent with its tall

chimneys, and 18th-century Painswick House. South of town a few old cloth mills have survived on Painswick stream.

▶ *Return to Gloucester on the B4073.*

SCENIC ROUTES

Cotswold villages and towns are all attractive but the view over Cranham from the unclassified road to Painswick is one of the most exciting. The Malvern Hills and the dramatic silhouette of the Herefordshire Beacon (the British Camp) are best seen along the A449 from Ledbury.

RECOMMENDED WALKS

Footpaths on this tour range from very easy gentle strolls to much longer and arduous walks. A climb to the top of the Worcestershire Beacons in the Malverns will give one of the finest views in England, with the green undulations of Hereford to the west and the flatter Severn Valley to the east.

Old Volcanoes
& Bridges in
Shropshire

1/2 DAYS • 102 MILES • 165KM

The Welsh border counties are among the greenest parts of Britain. Gentle hills and steep-sided volcanic cones add variety to the scenery. The Severn Valley is the birthplace of the industrial revolution.

ITINERARY		
SHREWSBURY	►	**Acton Burnell (8m-13km)**
ACTON BURNELL	►	**Church Stretton**
		(9m-14.5km)
CHURCH STRETTON	►	**Craven Arms (8m-13km)**
CRAVEN ARMS	►	**Ludlow (7m-11km)**
LUDLOW	►	**Cleehill (6m-10km)**
CLEEHILL	►	**Bewdley (15m-24km)**
BEWDLEY	►	**Bridgnorth (14m-23km)**
BRIDGNORTH	►	**Shipton (10m-16km)**
SHIPTON	►	**Much Wenlock (6m-10km)**
MUCH WENLOCK	►	**Ironbridge (4m-6.5km)**
IRONBRIDGE	►	**Wroxeter (10m-16km)**
WROXETER	►	**Shrewsbury (5m-8km)**

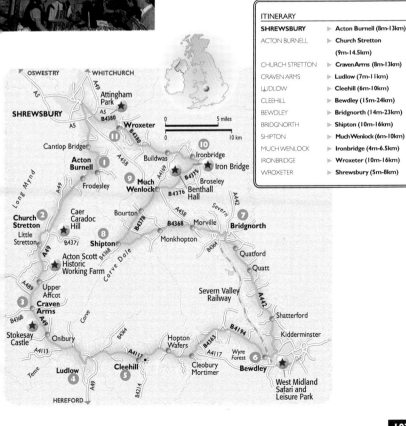

i *The Music Hall, The Square, Shrewsbury*

▶ *Take the A458 to the ring road where unclassified roads lead to Cantlop Bridge and Acton Burnell, 8 miles (13km).*

❶ Acton Burnell, Shropshire
On the edge of this picturesque village, with its timber-framed black-and-white cottages and grey-green stone buildings, is a cast-iron bridge, built in 1810 to a design by Thomas Telford. Acton Burnell Castle is a red sandstone ruin, which dates from the 13th century; it is said the first English Parliament met here in 1283. The Church of St Mary is almost entirely 13th-century, apart from its Victorian tower, and contains memorials to the Burnell family who held the manor in 1183. It also houses memorials to the Lees family, who owned the village in the 17th century and who were ancestors of General Robert E Lee, chief commander of the Southern forces in the American Civil War.

▶ *Follow unclassified roads via Frodesley then the A49 to Church Stretton, 9 miles (14.5km).*

❷ Church Stretton, Shropshire
Church Stretton is in fact three settlements. All Stretton lies to the north of the main town, and Little Stretton stands 1½ miles (2.5km) south. The town's medieval remains are in the High Street, along with its 18th- and 19th-century buildings. The Church of St Laurence is partly 12th-century Norman with a 14th-century roof. In the south transept is a memorial to Sarah Smith, the Victorian novelist who wrote under the name of Hesba Stretton. The town was popular with Victorians, who came to sample its natural spring water.

▶ *Continue south along the B4370, joining the A49 to Craven Arms.*

---

❸ Craven Arms, Shropshire
This small village was originally the hamlet of Newton, but in the 19th century it developed and was named after a coaching inn. Today it is a centre for live-stock auctions, at the foot of Wenlock Edge, a steep outcrop of limestone. Stokesay Castle, half a mile (1km) along the road, is the best preserved and the oldest example of a fortified manor house in England.

▶ *Keep on with the A49 a further 7 miles (11km) to Ludlow.*

❹ Ludlow, Shropshire
Ludlow is a pearl in a sea of riches and has been described as 'the perfect historic town', with nearly 500 listed buildings. Two buildings worthy of a visit are

---

Ludlow Castle, which dates from Norman times, and the magnificent sandstone Church of St Laurence. Mainly 15th-century, it is the largest in the county and the ashes of the poet A E Housman lie in its churchyard. Near by are the 17th-century Feathers Hotel and the beautiful black-and-white Reader's House. Ludlow Museum, in Buttercross, tells the story of the town from Norman times, and a major arts festival takes place here in late June and early July.

i *Castle Street*

▶ *Take the A4117 going east for 6 miles (10km) to Cleehill.*

Reader's House, Ludlow, has a three-storey Jacobean porch

5 Cleehill, Shropshire

East of Cleehill, on the A4117, is an AA Viewpoint which offers amazing views over Tenbury and the Teme Valley, towards the hills in the distance. The strange 'golf ball' on 1,750-foot (533m) Titterstone Clee Hill, north of the village, is part of a satellite tracking station. Further along the A4117, running east, is Cleobury Mortimer, with its remarkable twisted wooden church tower. Hugh de Mortimer built a fortress here in 1160 and its earthworks can still be seen near the church.

▶ *Follow the B4363 turning right on to the B4194 through Wyre Forest to Bewdley.*

6 Bewdley, Hereford and Worcester

This elegant Georgian town was a major port of England in the 17th and 18th centuries. For many years boats were man-handled up the River Severn by a hardy breed of boatmen called 'bow hauliers'. There are pleasant walks in the Wyre Forest, and the Severn Valley Railway runs to Bridgnorth through fields and woods. Near by is West Midland Safari and Leisure Park, with animal reserves and amusements.

BACK TO NATURE

West of Bewdley is Wyre Forest, all that remains of a vast royal hunting forest mentioned in the Domesday Book. It is an area of mixed heath, scrub and oak woodland, with plantations of Douglas fir and larch, where fallow deer roam and silver-washed fritillary butterflies glide.

ⓘ *Bewdley Museum, Load Street*

▶ *Take the B4190 towards Kidderminster turning left on to unclassified roads towards Shatterford, then turning left on to the A442 to Bridgnorth.*

7 Bridgnorth, Shropshire

There are two parts to this historic market centre, connected by a winding main road, a cliff railway and a steep flight of steps. The original settlement was in the High Town, where Bridgnorth Castle was built. The only remaining fragment is the leaning tower, which is set at a steeper angle than the Leaning Tower of Pisa. The most graceful building is Italianate St Mary Magdalene's Church, built in 1792 by Thomas Telford. For railway enthusiasts there is not only the Severn Valley Railway, but also the funicular, linking the upper and lower parts of the town. In Low Town is Bishop Percy's House, a fine half-timbered building of 1580.

ⓘ *The Library, Listley Street*

▶ *Leave Bridgnorth on the A458, then after 3 miles (5km) turn left at Morville on to the B4368 to Shipton.*

8 Shipton, Shropshire

Set in the heart of Corve Dale, with views of Brown Clee Hill to the south, this small village sits

Stokesay Castle is really a fortified manor house

The town of Ironbridge, famous for its bridge, took a leading role in the Industrial Revolution

snugly in the midst of the green fields and valley. Shipton Hall is the focal point, a beautiful complex of stone buildings dating from 1587. There is an attractive walled garden, medieval dovecote and old parish church, as well as a fine 18th-century stable block.

▶ Take the **B4378** to Much Wenlock

🖲 Much Wenlock,
Shropshire
This charming market town has many half-timbered buildings, notably the Manor House, the Guildhall and Raynald's Mansion. Ruined Wenlock Priory was founded by St Milburga in the 7th century as a convent and destroyed by Danes in the 9th century. It was rebuilt by Lady Godiva and her husband, in the 11th century, though it was soon destroyed again by the Normans. Benthall Hall, 4 miles (6.5km) northeast, is a 16th-century house with fine panelling and mullioned windows.

[i] The Museum, High Street

▶ Leave Much Wenlock on the **B4376**, turning left on to the **B4375**. In a short distance turn left on to an unclassified road to Ironbridge.

🔟 Ironbridge, Shropshire
Ironbridge was at the forefront of the Industrial Revolution. Its splendid iron bridge over the River Severn, the first of its kind in the world, was built in 1778 by Abraham Darby to enable traffic to pass across the river without interrupting its navigation. West of Ironbridge, the B4380 brings you to Buildwas, where the bridge over the Severn is a 1906 replacement of Telford's original one. The ruins of nearby 12th-century Buildwas Abbey, now roofless and without its aisle walls, are a striking contrast to the enormous cooling towers of the power station downstream. Stone from the ruin was incorporated in the local church.

⟨i⟩ *Tollhouse*

▶ *Continue for 2 miles (3km) on an unclassified road to take the B4380 to Wroxeter.*

Ⅲ Wroxeter, Shropshire
Near this quiet little village is the Roman town of Viroconium, which was the fourth largest town in Roman Britain. A walk round the site reveals the baths, a market hall and fragments of other buildings. The most impressive relic of the baths is the 20-foot (6m) wall, where a square entrance once had double doors leading to the *frigidarium* or 'cooling off' room. A museum displays pottery, painted plaster and coins from the site.

Two miles (3km) northwest on the B4380 is Atcham, where Attingham Park features magnificent gardens, woodlands and a deer park. The gardens are open throughout the year, and the house contains a fine collection of early 19th-century English and Italian furniture. Parts of the red sandstone 13th-century Church of St Eata were built with stones from the ruins of *Viroconium*.

▶ *Continue along the B4380 to return to Shrewsbury, 5 miles (8km).*

SCENIC ROUTES

In the Shipton area the scenery is gentle and the B4378 to Much Wenlock runs through Corve Dale, with fine views of the River Corve. From Acton Burnell to Church Stretton, along the A49 and the unclassified road, the views are spectacular, with Long Mynd to the west and Caer Caradoc Hill, where it is thought the Romans defeated the British leader Caractacus in AD 50, to the east.

RECOMMENDED WALKS

The Shropshire Way is a long-distance walk from Whitchurch through Shrewsbury to Clun and the Clee Hills. There are several walks around Ludlow, notably across the Teme and on to Whitcliffe Common, which was the town's common land in the Middle Ages, and the Forestry Commission have several attractive, clearly marked walks, such as from the Wyre Forest centre near Bewdley.

The ruins of Wenlock Priory

SPECIAL TO...

Six miles (10km) of the Severn Valley changed the world as a result of industrial developments in the late 18th and 19th centuries. Here, the past is portrayed in the museums of Ironbridge, Coalbrookdale, Jackfield and Coalport.
The Ironbridge Gorge Museum was one of the first World Heritage Sites in Britain, and one ticket admits you to the bridge, the Darby furnace, Blists Hill, Coalport China Museum, the tile museum, Rosehill House and elsewhere. The ticket is valid indefinitely.

THE NORTH

The North of England is noted for the old industrial towns of Lancashire and Yorkshire, where communities developed in the wake of the coal mining, engineering, woollen and cotton manufacturing industries. They have become modern thriving towns, while retaining much of historical interest, including relics of the industrial revolution. Surrounding these urban areas are some of the finest expanses of British countryside, especially in the Lake District, which has spellbound the adventurous traveller since the earliest days of tourism, and the Pennines, known as 'the backbone of England'.

Visitors from all over the world are attracted by the scenic beauties of the Lake District, with its mountains, still lakes and villages which seem to have grown out of this rocky landscape. Stone walls can be seen stretching skywards over all but the highest hills, in an area where beauty inspired Wordsworth and other writers and poets, bringing walkers and climbers in their droves.

Dry stone walls at Grassington

The Lake District villages are generally built of lava or slate, except in Eskdale, to the west, where pink granite is found, but those in the Pennines are quite different: dark and somewhat forbidding in areas of millstone grit, or light and cheery where carboniferous limestone is the local rock. Old quarries and mines are dotted around the hills, and the higher parts of the Pennines become moorland, often bleak and isolated.

Down in the valleys, conditions are kinder to man and animals, and on the lowlands which surround these hill masses there is much rich farming, generally of cattle and sheep, which appreciate the lush grasslands. The larger lowlands, such as the Vale of York, the Lancashire and Cheshire Plain and lowlands of Solway, are where most of the large towns have grown up.

Carlisle

The regional capital of Cumbria is a well-placed city, with the Lake District to the south and Hadrian's Wall to the north. Carlisle's castle has been a border fortress since Norman times, and its detailed history is portrayed in an exhibition in the keep. A military museum, dedicated to the Border regiments, is also housed here. The cathedral is one of England's smallest, and has remarkable carved choir stalls. Near by is the Carlisle Cross, where servants were once hired, and where Bonnie Prince Charlie stood to claim the throne of England in 1745.

Ripon

Ripon is a busy little town, dominated by its cathedral, one of the oldest in England. An ancient Saxon crypt, thought to date from AD 672, lies beneath the cathedral, and inside fine features include a 16th-century Gothic nave. Another ancient building is the Wakeman's House, built in the 14th century for the man who would 'set the watch' by blowing a horn at 9pm every evening – a practice which continues today. An inscription on the 19th-century Town Hall reminds residents that 'Except ye Lord keep ye cittie, ye Wakeman waketh in vain'. The Prison and Police Museum is well worth a visit.

Morecambe

This Victorian seaside resort overlooks Morecambe Bay, with its miles of sand, and the Lake District hills are clearly visible to the north. Traditionally a holiday centre for visitors from northern England, Morecambe retains its popularity, and the late weeks of the summer season have the added attraction of 'illuminations'. Another feature Morecambe has to offer its visitors is the new seafront promenade where sculptures are displayed.

Ashness Bridge, Derwent Water

Macclesfield

This old textile town made its name from the manufacture of silk, and there are still some of the 18th- and 19th-century mills on the steep streets overlooking the Bollin Valley. The story of silk can be seen in the award-winning Silk Museum, and you can visit the Paradise Mill, a working mill until 1981. Macclesfield's other outstanding attraction is the church, originally founded in the 13th century, which sits high above the town and can be reached by climbing 108 steps.

York

It was the Vikings who established the settlement of Jorvik, which was developed by the Normans as the capital of the north. History lives in every street of this glorious city, which celebrates its 10th-century origins in the time-travelling Jorvik Viking Centre and re-creates whole streets from the past in the York Castle Museum. But the greatest treasure is York Minster, the largest medieval cathedral in northern Europe, whose grandeur and beauty are unsurpassable. You will need a long stay to see everything of interest in York: medieval houses overhanging the narrow Shambles; the extensive city walls; and the National Railway Museum, a favourite with children and railway buffs, are only a few of its wealth of attractions.

The Heart of
Lakeland

Leave the soft red sandstones of Carlisle and the Eden Valley to weave through hills of volcanic rocks and lakes carved out during the last Ice Age, before heading into the Pennines, with their different, gentler beauty.

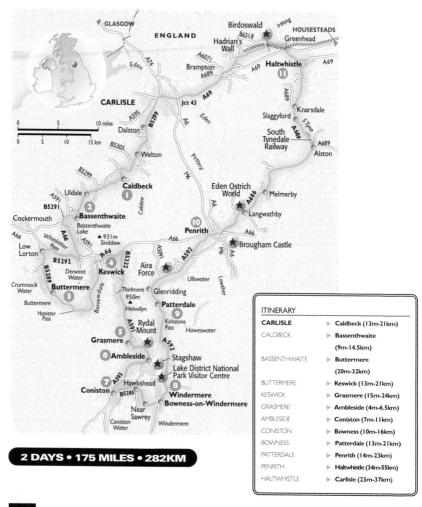

ITINERARY

CARLISLE	▶	**Caldbeck** (13m–21km)
CALDBECK	▶	**Bassenthwaite** (9m–14.5km)
BASSENTHWAITE	▶	**Buttermere** (20m–32km)
BUTTERMERE	▶	**Keswick** (13m–21km)
KESWICK	▶	**Grasmere** (15m–24km)
GRASMERE	▶	**Ambleside** (4m–6.5km)
AMBLESIDE	▶	**Coniston** (7m–11km)
CONISTON	▶	**Bowness** (10m–16km)
BOWNESS	▶	**Patterdale** (13m–21km)
PATTERDALE	▶	**Penrith** (14m–23km)
PENRITH	▶	**Haltwhistle** (34m–55km)
HALTWHISTLE	▶	**Carlisle** (23m–37km)

2 DAYS • 175 MILES • 282KM

i Carlisle Visitor Centre, Old Town Hall, Green Market, Carlisle

► Take the **B5299** south from Carlisle to Caldbeck.

1 Caldbeck, Cumbria
This stone-built village is set in undulating countryside with the Lake District hills to the south. In the churchyard is the grave of John Peel, who was buried here in 1854. The famous huntsman inspired his friend, John Woodcock Graves, to write the song '*D'ye ken John Peel*'. There is a plaque outside the house where Graves composed the song.

► Continue on the **B5299** before branching left on to unclassified roads through Uldale to Bassenthwaite.

2 Bassenthwaite, Cumbria
Bassenthwaite is situated off the A591. 'Thwaite' is a Norse word for a clearing in the forest, and is found in many village names in the area. Bassenthwaite Church, 3 miles (5km) south, was founded in the 12th or 13th century and retains its Norman chancel arch and many Early English features. Nearby Lake Bassenthwaite is a large ice-cut lake, and towering above its western shore is Skiddaw, one of only three Lake District hills higher than 3,000 feet (931m).

► Leave Bassenthwaite on unclassified roads towards the **B5291** round the northern shores of the lake, then take the **A66** south to Braithwaite. Continue on the **B5292** and over Whinlatter Pass to Low Lorton then left on to the **B5289** to Buttermere.

3 Buttermere, Cumbria
The tiny village of Buttermere stands in the heart of spectacular landscape. A stiff climb to Whinlatter Pass, beyond the Forestry Commission's Visitor Centre, takes you on to wild moorland. The surrounding hills, Red Pike and High Stile, tower over the flat green valley floor, with impressive waterfalls such as Scale Force. The B5289 takes you through Borrowdale, a valley which is reached by crossing 1,174-foot (358m) Honister Pass. Dark rocks tower above the skyline and quarries scar the landscape where Borrowdale rock, formed by volcanic activity about 500 million years ago, is extracted. This famous rock is used in buildings as far away as Dallas and Hong Kong, and you can buy small souvenirs from many of the local shops. The southern end of the valley is dominated by the summits of 2,560-foot (780m) Glaramara and 2,986-foot (910m) Great End.

► Take the **B5289** to Keswick.

Crummock Water, Buttermere

4 Keswick, Cumbria
The capital of the northern Lake District now caters for walkers, climbers and holiday-makers, but one of its oldest industries is the manufacture of coloured pencils, which originally used local graphite. The Cumberland Pencil Factory has a museum and among its exhibits is the world's largest pencil.

On a hill to the east of Keswick is Castlerigg Stone Circle, a prehistoric monument in a setting of magical beauty. Cumbrian folklore claims that the famous great stones were once men who were turned into boulders by witches.

i The Moot Hall, Market Square

► Take the **A66** for 4 miles (6.5km), then turn right on to the **B5322** through St John's in the Vale and then the **A591** south to Grasmere.

5 Grasmere, Cumbria
Grasmere's hills and lakes are a real tourist magnet. William Wordsworth wrote much of his greatest verse here, and his friends Coleridge, de Quincey and Southey were inspired by the location. Dove Cottage, where Wordsworth lived with his sister Dorothy, is open to the public and contains relics of his

life and times. A few miles further along the A591 is Rydal Mount, where Wordsworth lived from 1813 until his death in 1850. It houses many of the family's belongings and has a beautiful view of tranquil Rydal Water.

i Redbank Road

SPECIAL TO...

For over a hundred years, Grasmere gingerbread has been made in the village. The recipe is such a closely guarded secret it has to be kept in the vaults of a local bank!
The rush-bearing ceremony, held every year, involves the carrying of elaborately decorated bundles of rushes to the church, after which the bearers are rewarded with a piece of delicious gingerbread.

▶ Continue to Ambleside.

6 Ambleside, Cumbria
Ambleside is a major Lake District centre at the northern end of Lake Windermere. Its

Mysterious Castlerigg Stone Circle

many stone houses include Bridge House, the smallest in the Lake District. Built on a tiny bridge over the Stock Ghyll, it is now owned by the National Trust and is open to the public. In the town library are the relics excavated from the Roman site of Galava Fort, at Borrans Park, and the woodland gardens of Stagshaw, just south of the town, have superb views of the lake.

i Central Buildings, Market Cross

▶ Leave on the A593 to Coniston.

7 Coniston, Cumbria
Coniston Water is famous as the place where Donald Campbell set a new world record and later died in 1967. The Steam Yacht *Gondola*, an 1859 steam launch, has been restored, and now takes passengers on regular scheduled trips around the lake.

A little further on, at Hawkshead, is the Beatrix Potter Gallery; at Hill Top, in Near Sawrey, Potter wrote some of her world-famous children's stories. The house is open to the public.

i Ruskin Avenue

▶ Take the B5285 to the Windermere ferry.

8 Bowness and Windermere, Cumbria
The ferry across Lake Windermere to Bowness was restored in 1990 and leads to this small town with its narrow streets and fine 15th-century church.

Windermere, just north of Bowness, is a focal point in the Lake District for sailing and boating. The Steamboat Museum, at Rayrigg Road, has a collection of Victorian and Edwardian boats, many of which still float and are in working order. The lake has 14 islands, including Belle Isle, a privately owned estate with a round 18th-century mansion house.

i Glebe Road, Bowness-on-Windermere; Victoria Street, Windermere

---

RECOMMENDED WALKS

For a gentle walk, follow the footpath opposite the railway station in Windermere to the top of Orrest Head, 784 feet (239m), where there are fine views of the lake and Belle Isle.

Dove Cottage, Grasmere

▶ *Take the A592 north to Patterdale.*

9 Patterdale, Cumbria
Patterdale was named after St Patrick, who is said to have walked here after being shipwrecked on Duddon Sands in AD 540. St Patrick's Church, built in 1853, is notable for its tapestries by embroidress Ann Macbeth, who lived here until her death in 1948. This attractive village is at the head of Ullswater, a popular boating lake. A steamer plies from the pier at Glenridding to the opposite end of the lake, and the scenery is dominated by 3,117-foot (950m) Helvellyn. At the foot of the sheer eastern slopes is

Red Tarn, a corrie lake in a hollow scooped out of solid rock during the Ice Age. Two miles (3km) from Glenridding is Aira Force, and it was here that Wordsworth was inspired to write his 'host of golden daffodils'.

[i] *Main Car Park, Glenridding*

▶ *Take the A592 alongside Ullswater to Penrith.*

10 Penrith, Cumbria
Penrith was the capital of Old Cumbria, and there are remains of buildings suggesting its former importance. The 12th-century ruins of Brougham Castle are just outside the town, and remnants of a Roman fort built by Agricola are near by. The Gloucester Arms, dating from 1477, is one of the oldest inns in England, and the Duke of Gloucester, later Richard III, is said to have lived here. Three miles north at Langwathby is Eden Ostrich World, with rare farm animals, a giant maze and tractor rides. The wild, open spaces round Penrith may be bleak, even in summer, and crossing the Pennines can prove difficult in winter.

[i] *Robinson's School, Middlegate*

▶ *Follow the A686 through Langwathby towards Alston. Turn left on to the A689 then*

right along an unclassified road to Haltwhistle.

11 Haltwhistle,
Northumbria
This small, grey market town is a good starting point for Hadrian's Wall, built in the 2nd century AD to ward off Scottish tribes. Holy Cross Church, founded in 1178, is a fine example of Early English architecture. There is no tower, and the sanctuary preserves three carved coffin lids, thought to date from the 14th century. The South Tynedale Railway, England's highest narrow-gauge railway, runs from Alston towards Haltwhistle. Further along the A69, at Greenhead, the Roman wall, turret, fort and museum recall life 2,000 years ago.

[i] *Railway Station, Station Road*

▶ *From Greenhead take the B6318 and unclassified roads to rejoin the A69. Continue through Brampton to Carlisle.*

Across the
Backbone of England

The green valleys and wild, often wind-swept moorland of Yorkshire provide a rich variety of scenery, with ever-changing views. Curiously weathered rocks add an eerie atmosphere to the landscape of hills and vales, and castles and monastic ruins recall the prosperity of the Middle Ages on this tour.

2 DAYS • 153 MILES • 247KM

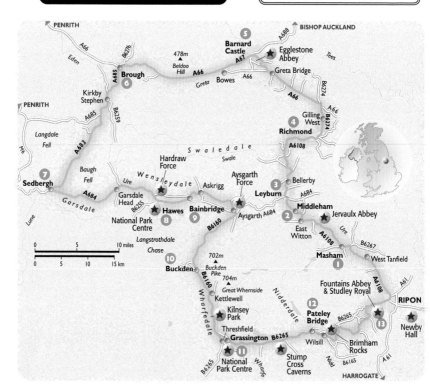

ℹ️ *Minster Road, Ripon*

FOR CHILDREN

Four miles (6.5km) southeast of Ripon is Newby Hall and Gardens. The grounds cover about 25 acres (10 hectares) and include thrilling adventure gardens for children, a memorable ride on a miniature train and woodland discovery walks.

▶ *Take the **A6108** to Masham.*

❶ Masham, North Yorkshire
Masham's importance as a market town is illustrated by the huge market square, dominated by its Market Cross. Masham Market is held every Wednesday and Saturday. The town is full of interesting features: a four-arched bridge over the Ure dates from 1754, and St Mary's Church is older, its 15th-century spire standing on top of a Norman tower. The town is the home of Theakston's brewery, famous for its 'Old Peculier' ale.

Five miles (8km) from town is Jervaulx Abbey, in an attractive riverside setting. This Cistercian abbey was founded in 1156 and later destroyed in the 15th century, though enough of it remains to show how impressive it once was.

▶ *Follow the **A6108** for 8 miles (13km) to Middleham.*

❷ Middleham, North Yorkshire
Grandiose building traditions of the past can be seen in the ruins of 12th-century Middleham Castle, a former seat of the Neville family, where some of the walls are 12 feet (3.5m) thick. This was the childhood home of Richard III and its massive keep is one of the largest ever built. The view from the top is magnificent, looking out across Wensleydale over wild but beautiful moorlands. Now an important horse breeding and training centre, Middleham is a good base for exploring Wensleydale.

▶ *Continue north to Leyburn.*

❸ Leyburn, North Yorkshire
Leyburn is a major commercial centre for the area. Its appearance is that of a prosperous late Georgian market town, and even though most shop fronts have become largely modern, some 18th-century houses survive, notably around Grove Square; the Bolton Arms and Leyburn Hall are probably the best examples. This is another good Wensleydale centre, and there are fine views from The Shawl, a 2-mile (3km) limestone scar not far from the town centre.

ℹ️ *Central Chambers, Railway Street*

▶ *Keep on the **A6108** to Richmond.*

❹ Richmond, North Yorkshire
There is much to see in this capital and gateway to Swaledale, thought to be the finest of all Yorkshire Dales. From every angle Richmond Castle dominates the town. This fine Norman fortress, built on to solid rock, was started in 1071 overlooking the Swale, Britain's fastest river, but was never finished. The large, cobbled market-place is surrounded by such architectural gems as the Georgian Theatre Royal, built in 1788, which was restored and reopened in 1962. You can see the home of the original 'sweet lass of Richmond Hill', of whom the famous song was written in 1785, and the award-winning Green Howards Museum covers the history of the regiment, including a unique collection dating from 1688 of war relics, weapons, medals and uniforms. Other interesting sights include Greyfriars Tower, the one surviving feature of an old abbey, and the Holy Trinity Church.

ℹ️ *Friary Gardens, Victoria Road*

FOR HISTORY BUFFS

Lead mining helped the growth of Richmond and many of the surrounding villages in the 17th and 18th centuries. There are numerous footpaths leading to the old mine workings, where you can see the crushing floors and other remnants, and perhaps find tiny fragments of lead glistening in the sunlight.

▶ *Take the **B6274** to the junction with the **A66** and continue to Greta Bridge. After crossing the River Greta turn right on to unclassified roads to Barnard Castle.*

❺ Barnard Castle, Durham
Medieval Barnard Castle, after which the town is named, is now

Middleham's impressive castle ruins

Bainbridge was the centre of the once-great Forest of Wensleydale a ruin, but in its great days it stood guard over a crossing point of the River Tees. The town boasts one of the finest museums in Britain, Bowes Museum, in a splendid French château-style mansion which was built in 1869 by John Bowes, son of the Earl of Strathmore. It contains an outstanding collection of paintings, porcelain, silver, furniture and ceramics.

A few miles south, off the B6277, are the ruins of Egglestone Abbey, in a delightful setting on the bank of the Tees, and southwest, along the A67, is the village of Bowes, where the local boarding schools gave author Charles Dickens the idea for Dotheboys Hall in his novel *Nicholas Nickleby*. William

Shaw, the unfortunate model for sadistic schoolmaster Wackford Squeers, is buried in the churchyard. The Church of St Giles contains a Roman dedication stone, one of many relics of the Roman invasion in the area. Bowes Castle, like the church, used Roman stone for its building.

i Woodleigh, Flatts Road

▶ Take the **A67** to Bowes and follow the **A66** west along the line of an old Roman route to Brough.

6 Brough, Cumbria
Standing on the site of Roman *Verterae*, Brough Castle, now in ruins, was built by William II and later restored by Lady Anne Clifford in the 17th century. During the 19th century this old

settlement was a coaching town, and used to hold an annual horse fair. The area has many miles of good walking.

▶ Take the **A685** to Kirkby Stephen, then the **A683** to Sedbergh.

7 Sedbergh, Cumbria
Sedbergh is an old weaving town, and the Weavers' Yard still exists behind the King's Arms. The town is now more important as a tourist centre, and the rich natural history of the area is now augmented by the town's official status as England's Book Town. The Public School has gained a national reputation for its academic standards and sporting traditions. The A684 east takes you through Garsdale, whose only community is a line of houses called The Street.

i *Dales Countryside Museum, Station Yard*

▶ *Take the **A684** for a further 4 miles (6.5km) to Bainbridge.*

9 **Bainbridge,** North Yorkshire

This little Dales village, with its lovely stone buildings set round the green, was the former centre of the once great Forest of Wensleydale. Low Mill, on the east side of the green, has been restored and is occasionally open to the public. Brough Hill, a natural grassy hillock to the east is the setting for a Roman fort, and gives fine views of Wensleydale and the village.

A little further along is Askrigg, another charming village, built of local stone and set among hills, valleys and waterfalls. Most of the buildings are 18th- and 19th-century, built as a result of increasing prosperity in the clock-making, lead-mining and textile industries. Waterfalls are numerous, but especially dramatic is Aysgarth Force.

▶ *From Bainbridge cross over the River Ure and then turn right. From here, continuue on unclassified roads, then at Aysgarth take the **B6160** to Buckden.*

10 **Buckden,** North Yorkshire

Buckden, in Wharfedale, is a very popular holiday and walking area. Kettlewell, further down the valley, was formerly part of the estate of the Percy family, ancestors of the Dukes of Northumberland.

This stretch of road passes the imposing limestone outcrop of Kilnsey Crag, one of Yorkshire's most distinctive landmarks, alongside the all-weather attraction of Kilnsey Park, which has been established as a Visitor Centre.

▶ *Follow the **B6160** south and turn left at Threshfield on to the **B6265** into Grassington, a distance of 11 miles (18km).*

SPECIAL TO...

This area of the Dales was chosen as the location for the successful BBC TV series *All Creatures Great and Small*, the story of a country vet's practice based on the autobiographical books by James Herriot. Cringley Hall, in the centre of the village of Askrigg is 'Skeldale House' and Askrigg itself is 'Darrowby', where the vets had their surgery. For thousands of visitors 'Herriot Country' is every bit as important as 'Brontë Country'.

11 **Grassington,** North Yorkshire

This is Wharfedale's principal village and another National Park Centre, for the North York Moors. Its small passageways, cobbled market-place, medieval bridge and interesting old buildings all add to the appeal. There are Bronze and Iron Age settlements at Lea Green, north of the village, and further east, along the B6265, are the underground caverns of Stump Cross. The main cave has been developed into an impressive floodlit show cave, with wonderful stalagmite and stalactite formations.

i *Grassington National Park Centre, Hebden Road*

▶ *Continue along the **B6265** to Pateley Bridge.*

12 **Pateley Bridge,** North Yorkshire

This pleasant town has been the focus of everyday life in Nidderdale since ancient times. The picturesque ruins of Old St Mary's Church stand above the village on the hillside, and the Nidderdale Museum has fascinating exhibits including the Victorian Room and a replica cobbler's shop. A mile (1.6km) from town is the former Foster Beck Hemp Mill, now a restaurant, which features a huge 17th-century water wheel, the second largest in the country.

▶ *Continue east along the **A684** to Hawes.*

8 **Hawes,** North Yorkshire

Hawes is a centre for sheep-marketing and a focal point of Upper Wensleydale life. Just off the main street are quaint alleyways and old cottages which have not changed much for 200 years. The National Park Centre is located at the Dales Countryside Museum, which is housed in an engine shed of the old railway.

Hardraw Force, the highest waterfall in England, is also considered to be the most spectacular, and is accessible only by foot through the grounds of the Green Dragon Inn. The water drops 90 feet (27m) over the limestone Hardraw Scar, into a narrow valley, once the venue for brass band competitions.

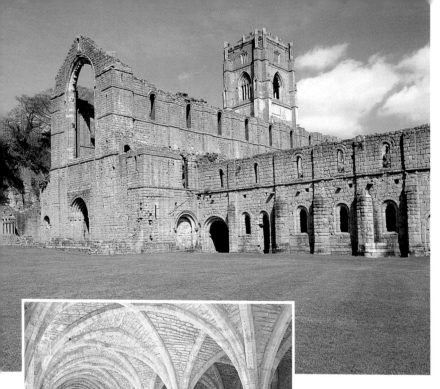

Above and inset: Fountains Abbey, perhaps England's finest abbey

East of town, along the B6165 (turn off at Wilsill) and unclassified roads are Brimham Rocks. These curious rock formations have been sculpted out of the millstone grit by wind and rain over thousands of years, and there are wide views from the surrounding moorlands.

ⓘ *18 High Street*

▶ *Leave by the B6265 turning right after 1 mile (1.6km) on to the B6165. At Wilsill turn left and follow unclassified roads past Brimham Rocks to Fountains Abbey.*

🔟 Fountains Abbey, North Yorkshire

Founded by Cistercian monks in 1132, Fountains is the largest and perhaps the finest abbey in England. Particularly notable are the tower, nave and lay brothers'

quarters. It was acquired by William Aislabie in 1768 and became the focal point of his magnificent landscaped gardens at nearby Studley Royal Park, which contains typical ornaments of the period, such as a lake, a temple and statues. The park's original house burned down in 1945, but there are still estate cottages, huddled round a 19th-century church designed by William Burges. Deer and other livestock can be seen grazing in the park.

▶ *Return to the B6265 for the journey back to Ripon.*

RECOMMENDED WALKS

The various National Park Centres provide a programme of guided walks on Bank Holidays and during July and August. These start at 2pm and usually last 2½ to 3 hours. Local people with a special interest in some aspect of the Dales act as guides. Information about these walks is given in *The Visitor*, a free publication.

BACK TO NATURE

In the gritstone area of the Yorkshire Dales, above Nidderdale and Swaledale, purple heathers dominate the scene, but in the limestone country round Wharfedale you will find more variety, with the tiny coloured flowers which thrive in the calcite-rich soils. Plants such as yellow pimpernel, giant bell-flower, lily of the valley and ramson grow well in the light shade cast by ash, which grows on the limestone scars, while the unmown roadside verges and hay meadows are favoured by knapweed, sneezewort, early purple orchids and cowslips.

Over Hills
& Plains

Lush green valleys, wild grouse moorland and one of the liveliest seaside resorts in the country are included in this tour, which starts at Morecambe, on the edge of the Irish Sea, and climbs to the Pennines, before returning to the coast.

1/2 DAYS • 152 MILES • 246KM

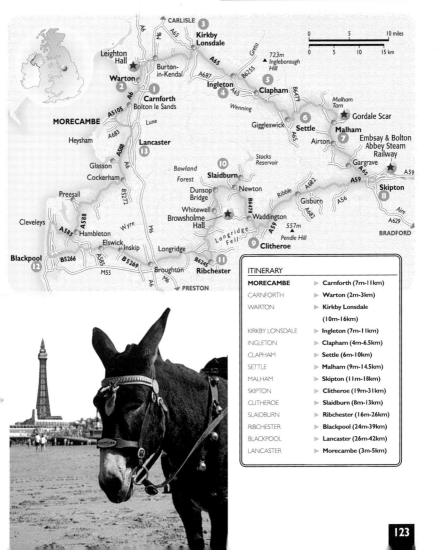

ITINERARY	
MORECAMBE	▶ **Carnforth (7m-11km)**
CARNFORTH	▶ **Warton (2m-3km)**
WARTON	▶ **Kirkby Lonsdale (10m-16km)**
KIRKBY LONSDALE	▶ **Ingleton (7m-11km)**
INGLETON	▶ **Clapham (4m-6.5km)**
CLAPHAM	▶ **Settle (6m-10km)**
SETTLE	▶ **Malham (9m-14.5km)**
MALHAM	▶ **Skipton (11m-18km)**
SKIPTON	▶ **Clitheroe (19m-31km)**
CLITHEROE	▶ **Slaidburn (8m-13km)**
SLAIDBURN	▶ **Ribchester (16m-26km)**
RIBCHESTER	▶ **Blackpool (24m-39km)**
BLACKPOOL	▶ **Lancaster (26m-42km)**
LANCASTER	▶ **Morecambe (3m-5km)**

i *Old Station Buildings,*
Morecambe

▶ *From Morecambe take the*
A5105, then the A6 for 7
miles (11km) northwards to
Carnforth.

1 **Carnforth,** Lancashire

Carnforth is a small Victorian
market town on the west coast
railway line to Scotland. The
Lancaster Canal threads through
the town providing fascinating
towpath walks that quickly take
you into the surrounding countryside.

    Here, close to the A6 and the
town centre, the marina is popular with canal enthusiasts and
those just seeking peace and
quiet. Craft can be hired here by
the day or the week.

▶ *Follow the unclassified road*
2 miles (3km) to Warton.

The Devil's Bridge at Kirkby
Lonsdale is one of the most
ancient bridges in the country

2 **Warton,** Lancashire

Warton has an unusual claim to
fame. George Washington had
ancestors living here, and legend
has it that the famous 'Stars and
Stripes' come from the family's
coat of arms, which can be found
in the 14th-century church.

    Near Warton is 18th-century
Leighton Hall, built on the site

of an earlier medieval house. In
1826 the estate was bought by
Richard Gillow, a distinguished
maker of fine furniture, and the
house is a treasure chest of
priceless pieces.

▶ *Continue on unclassified roads,*
across the A6 just south of
Burton-in-Kendal then join the
B6254 at Whittington and
follow to Kirkby Lonsdale.

3 **Kirkby Lonsdale,**
Cumbria

Kirkby Lonsdale is a fascinating
town to explore. Look out for
the three-arched Devil's Bridge
spanning the River Lune.
Possibly 13th-century, it is one
of the finest ancient bridges in
the country. John Ruskin, the
19th-century writer and painter,
loved this area of the Lune
valley. The 'Ruskin Walks',
which start near the churchyard,
are well signposted. Cowan
Bridge, just down the road, has
further literary links, for it was
here that novelists Charlotte and

Emily Brontë endured a harsh boarding school education from 1823 to 1825. Now only a few cottages mark the site of the Clergy Daughters' School, immortalised by Charlotte as Lowood in her novel *Jane Eyre*.

ⓘ *24 Main Street*

▶ *Continue on the A65 for 6 miles (10km), then turn left on to the B6255 into Ingleton.*

4 Ingleton, North Yorkshire
Ingleton thrives as a centre for visitors to the Yorkshire Dales. The limestone hills to the north are honeycombed with caves, many accessible only to experienced potholers, but White Scar Cave is open to everyone. It is below the heights of 2,373 feet (723m) Ingleborough which, with Whernside at 2,419 feet (737m) and Pen-y-ghent at 2,273 feet (693m), forms the most formidable trio of peaks in the Dales.

ⓘ *Community Centre, Main Street*

▶ *Take the unclassified road along the foot of Ingleborough to Clapham.*

5 Clapham, North Yorkshire
Tiny Clapham is the unlikely Fleet Street of the Dales, for it is here that *The Dalesman* magazine is published. The village has a Yorkshire Dales National Park Information Centre, and like Ingleton is a noted potholing centre. To the north of the village is Ingleborough Cave, and the famous Gaping Gill pothole, 378 feet (123m) deep, with a central chamber large enough to hold a small cathedral.

▶ *From Clapham take the B6480 to the A65 and follow before branching off left to Settle.*

6 Settle, North Yorkshire
Settle is an attractive town, with its picturesque narrow streets, secluded courtyards and Georgian houses. By far the most outstanding building is The Folly (1675), an extravaganza of windows and fine masonry. The 71-mile (114km) railway line from Settle to Carlisle runs through the Ribblesdale valley and is one of the most scenic routes in the country. Just outside the town is Giggleswick Scar, a rock wall caused by massive earth move-

St Mary's Church, Ingleton

ments millions of years ago. In 1838, the chance discovery of Victoria Cave led to the retrieval of many bones of prehistoric animals long extinct in the British Isles.

ⓘ *Town Hall, Cheapside*

▶ *Take the B6479 north from Settle, turnf off right at Langcliffe on to unclassified roads to Malham Tarn and Malham.*

7 Malham, North Yorkshire
Malham is a focal point for geographers and geologists, and the Yorkshire Dales National Park Interpretation Centre is based here. Stroll up the Pennine Way to Malham Cove, a 250-foot (76m) limestone amphitheatre. It used to be a spectacular waterfall, but the river now crawls out at the foot of the cliff. To the east is Gordale Scar, an almost vertical gorge thought to be a collapsed cavern and boasting a dramatic waterfall.

▶ *Follow the road from Malham to Gargrave, then take the A65 to Skipton.*

The geological curiosity of Malham Cove lends an otherworldly air to this spectacular area

today it still stands boldly on its limestone knoll overlooking the town. The town itself was once filled with the sound of looms – first wool, then cotton brought prosperity in the last century. Pendle Hill, associated with the trial of several Lancashire women accused of being witches, rises to 1,828 feet (557m) on the east side of Clitheroe.

i 12–14 Market Place

▶ Follow the **B6478** north for 8 miles (13km) to Slaidburn.

RECOMMENDED WALKS

Malham village is close to the highly dramatic Malham Cove and Gordale Scar. Walk up the steep path to the top of the cove, and continue along the route of the old river, now dried up. You will soon reach the point at which the stream disappears underground through a series of holes. Retrace your steps or turn right and follow the signs to Gordale, where you can scramble down a waterfall and walk through a gorge on the way back to the village.

8 Skipton, North Yorkshire
This pleasant market town is dominated by Skipton Castle, one of the most complete medieval castles in England. It was originally built in Norman times and was partly rebuilt in the 1650s after being damaged in the Civil War. Opposite the castle entrance is the Craven Museum, with exhibits on geology and local folk history. Near by, at Embsay, is the Embsay and Bolton Abbey Steam Railway which runs 20 locomotives.

i 35 Coach Street

▶ Take the **A59** to Clitheroe.

9 Clitheroe, Lancashire
After the Civil War the small keep of Clitheroe Castle was presented to General Monk, and

10 Slaidburn, Lancashire
The little village of Slaidburn, on the River Hodder, was for centuries the administrative 'capital' of the Forest of Bowland. This wild region of grouse moor and high fells was one of the ancient royal forests of Saxon England. At the centre of the village is an inn called Hark to Bounty. Legend says

Bounty was a foxhound belonging to a local vicar, and that its barking was easily distinguishable from the rest of the pack. Gisburn Forest, northeast of the village, is an extensive coniferous plantation sloping down to Stocks Reservoir, that takes its name from the village which was drowned to create it during the 1930s.

▶ Take the **B6478** back to Newton, then branch off on to unclassified roads through Dunsop Bridge, Whitewell and over Longridge Fell to Ribchester.

⓫ Ribchester, Lancashire
The country round Ribchester was guarded by a Roman fort called Bremetennacum, built around AD 70. In the 18th century a schoolboy found a Roman ceremonial helmet, and since then the extensive remains have been excavated and you can see many of the finds, including pottery, coins, a bathhouse and granaries, in the Ribchester Roman Museum. Two Roman columns support the oak gallery in 13th-century St Wilfred's Church, and the pillars at the entrance of the White Bull Inn are said to come from a Roman temple.

▶ Take the **B6245** to Longridge and then the **B5269** west via Broughton and Elswick to join the **B5266** to Blackpool.

⓬ Blackpool, Lancashire
Blackpool stretches in a long, multicoloured ribbon by the sea, punctuated with three piers and dominated by its 519-foot (158m) tower. Built between 1891 and 1894, Blackpool Tower was for many years the highest building in Britain, and it gives a breathtaking view of the surrounding coast. The heart of Blackpool, the Golden Mile, is more like a quarter of a mile (0.4km). It is possible to walk the whole length of the seafront between Fleetwood in the north and Squires Gate in the south, but it is more fun to go on one of

the trams which still run along the promenade. During autumn evenings, the whole front is ablaze with more than 375,000 bulbs, laser beams, animated displays and tableaux.

ⓘ *I Clifton Street*

▶ Follow the trams to Cleveleys, before turning inland on the **B5412** then right taking you on to the **A585**. Turn left on to the **A588** to Lancaster via Pilling and the Cockerham marshes.

Blackpool's famous roller-coaster

FOR CHILDREN

The Pleasure Beach amusement park, with the first 360-degree 'loop the loop' roller-coaster in Britain, and Sandcastle Waterworld, the world's greatest 'inside seaside' with tropical fun pools and a 300-foot (91m) water slide are popular with children, as are the Blackpool Sea Life Centre and Blackpool Zoo

⓭ Lancaster, Lancashire
This county town was England's chief port for the American trade throughout the 18th century. The elegant Customs House, designed by Robert Gillow now houses the Lancaster Maritime Museum. The massive Norman

keep of Lancaster Castle now serves to keep people in rather than out: it is the county gaol. It contains a well tower where prisoners languished while awaiting trial – including 10 Lancashire witches convicted and hanged in 1612. On show are grim relics such as the clamp and iron used to fasten a criminal's arm while the initial 'M' (for malefactor) was burned on to his hand. The City Museum in Market Square is also the Museum of the King's Own Royal Lancashire Regiment, and the Judges'

Lodgings on Castle Hill contain a Museum of Childhood.

ⓘ *29 Castle Hill*

▶ Cross the River Lune on the **A588**, and a short drive takes you back to Morecambe.

SCENIC ROUTES

Spectacular views can be found as you pass through the mountainous spine of England, the Pennines, on the road from Malham to Skipton before it joins the A65. The dramatic form of Ingleborough dominates the landscape, especially from Kirkby Lonsdale and along the A65.

Derbyshire's
White Peak

This tour of the Peak District explores the gentler southern side, the White Peak, with its high close cropped sheep pasture, limestone dry walling and pretty wooded valleys, but our route also offers a small glimpse of the Dark Peak – bleaker moorland and angular outcrops of blackened millstone grit.

1/2 DAYS • 85 MILES • 138KM

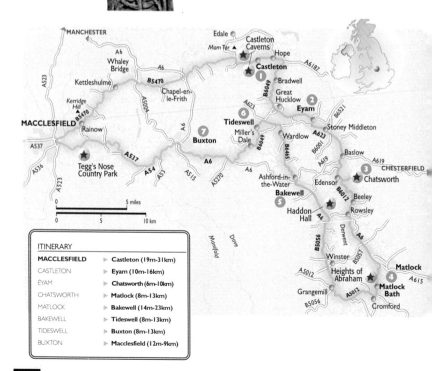

ITINERARY

Stalagmites in Treak Cliff Cave, near Castleton
Left: Saxon cross, Eyam

[i] *Town Hall, Macclesfield*

BACK TO NATURE

Situated near Macclesfield, Goyt Valley is an area of bog, moorland, forest and open water. The two reservoirs – Errwood and Fernilee – have wintering wildfowl and species such as red grouse, curlew, lapwing and redshank breed on the open moorland.

▶ *Leave Macclesfield by the **B5470** to Rainow, then in 4 miles (6km) cross the **A5004**, taking the **B5470** to Chapel-en-le-Frith. Take the unclassified road signed Rushup and Edale, then turn right and shortly left signed Castleton Caverns for Castleton.*

❶ Castleton, Derbyshire
Dominating this pretty Peak village is Peveril Castle, built by William Peveril, illegitimate son of the Conqueror, and immortalised in Sir Walter Scott's 1825 novel *Peveril of the Peak*. Although roofless, Henry II's huge keep still stands. Castleton has a 200-year history of visitors, who come mainly to see the spectacular caverns in the limestone hills. Follow the stream to Peak Cavern, which has Britain's largest natural cave entrance. You can still see evidence here of the rope-makers who lived and worked in the cavern: their speciality was hangmen's nooses. There are other local caverns, carved out by miners looking for lead and the lovely Blue John Fluorspar. Treak Cliff, Speedwell (explore it by boat) and Blue John Caverns are all open to visitors.

A trip behind Mam Tor, 'the shivering mountain', leads to nearby Edale, which lies snugly in the Noe Valley and is the starting point of the Pennine Way footpath.

▶ *Go east on the **A625**, then turn right on to the **B6049**. Soon turn left on unclassified roads to Great Hucklow, through Foolow to Eyam.*

❷ Eyam, Derbyshire
In 1665, the year of the Great Plague in London, a chest of clothes was sent from the capital to the village of Eyam, high up among the moors. Soon four out of every five villagers were dead. But what made Eyam special was the extraordinary sacrifice that these villagers made. Led by the rector, William Mompesson, they resolved to isolate themselves and prevent the disease from wiping out neighbouring communities. The churchyard's graves reflect this sad story and every August a service is held in a nearby dell, known as Cucklet Church, where Mompesson held his open-air services. Near his wife's grave is a unique sundial, telling the time throughout the world.

▶ *Turn right on to the **B6521**, then left on to the **A623**. At Baslow turn right on to the **A619**, then shortly left on to the **B6012**. In 5 miles (8km) turn left again at Edensor for Chatsworth.*

❸ Chatsworth, Derbyshire
Chatsworth is one of the grandest country houses in England, popularly known as the 'Palace of the Peak'. The Elizabethan house, built in 1555 by Bess of Hardwick, was virtually replaced with the 1st Duke of Devonshire's baroque mansion of the late 17th century, finished by the 6th Duke in the 1820s. Although Capability Brown landscaped the grounds, their crowning feature is Joseph Paxton's stunning Emperor Fountain, at 260 feet (80m) the tallest in Britain. When you rejoin the main road, take a look at the golden stone village of Edensor. Before 1839 the village

lay in full view of the big house, so the 6th Duke had Paxton demolish it and rebuild it out of sight!

▶ *Leave Chatsworth and turn left on to the B6012. At Rowsley turn left on to the A6 for Matlock.*

4 Matlock and Matlock Bath, Derbyshire

Matlock is the administrative centre of Derbyshire, a busy town built around an ancient stone bridge across the river. Next door is Matlock Bath, a 19th-century spa town, where the water still bubbles up at a constant 20°C, although the Pavilion where Victorians used to take it is now an entertainment centre. Commanding the heights above Matlock Bath are the Victoria Prospect Tower and the strange folly of Riber Castle. The Peak District Mining Museum can be found alongside the River Derwent.

A mile (1.6km) from Matlock is Cromford, an important benchmark in the development of England as an industrial nation. Here, in 1771, Richard Arkwright built the world's first mechanised textile factory. It survives today, with the new village he built for his workers.

ⓘ *The Pavilion, Matlock Bath*

FOR CHILDREN

A spectacular cable-car journey takes you from the river at Matlock Bath to the 1,000-foot (305m) Heights of Abraham. At the top, you can climb the Victoria Prospect Tower, and below ground there are two huge caverns to explore, the Great Rutland and the Great Masson.

▶ *Leave Matlock Bath on the A6 and at Cromford turn right on to the A5012 signed Buxton. Turn right on to the B5056 then the A6 to Bakewell.*

Bakewell is famous for its puddings

SPECIAL TO...

The National Tramway Museum at Crich, just south of Cromford, is unique. Over 40 trams from all over the world, built between 1873 and 1953, are kept here in pristine condition by volunteers, and on any one day several trams run. For the price of admission you can hop on and off as much as you like anywhere along the 1 mile (1.6km) route.

5 Bakewell, Derbyshire

The fine five-arch stone bridge built in 1300 to span the River Wye, is the principal feature of this market town. The Romans came here first for the warm springs; the Saxons named it Bad Quell or 'bath well'. Most of the buildings are 17th- and 18th-century, but the Old House Museum, with its wattle-and-daub walls, is at least a hundred years older.

The town boasts more than 50 shops, including the Old Original Bakewell Pudding Shop. Bakewell Pudding – don't dare call it 'tart' here – is supposed to have originated in the kitchens of the Rutland Arms Hotel, when a cook poured an egg mixture on to the jam instead of the pastry.

ⓘ *Old Market Hall, Bridge Street*

FOR HISTORY BUFFS

Haddon Hall, near Bakewell, is reputed to be England's most complete and authentic medieval manor house, and is certainly one of Derbyshire's finest buildings. Unlike many large country houses, it remains very much as it was 300 years ago.

▶ *Go north on the A6 from Bakewell. At Ashford-in-the-Water turn right on to the B6465 and, in 4 miles (6.5km), left on to the A623, then turn left into Tideswell.*

6 Tideswell, Derbyshire

Tideswell grew with the medieval wool trade – being granted market status as early as the 13th century. Over the intervening years it has become a

sleepy backwater away from the main roads, and little remains to indicate the town's heyday, with one glorious exception. The 14th-century Church of St John the Baptist, with its soaring tower, is known as the 'Cathedral of the Peak'. Tideswell is a venue for well-dressing, the tradition of decorating wells with flowers, which takes place at the end of June or very early in July.

▶ From Tideswell go south on the **B6049**, then join the **A6** heading west to Buxton.

7 Buxton, Derbyshire
At 1,007 feet (307m), Buxton is one of the highest towns in England. People have sought the town out since Roman times for its springs of mineral water. Not only is it good for rheumatics, but it tastes nice too. Bring a bottle and help yourself, free,

from St Anne's Well; you can even swim in warm spa water in the Pavilion's indoor pool. It was in the 18th century that the town took off as a spa resort, thanks to the 5th Duke of Devonshire, who built the beautiful Doric-style Crescent and the huge domed riding school and stables, now the Royal Devonshire Hospital. The town has two golf courses, an elegantly restored Opera House and the lovely Pavilion Gardens. Walks are plentiful; one that offers a panoramic view of the town is the round trip up to Solomon's Temple, a folly on Grinlow.

ℹ️ The Crescent

▶ Leave Buxton on the **A53**, going right on to the **A54**. Turn right again on to the **A537** signed Macclesfield and in 5 miles (8km) turn left

Buxton is a sophisticated and elegant Georgian spa town

on to unclassified roads past Tegg's Nose Country Park into Macclesfield.

SCENIC ROUTES

The route between Macclesfield and Castleton offers a picturesque introduction to the Dark Peak. The road undulates up hill and down dale between drystone walls, through gritstone villages whose cottages have been blackened by centuries of industrial smoke. On a clear day there are lovely views across the Cheshire Plain. On your left as you approach Rainow on the B5470 is White Nancy, a curious monument at the end of prominent Kerridge Hill.

131

From Vale
to Moor

2 DAYS • 124 MILES • 201KM

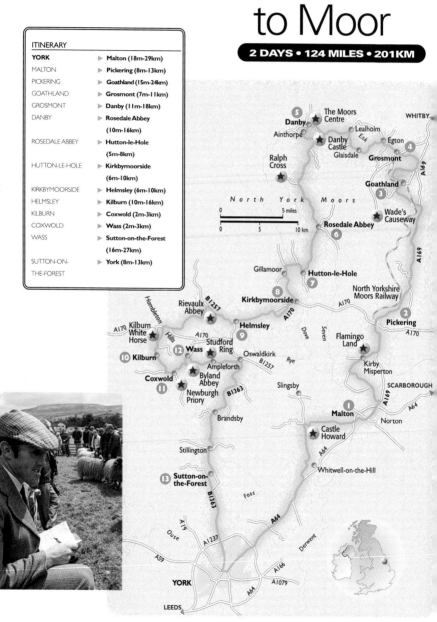

This area of North Riding extends from the gentle farmlands of the Vale of York to the wild beauty of the North York Moors, taking in delightful villages and evocative ruins.

Castle Howard is one of the architect Vanbrugh's finest works

i *York Railway Station*

▶ *Take the **A64** and turn left on to an unclassified road before Whitewell-on-the-Hill, passing Castle Howard, through Coneysthorpe to Malton.*

❶ Malton, North Yorkshire

Malton is divided in two by the site of a Roman station. New Malton is the busy market town, and Old Malton, a mile (1.6km) northeast, is a small village. Malton Museum, in the town, contains extensive Romano-British remains from the fort of Derventio and other settlements. Northwards is Eden Camp Modern History Museum, a former prisoner-of-war camp, where displays include women at war and the rise and fall of the Nazi Party.

Six miles (10km) southwest of Malton, on a signed road, is Castle Howard, a magnificent 18th-century house designed by Sir John Vanbrugh. It has been the home of the Howard family for nearly 300 years and notable features include the central dome, the Temple of the Four Winds and Hawksmoor's mausoleum.

i *Malton Museum, Market Place*

FOR CHILDREN

Kirby Misperton, near Malton, is the home of Flamingo Land. Over 1,000 animals include camels and polar bears, many of which have been bred here. Special attractions are organised, such as the parrot and dolphin shows.

▶ *Follow the road to Old Malton, cross the **A64** on to the **A169**, turning almost immediately left on to an unclassified road through Kirby Misperton, rejoining the **A169** north to Pickering.*

❷ Pickering, North Yorkshire

This ancient town is the starting point for the North Yorkshire Moors Railway, which runs between Pickering and Grosmont. Parts of the town's Church of St Peter and St Paul date from the 11th century and it contains splendid medieval wall paintings, notably *St George and the Dragon*. The ruins of Pickering Castle include a motte-and-bailey which was founded by William the Conqueror, and the Beck Isle Museum of Rural Life, in a fine Georgian building, and is packed with bygones of the Victorian era.

i *The Ropery*

▶ *Continue along the **A169** for about 12 miles (19km), then turn left on to an unclassified road to Goathland.*

❸ Goathland, North Yorkshire

Goathland is a picturesque village in the North York Moors and the area is renowned for spectacular waterfalls, including Nelly Ayre Foss, Mallyan Spout and Thomason Foss.

SPECIAL TO...

Goathland is the home of the Goathland Plough Stots, a sword dance team whose displays originated with Viking raiders over 1,000 years ago. It takes place on Plough Monday, the first Monday after 6 January, when a service is held to bless the Plough Stots ('stot' means bullock).

▶ *Return to the **A169** for a short distance, then turn left on to unclassified roads to Grosmont.*

❹ Grosmont, North Yorkshire

Grosmont is the northern terminus of the impressive North Yorkshire Moors Railway, and its

All aboard the North Yorkshire Moors Railway

popularity owes much to the railway. A trip on the Moorsrail will take you back to a gentler and slower age, and the locomotive sheds are worth a visit to see engines being prepared and restored.

▶ *Continue west along unclassified roads to Danby.*

FOR HISTORY BUFFS

A remarkably well-preserved stretch of an old Roman road, Wade's Causeway, passes near Grosmont. It was built 2,000 years ago as part of a Roman route from Malton to the coast near Goldsborough, and lay hidden until it was rediscovered in 1914.

---

5 Danby, North Yorkshire
The Moors National Park Centre is located in Danby in a former shooting lodge, with exhibitions and impressive gardens. Southeast of the village are the ruins of 14th-century Danby Castle, where Catherine Parr, Henry VIII's sixth wife, once lived. The route now goes on to the moors past two old

crosses, Fat Betty and the Ralph Cross, which is used as the symbol for the North York Moors National Park.

i *The Moors National Park Centre, Danby Lodge, Lodge Lane*

▶ *Follow unclassified roads south to Rosedale Abbey.*

6 Rosedale Abbey, North Yorkshire
Rosedale's 12th-century Cistercian abbey no longer exists: only a few stones remain in the village. Ruins of railways and kilns at Chimney Bank Top are reminders of the old 19th-century ironstone industry. The famous chimney, once visible for miles, was demolished in 1972 when it was declared unsafe.

▶ *Continue to Hutton-le-Hole.*

7 Hutton-le-Hole, North Yorkshire
Hutton-le-Hole's Ryedale Folk Museum, in an ancient cruck-type building, features a marvellous collection of farm equipment, and reconstructed buildings. There are two 3½-mile (6km) walks signposted from the centre of the village into the countryside.

▶ *Continue on unclassified roads, crossing the River Dove and through Gillamoor to Kirkbymoorside.*

8 Kirkbymoorside, North Yorkshire
Situated at the edge of the moor, this small town is just off the main road, with quiet streets and squares. The church dates from the 12th century and retains some fine Norman masonry and fragments of a Saxon cross.

▶ *Take the A170 for 6 miles (10km) to Helmsley.*

9 Helmsley, North Yorkshire
Roads from Cleveland, Thirsk and York converge upon the town square, making Helmsley a busy trade centre. Helmsley Castle dates from 1186 and was

once inhabited by the Duke of Buckingham, court favourite of James I and Charles I.

Two miles (3km) west of Helmsley is Rievaulx, one of the largest Cistercian abbeys in England. The 12th-century ruins are surrounded by wooded hills, and above the abbey wall is Rievaulx Terrace, a beautiful landscaped garden with mock-Greek temples completed in 1758.

i *Helmsley Castle*

RECOMMENDED WALKS

Highly recommended is the 3½-miles (6km) walk from Helmsley to Rievaulx, which runs along the richly wooded valley of the River Rye.

▶ *Follow unclassified roads from Rievaulx through Scawton to rejoin the A170, then turn left to White Horse Bank and Kilburn.*

10 Kilburn, North Yorkshire
Kilburn White Horse is the only turf-cut figure in the north of England. Almost 314 feet (96m) long by 228 feet (70m) high, it can be seen from the central tower of York Minster, 19 miles (31km) away. The village is well known for its woodcarvings, the work of Robert Thompson, who died in 1955. His trademark, a mouse, is still carved into the items produced by craftsmen at his works.

i *Sutton Bank Visitor Centre*

▶ *Continue on unclassified roads for 2 miles (3km) to Coxwold.*

11 Coxwold, North Yorkshire
Coxwold's most outstanding building is the 15th-century octagonal-towered church. In the churchyard is the gravestone of the 18th-century author Laurence Sterne, who named his house Shandy Hall, after the hero of his novel *The Life and*

Opinions of Tristram Shandy; today it is a museum devoted to his life and works. Just beyond the village is Newburgh Priory, a 17th- and 18th-century house with a lake and gardens.

▶ *Return to Coxwold, then take an unclassified road to Wass.*

12 Wass, North Yorkshire
Wass was partly built from the ruins of nearby Byland Abbey, the largest Cistercian church in the country, with a 26-foot (8m) diameter window dating from the 13th century.

Two miles (3km) east of Wass is Ampleforth, which was chosen as the site of a school by English monks escaping from the French Revolution. Ampleforth College is now England's premier Roman Catholic public school.

Nearby Studford Ring is thought to date from the Bronze Age and is probably the finest earthwork enclosure in the area.

▶ *Continue east on unclassified roads to Oswaldkirk. Turn right on to the B1363 and continue south to Sutton-on-the-Forest.*

13 Sutton-on-the-Forest, North Yorkshire
Set in the undulating Howardian Hills, this is an unusual brick-built village with a stone church. Sutton Park, an early Georgian house, contains antique furniture by Chippendale and Sheraton and a collection of porcelain.

▶ *Return to York via the B1363, 8 miles (13km).*

Helmsley nestles beneath the southern rim of the moors

RECOMMENDED WALKS

The 100-mile (160km) Cleveland Way curves round the edge of the Moors, and certain stretches along it make ideal short walks.

BACK TO NATURE

The North York Moors are managed primarily to encourage the numbers of red grouse, but birds such as golden plovers, dunlins, curlews and lapwings also take advantage of the varied habitat.

SCOTLAND

Cross the border from England to Scotland, and you will find that the landscape, architecture and historical emphasis all change. This is part of the United Kingdom which retains its own educational and legal systems and parliament, banknotes and established church. Scotland joined the Union in 1707, but many of its castles and historic houses, heroes and battlefields are from the time when England was 'the auld enemy'. Football and rugby internationals retain something of that ancestral rivalry.

The ruined Border abbeys are evidence of the old raiding days. Along the Galloway coast, revenue duties on brandy, wine, silks and other goods were so resented that generations of Solway men made their living by smuggling. This was no casual trade. Several smuggling companies were proper businesses, with shareholders and accurate, if secret, books of accounts. Further north, in the Highland and Grampian glens, it was whisky taxes that were bitterly disliked. Pure mountain water, often flavoured by the peaty ground through which it flowed, was the basis of hundreds of illicit whisky stills. Some respectable modern distilleries happily admit to a raffish past.

Scotland has its own character and its own history. At the turn of the 13th and 14th centuries the story was one of avoiding an English conquest, and Scotland's independence was re-asserted during the reign of Robert I – Robert the Bruce. His descendants founded the dynasty of the Stuart kings and queens, and the story of the Highlands in the first half of the 18th century is largely bound up with the efforts of the Stuarts to regain the British throne. All their attempts were failures, but the history of the Jacobites is still well remembered.

The tours take you to Jacobite country, to the land of the Solway smugglers, to ground fought over in the Border wars, and to lonely northwestern districts, where the people were forced off their holdings by 19th-century landlords wanting the larger rents offered first by incoming sheep farmers and then by wealthy deerstalkers. In places you will wonder why the land seems so empty: it was not always so.

Neidpath Castle was battered by Cromwell during the Civil War

Gentle hills slope away from the banks of Loch Lomond

Inverness

Inverness is the capital of the Highlands. Industry is confined to one area, and the town can boast some fine old buildings among clumsy modern developments. Inverness makes a feature of its riverside walks, overlooked by a 19th-century castle, and footbridges cross to the Ness Islands. There are cruises on the Caledonian Canal, a good local museum, and the curious claim – which you can judge at Tomnahurich Hill – that the town has the most beautiful burial ground in the country!

Aberdeen

Aberdeen is the grey Granite City, the capital of North Sea oil, but the granite of its buildings comes to life and sparkles in the sun. There are excellent museums and galleries, such as Provost Skene's House, golf courses and a long beach, while its parks rival any in Britain. Aberdeen is a regular top prizewinner in the Britain in bloom competition: look for the 100,000 roses planted along one city dual-carriageway.

Edinburgh

Once again Scotland's seat of government, Edinburgh is obviously a capital city. The New Town is one of the most graceful examples of Georgian planning, and few shopping streets have such an imposing backdrop as Princes Street, dominated by the castle rock. Edinburgh houses Scotland's national galleries and some splendid museums, as well as being, every August and September, a world-famous festival city.

Within the city limits, look for Dean Village, a remarkable survival of lovely buildings by the Water of Leith, and for Cramond, once an oyster-fishermen's village, where the Almond Water flows into the Forth.

Dumfries

Dumfries is the Queen of the South, the principal town in the region which stretches from the English border to the Mull of Galloway. Its museums are varied and impressive, one featuring an old windmill adapted to house a camera obscura. Robert Burns is remembered affectionately in Dumfries; it was his home in later years. His house is one of the town museums, and his favourite pub, the Globe Inn, retains many Burns mementoes.

Dumbarton

Dumbarton was once the capital of the Celtic kingdom of Strathclyde. Later, it became an innovative shipbuilding centre and, almost in passing, a pioneer of the helicopter and the hovercraft. It is still an exhilarating experience to climb to the viewpoint summit of Dumbarton Rock, the old Celtic stronghold and later a fortress of the Crown. Although the shipyards have been abandoned, the Denny Experiment Tank, where scale models of hulls were tested to see how they performed in miniature storms, still survives.

History &
Mystery

History and magnificent scenery are ever present on this tour.
Just outside town lies Culloden, where Bonnie Prince Charlie's
defeat in 1746 ruined the last hope of a Stuart restoration to the
British throne. There are glorious sea, loch, island and mountain
views, and who knows what may be lurking in Loch Ness?

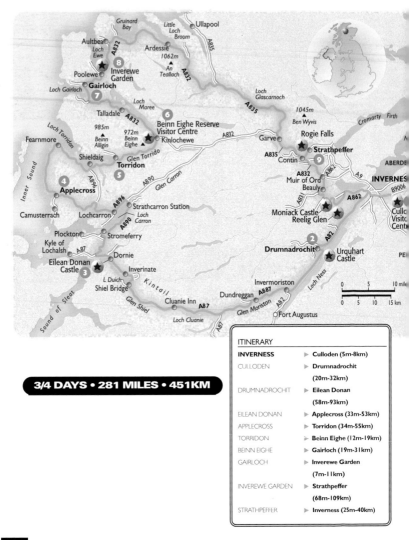

3/4 DAYS • 281 MILES • 451KM

ITINERARY		
INVERNESS	▶	**Culloden (5m-8km)**
CULLODEN	▶	**Drumnadrochit**
		(20m-32km)
DRUMNADROCHIT	▶	**Eilean Donan**
		(58m-93km)
EILEAN DONAN	▶	**Applecross (33m-53km)**
APPLECROSS	▶	**Torridon (34m-55km)**
TORRIDON	▶	**Beinn Eighe (12m-19km)**
BEINN EIGHE	▶	**Gairloch (19m-31km)**
GAIRLOCH	▶	**Inverewe Garden**
		(7m-11km)
INVEREWE GARDEN	▶	**Strathpeffer**
		(68m-109km)
STRATHPEFFER	▶	**Inverness (25m-40km)**

⬜ *Castle Wynd, Inverness*

FOR CHILDREN

Before leaving Inverness, pay a visit to Whin Park, one of the finest children's play areas in the Highlands.

▶ *Leave Inverness on the B9006 to the battlefield of Culloden.*

❶ Culloden, Highland

Cared for by the National Trust for Scotland, Culloden Moor is a place of sombre memories. It was here, on 16 April, 1746, that the Duke of Cumberland's army crushed the Jacobite rising led by Prince Charles. The battlefield is laid out with plaques showing the disposition of the opposing forces, and in the visitor centre you can follow the story of this last major battle on British soil. Displays illustrate the confusing political climate of the times, when there were Scots – and even different Highland clans – fighting on both sides. The bitter aftermath of the battle, when government troops were sent on a murderous rampage through the glens, is also described.

▶ *Return to Inverness and take the A82 as for Fort William.*

❷ Drumnadrochit, Highland

This is the site of the Loch Ness Centre, with its exhibition about the search for the world's most famous monster, said to lurk in the chill waters. You may arrive feeling sceptical, but you will almost certainly leave with the feeling that there is *something* here to be explained. Follow the 'Divach' sign off the A82 to the graceful Falls of Divach, and visit the striking lochside ruins of 13th-century Urquhart Castle, and the roadside monument to John Cobb, the land-speed record holder who was killed on Loch Ness in 1952 trying for the water-speed record.

⬜ *The Car Park*

▶ *Continue on the A82 to Invermoriston, then take the A887 and go straight on along the A87. Continue through*

Eilean Donan Castle, built by Alexander II of Scotland in 1220

Inverinate and turn right up Carr Brae. Go into Dornie and turn left for Eilean Donan Castle.

❸ Eilean Donan, Highland

Probably the most photographed castle in Scotland, Eilean Donan was rebuilt on its splendid islet site between 1912 and 1932, after lying in ruins since the Jacobite Rising of 1719. The MacRaes have been its Constables since 1509. Principal apartments open to visitors are the barrel-vaulted billeting room and the small but impressive banqueting hall. In the hall, look for the letter from Bonnie Prince Charlie – 'Being fully persuaded of yr loyalty and zeal for the King's service…' – sent to clan chiefs on behalf of his father, seeking their support in the 1745 Rising.

▶ *Leave Dornie on the A87 as for Kyle of Lochalsh, then turn right on to the A890, left on to the A896 through Lochcarron and Kishorn, and left for Applecross.*

Loch Maree, one of Scotland's most beautiful inland lochs

FOR HISTORY BUFFS

Beside the A87 in wild Glenshiel a plaque describes the battle fought there during the short-lived Jacobite Rising of 1719. The defeated Jacobite army included a company of Spanish troops – the last foreign soldiers to fight on Scottish soil.

RECOMMENDED WALKS

Lochcarron Environmental Group publishes a guide to 15 hill, coast and forest walks. One climbs the Allt nan Carnan gorge above three waterfalls, with glorious views over Loch Carron and the Attadale hills.

4 Applecross, Highland
If you don't like narrow mountain roads, skip Applecross; if you do you will find a beautifully located crofting village, facing the splendid skyline of the Cuillin Hills on Skye. St Maelrhuba is the local saint, and after his death in AD 722, villagers carried soil from his grave on long or perilous journeys. Potter southwards to the lovely rocky bay beyond Camusterrach and take a picnic behind the rippled sandbanks of Applecross Bay. On the lonely road north, look for the pathway which, until a generation ago, was the only land link between the scattered settlements of North Applecross.

i Main Street, Lochcarron

▶ Leave Applecross following the 'Shieldaig' sign. Turn left at a T-junction to rejoin the **A896**.

5 Torridon, Highland
The Torridon landscape has no peers in mainland Scotland, with shapely Beinn Alligin and its outliers soaring from the sea-loch and, further east, Liathach's seven-peaked pinnacled ridge towering over Torridon village and glen. Both ranges are owned by the National Trust for Scotland, and a classic 9-mile (14.5km) walk on Trust ground explores the wild country behind Liathach. In summer, the Trust Visitor Centre explains the history, geology and wildlife of this glorious district, and there is an exhibition and audio-visual presentation on red deer near by.

i NTS Visitor Centre

▶ Continue on the **A896**. Turn left on to the **A832**.

6 Beinn Eighe, Highland
This magnificent mountain range, with quartzite summit rocks which give the impression of a permanent dusting of snow, was Britain's first National Nature Reserve. The Visitor Centre on the A832 illustrates the fascinating wildlife of the mountain – warblers and redstarts in the birchwoods, crossbills among the pines, otters and black-throated divers on the margins of Loch Maree. Two waymarked trails – one to 1,700 feet (518m) – offer tremendous views over the loch.

i Beinn Eighe Reserve Visitor Centre

BACK TO NATURE

Beinn Eighe National Nature Reserve, near Kinlochewe, has some of the most dramatic scenery in Britain. Remnants of Caledonian pine forest harbour interesting plants such as creeping lady's tresses, lesser twayblade orchid, twinflower and chickweed wintergreen.

▶ Continue on the **A832** to Gairloch.

7 Gairloch, Highland
Gairloch is really a cluster of crofting settlements on the shores of an attractive sea loch,

which has become a resort with fine sands, a fishing harbour and one of the most beautifully located golf-courses in Scotland. Gairloch Heritage Museum has fishing boats in its courtyard, an old lighthouse tower installed at ground level, and indoor displays on the fishing, crofting and archaeological history of the heartland of the MacKenzies.

ℹ️ *Auchtercairn, Gairloch*

▶ *Continue through Poolewe.*

8 **Inverewe Garden,** Highland

This is perhaps the most famous garden in the whole of Scotland. Its Victorian creator transformed a bare, windswept promontory into a pine-sheltered woodland where, helped by the benign effect of the Gulf Stream, a spectacular collection of rhododendrons, primulas, deep blue meconopsis and hundreds of other plants and flowering shrubs now flourishes.

FOR HISTORY BUFFS

Turn off the A832 into Aultbea and behind Pier Road is a board describing how, during World War II, the anchorage of Loch Ewe was the gathering point for Arctic convoys to the Soviet port of Murmansk.

▶ *Continue on the A832, turn right on to the A835 then left at Contin on the A834.*

9 **Strathpeffer,** Highland

What was once Europe's most northerly spa remains a fine looking resort centred on a gathering of sturdy Victorian hotels and villas in wooded grounds. Strathpeffer's redundant station has been restored to house craft shops, and in a pavilion in the square, you can sample some of the mineral-rich waters from local springs. Be prepared for a strong taste of sulphur! In the old days, spa visitors were expected to take vigorous exercise; so there is an excellent golf-course, as well as a network of paths in a pleasant pinewood and, on the southern hills patrolled by kestrels and sparrowhawks, to the commanding viewpoint summit of Knock Farril.

ℹ️ *The Square*

RECOMMENDED WALKS

Turn off the A835 after Tarvie for the Rogie Falls. Footpaths cross a bridge over the rock pools and rapids, and pass a salmon ladder built to allow fish to swim upstream in the spawning season.

FOR CHILDREN

At Strathpeffer, ask the children to find the street names in the Victorian heart of the town. Apart from 'The Square', there are none: in its heyday as a spa, house names were the only addresses.

▶ *Return to Contin and turn left on the A835. Turn right on the A832 then right on the A862 through Beauly. Turn right to Moniack and pass Moniack Castle. Turn right at a T-junction following the Rebeg sign, pass the start of the Reelig Glen forest walk, then continue over a bridge and uphill. Take the first tarred road left, past a house called Kilninver, turn left at a T-junction and immediately first right, then right at a Give Way sign to go to Inverness.*

SCENIC ROUTES

Down Glenshiel, the A87 slices through a landscape of steep green mountainsides. After Inverinate, Carr Brae leads to a wonderful viewpoint, and, later, the A890 opens up dramatic views around Loch Carron.

Inverness Castle: Macbeth is thought to have lived on the site of the first castle here

The Castles
of Mar

Aberdeen is the gateway to Royal Deeside and to the great spread of historic houses known as the Castles of Mar. The Royal Family's Scottish home is here, where pine and birchwoods line the riversides and heathery grouse moors rise to the skyline hills. Salmon and trout anglers fish the Dee and its companion river, the Don. Gliders soar above Aboyne and Dinnet, while older transport is the fascination at Alford.

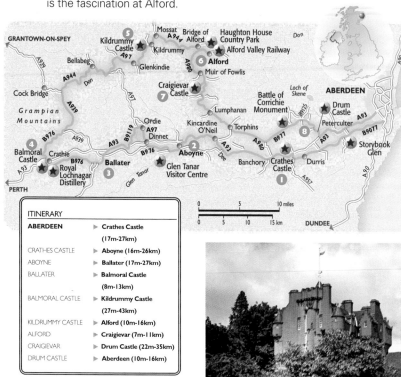

ITINERARY

ABERDEEN	▶ **Crathes Castle** (17m-27km)
CRATHES CASTLE	▶ **Aboyne** (16m-26km)
ABOYNE	▶ **Ballater** (17m-27km)
BALLATER	▶ **Balmoral Castle** (8m-13km)
BALMORAL CASTLE	▶ **Kildrummy Castle** (27m-43km)
KILDRUMMY CASTLE	▶ **Alford** (10m-16km)
ALFORD	▶ **Craigievar** (7m-11km)
CRAIGIEVAR	▶ **Drum Castle** (22m-35km)
DRUM CASTLE	▶ **Aberdeen** (10m-16km)

3 DAYS • 134 MILES • 214KM

ⓘ *23 Union Street, Aberdeen*

▶ *Leave Aberdeen on the B9077. Turn right on the A957, then left on the A93 to Crathes Castle.*

❶ Crathes Castle,
Grampian

Sixteenth-century Crathes Castle was the home of generations of the Burnett family. It is a typical design by the Bells, master masons of Aberdeen and its hinterland, with a tower-like structure and an intriguing ornamented roofline. Look out for the lovely painted ceiling of the Nine Nobles Room, and in the Green Lady's Room ponder the story of the Crathes ghost.

There are eight individual gardens, and one of their major attractions is the array of massive yew hedges, planted in 1702. Topiarists trim them into sweeping shapes, a task which takes three weeks every year.

FOR CHILDREN

Turn left off the B9077 for Storybook Glen, with its tableaux of children's stories, ranging from *Jack and the Beanstalk* and *Little Jack Horner* to the *Incredible Hulk* and *ET*.

▶ *Continue on the A93 to Aboyne.*

❷ Aboyne, Grampian

Built in Victorian times round a spacious green, Aboyne was previously a base for the 'floaters', the intrepid characters who made rafts of timber, cut up-river, and then steered them down the Dee to Aberdeen. There is a well-kept golf-course not far from the water-skiing centre at Aboyne Loch. Anglers fish the Dee, and there are pleasant riverside walks backed by banks of broom.

Aboyne Highland Games, held every August on the green, are among the most famous in Scotland.

RECOMMENDED WALKS

After Aboyne, turn left off the B976 at the grand gateway by the Bridge o' Ess into beautiful Glen Tanar.
Call in at the Glen Tanar Visitor Centre for information on the footpath routes beside the Water of Tanar, to forest viewpoints and along part of the Firmounth road, one of the historic rights of way across the Grampians.

SPECIAL TO...

Aboyne is just one place which hosts annual Highland Games. Tossing the caber, shot-putting and hill races, as well as normal track events, are featured at Ballater and further up Royal Deeside. The Lonach Gathering at Bellabeg, on the A944 in Strathdon, is preceded by a march of the green-clad Lonach Highlanders.

▶ *Leave Aboyne to the south. Turn right on the B976, right on the A97 as far as Ordie. Turn left on to the B9119 and right on the A93 to Ballater.*

❸ Ballater, Grampian

Close to the Royal Family's Balmoral estate, this sturdy granite-built town has many shops showing the royal warrant. Golf, angling and walks by the Dee are favourite recreations here, but there are also enjoyable footpaths on Craigendarroch and Craig Coillich, the two wooded viewpoint hills which squeeze the town towards the river. In the now redundant railway station there is a display on the Deeside Line and its most celebrated passengers: the Royal Family used to arrive by train at Ballater and continue by road to Balmoral.

ⓘ *Station Square*

▶ *Leave Ballater to the south and turn right on the B976 to the car park for Balmoral Castle.*

SPECIAL TO...

Single malt whisky is a classic Highland product. Turn left off the B976 before Balmoral for a tour of Royal Lochnagar Distillery, which received its royal warrant after a visit from Queen Victoria.

Sixteenth-century Crathes Castle

Craigievar Castle rises six storeys high and is topped by turrets

4 Balmoral Castle, Grampian

The Royal Family's Scottish home is their private property, and not one of the great state houses. Prince Albert collaborated closely with the architect commissioned to build the present castle in Scottish Baronial style. From May till the end of July, the beautiful grounds are generally open to visitors. The ballroom houses an exhibition on the history of the estate. Across the river from the car park, Crathie parish church is where the Royal Family worship when they are in residence at Balmoral.

▶ *Turn left on the **A93**, right on the **B976**, left on the **A939**, right on the **A944**, then straight on along the **A97** to Kildrummy Castle.*

5 Kildrummy Castle, Grampian

Built in the 13th century, this was the first great stone fortress in the north of Scotland. Even in decay it remains an impressive place. Modern Kildrummy Castle, once a mansion house, is now a hotel. The quarry from which it was built was transformed in Victorian times into a Japanese-style rock and water-garden with woodlands, pools, waterfalls, shrubs and flower beds linked by paths and stairways in a narrow ravine.

> **FOR HISTORY BUFFS**
>
> Kildrummy Castle witnessed a gruesome deed in 1306, when its English besiegers promised to reward with gold the black-smith who betrayed it to them. They kept their promise by melting the gold pieces and pouring them down his throat to kill him.

▶ *Continue on the **A97**, then right on the **A944** to Alford.*

6 Alford, Grampian

If it runs on wheels, Alford welcomes it. The Grampian Transport Museum houses a fine collection of cars, commercial and farm vehicles, models and transport memorabilia. Look for the *Craigievar Express*, a steam wagon built in the 1890s by a local postman; and a Sentinel steam lorry from a distillery, whose wares it advertises as most suitable for medicinal purposes.

Outside, the museum operates a little motor-racing circuit where sprints for modern and vintage cars are held. Close by, the old station has been restored as a railway museum.

i Railway Museum

> **FOR CHILDREN**
>
> From Alford station the narrow-gauge Alford Valley Railway runs into Haughton House Country Park, where there is an adventure playground in the birchwoods.

▶ *Return from Alford along the **A944** straight on along the **A980**, then right to Craigievar Castle.*

7 Craigievar Castle, Grampian

Although they were not building for fairy-tales, the Bell family of master masons combined a firm grasp of technique with a glorious lightness of touch. With its

---

profusion of towers and turrets, Craigievar demonstrates this very clearly. Built for 'Danzig Willie' Forbes, who made his fortune in the Baltic trade, it was completed in 1626. Craigievar's five floors of rooms include such features as a grand heraldic fireplace carved from granite, pine and oak panelling, intricate plaster ceilings and the first of the Craigievar gaming tables which had a vogue among 18th-century card players.

▶ *Continue on the **A980** and go straight on along the **B977** and the **B9125**, then immediately after Flora's Shop, turn right, following the 'Hopeton' sign. Turn right at a crossroads, avoiding a farm road straight ahead, then follow signs to Drum Castle.*

> **FOR HISTORY BUFFS**
>
> On the B977, look to the left for the granite monument to the Battle of Corrichie in 1562. Mary, Queen of Scots' army crushed the Gordons, the most powerful family in the northeast, in this battle. The Earl of Huntly, the head of the family, died in the battle, and his corpse was taken to Edinburgh to 'hear' the sentence that forfeited his lands and titles.

8 Drum Castle, Grampian

The Irvine family have been lairds at Drum Castle for 24 generations before giving the property to the National Trust for Scotland. They lived in a complex of linked buildings: a 13th-century keep, a Jacobean mansion and Victorian additions. Drum is well furnished with valuable pieces from different centuries. Among the portraits is one of Washington Irving, author of the classic *Rip van Winkle*, whose family left Scotland to live in America.

▶ *Rejoin the public road, then turn left on to the **A93** to return to Aberdeen.*

Exploring the
Tweed Valley

Hills are an important part of this tour, which visits the Pentlands, the Eildons and the Lammermuirs, and looks south to the Cheviots. But the valley of the River Tweed, one of Scotland's great trout and salmon waters, is the most significant element as the journey reaches the Border country.

2/3 DAYS • 134 MILES • 216KM

ITINERARY		
EDINBURGH	▶	**Hillend Country Park** (5m-8km)
HILLEND COUNTRY PARK	▶	**Peebles (18m-29km)**
PEEBLES	▶	**Traquair (8m-13km)**
TRAQUAIR	▶	**Innerleithen (2m-3km)**
INNERLEITHEN	▶	**Melrose (16m-26km)**
MELROSE	▶	**Kelso (14m-23km)**
KELSO	▶	**Coldstream (9m-14.5km)**
COLDSTREAM	▶	**Haddington (37m-59.5km)**
HADDINGTON	▶	**Aberlady (5m-8km)**
ABERLADY	▶	**Edinburgh (20m-32km)**

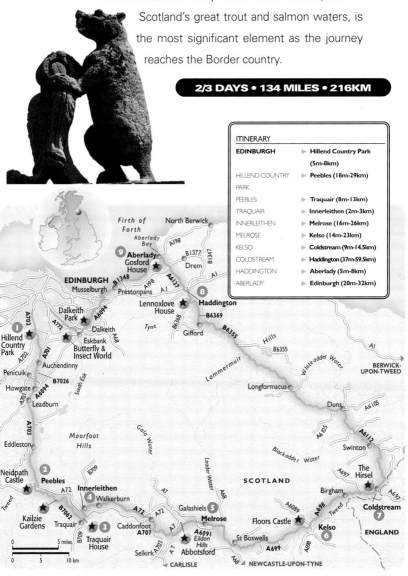

Edinburgh Castle perches on Castle Rock, possibly the site of an Iron-Age fort

i 3 Princes Street, Edinburgh

▶ *Leave Edinburgh on the A702 and turn right into Hillend Country Park, 5 miles (8km).*

1 Hillend Country Park, Lothian

This is one of two similar parks in the exhilarating Pentland Hills, which rise directly from Edinburgh's southern suburbs. Footpaths climb steeply to the grassy viewpoint summits of Caerketton and Allermuir, the boyhood hills of Robert Louis Stevenson. These paths link up with others across the rounded passes in the Pentlands, and alongside the many reservoirs which supply the city. Midlothian Snowsports Centre, with its extensive artificial ski-slope, is a year-round mountain resort in miniature.

i Pentland Hills Ranger Service Office

▶ *Continue on the A702, then straight on along the A703 and follow the A701 and B7026 through Auchendinny. Take the A6094 and the A703 again to Peebles.*

FOR CHILDREN

Hillend Snowsports Centre is the largest of its kind in Europe. Children's courses start for those aged six. On the return to Edinburgh, the Butterfly and Insect World on the A7 houses hundreds of exotic butterflies as well as scorpions, tarantulas and stick insects.

---

2 Peebles, Borders

No development is allowed to encroach upon Peebles' tree-lined riverside walks by the Tweed, and the town itself has a traditional charm. The Tontine Hotel in the High Street retains the old front yard where stage-coaches used to sweep to a halt. There is a well-stocked Tweeddale Museum, and the Cornice Museum of Ornamental

Plasterwork is close by, where you will be encouraged to don wellies and an apron, and try your hand at the craft. Peebles has extensive public parks and an interesting town walk.

Medieval Neidpath Castle stands dramatically above an up-river wooded curve of the Tweed, to the west of Peebles. Its walls still show signs of the bombardment in 1650 by Cromwell's artillery.

RECOMMENDED WALKS

The Sware Walk at Peebles heads west along the wooded river bank below Neidpath Castle, crosses Manor Bridge and Old Manor Bridge, then climbs to the wide-ranging Tweeddale viewpoint at Manor Sware.

---

i 23 High Street

▶ *Leave Peebles on the B7062 and turn left for Traquair House.*

3 Traquair, Borders
Twenty generations of Stuart lairds made Traquair House their home, but it dates from well before their time – from 1107 at least – and is the oldest inhabited house in Scotland. Traquair retains mementoes of such famous Stuarts as Mary, Queen of Scots and Bonnie Prince Charlie. As well as having valuable collections of glass, porcelain and embroideries, it is famous for its one derelict 18th-century estate brew-house. The present laird restored the copper, the mash tun, the coolers and fermenters, and now brews the rare Traquair Ale in quantities of no more than 210 barrels every year.

▶ *Continue on the **B7062** then turn left on the **B709** to Innerleithen.*

4 Innerleithen, Borders
The founder of this little textile town had the idea of using London names so addresses here include The Strand and Bond Street. Cashmere cloth is still woven in Innerleithen's mills, and the National Trust for Scotland has completely restored Robert Smail's Printing Works, closed as a family business only in 1986. A tour of this fascinating place recalls the otherwise lost technology of planers, reglets, quoins and sidesticks, and you may be given the chance to hand-set some type.

At a glorious viewpoint high in the town, the little blue-and-white spa pavilion of St Ronan's Well can be found. The spring was originally known as the 'Doo Well' because of the number of wood pigeons which frequented the area. St Ronan was thought to be a saint from France or Ireland and was adopted as patron saint of Innerleithen. The well became famous when, in 1824, Sir Walter Scott used it as a setting for his novel *St Ronan's Well*.

▶ *Leave Innerleithen on the **A72**. Bear right on the **A707**, then left on the **B7060**. Turn right on the **A7**, left on the **B6360**, right on the **A6091** as for Jedburgh, and left on the **B6374** into Melrose.*

FOR HISTORY BUFFS

Abbotsford, on the way to Melrose, was the home of Sir Walter Scott, author of the *Waverley* novels. He bought the site, on which he built Abbotsford, between 1811 and 1822. It took a long time to complete as he kept adding on bits. The tour includes his impressive library and study.

Robert Smail's print shop was started in 1840, when the original press was water-powered

5 Melrose, Borders
One of the most pleasant of the Border towns, Melrose is notable for the mellow ruin of its abbey, where the heart of Robert the Bruce is buried, and for Priorwood Garden, in which something like the old monks' orchard has been revived. Harmony Garden is an attractive walled garden with magnificent views over Melrose Abbey and the Eildon Hills.

Two walks explore the town, and the Southern Upland Way includes a lovely riverside stretch along the meadows by the Tweed.

RECOMMENDED WALKS

Starting from the B6359 in Melrose, the waymarked Eildon Walk climbs to the 1,325-foot (404m) Eildon North Hill, a magnificent viewpoint where a Roman signal station overlooked the Dere Street route from the Cheviots to the Forth. Here is the legendary resting place of King Arthur and his knights, sleeping under a spell.

i *Abbey House*

▶ *Leave Melrose on the **A6091** as for Jedburgh. Turn right on to the **A68** then left on the **A699** and left on the **A698** into Kelso.*

6 Kelso, Borders
This is a Border market town with a ruined abbey, the oldest cricket club in Scotland, a racecourse and a reputation for providing some of the best angling beats on the Tweed. Kelso has an elegant Georgian centre, and its cobbled square retains a bull ring – a pattern of stones marking the place where bulls were tethered during livestock sales. Kelso Pottery is well worth a visit.

Outside the town, Floors Castle, home of the Duke of Roxburghe, is richly furnished

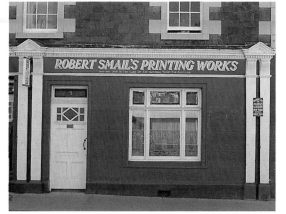

The Myreton Motor Museum at Aberlady

with paintings, tapestries and porcelain, and has a window for every day of the year. This huge mansion was built by William Adam between 1721 and 1725.

i Town House, The Square

▶ *Leave Kelso on the **A698** for Coldstream.*

7 Coldstream, Borders
This is the closest Scottish town to the English border. The Coldstream Guards, under an earlier name, were stationed in the town in 1660 when they marched south to assist in the restoration of King Charles II to the throne. There is a museum here dedicated to the regiment and its impressive heritage.

Just outside Coldstream, the Hirsel estate has a comprehensive museum and a craft centre, several walks and a colourful collection of rhododendrons in Dundock Wood.

▶ *Leave Coldstream on the **A6112** for Duns, then take the **A6105** as for Earlston. After leaving Duns, watch for the right turn to Gifford. Turn right*

*to Haddington on the **6355**, **B6369** and **B6368**.*

SPECIAL TO…

In Newtown Street, Duns, the Jim Clark Memorial Room commemorates the great Formula 1 World Champion who won 25 Grand Prix races and the Indianapolis 500.

FOR HISTORY BUFFS

Memorials at Gifford recall the Rev John Witherspoon, who signed the American Declaration of Independence and was president of the college which became Princeton University. Off the B6369, Lennoxlove House is the home of the Dukes of Hamilton. It contains many mementoes of Mary, Queen of Scots, including the ring which, on her way to the scaffold, she bequeathed to the Hamiltons.

8 Haddington, Lothian
Haddington is famous for the dozens of listed buildings along its streets, lanes and riverside walks. St Mary's Church contains the Lauderdale Aisle, scene of an annual ecumenical pilgrimage. Near by, St Mary's Pleasance is a garden laid out in an old Scottish style. Features to look for in Haddington include the town history display in Lady Kitty's Doocot (dovecote); Jane Welsh Carlyle's House, with its memories of the Victorian writer Thomas Carlyle; the Nungate Bridge; and the statue of two goats fighting. A goat eating grapes is Haddington's unusual coat of arms.

▶ *Leave Haddington on the **A6137** for Aberlady.*

9 Aberlady, Lothian
Once the trading seaport for Haddington, Aberlady is now a residential village with carefully preserved buildings, including a

medieval parish church with fine stained-glass windows, and attractive 18th- and 19th-century houses in the High Street. Aberlady's golf-course, Kilspindie, shared the ground with a rifle range when it was opened in 1898; hence the names of holes such as the Target and the Magazine. West of the village, Gosford House is the home of the Earl of Wemyss. The magnificent entrance hall houses Gosford's imposing portrait gallery.

BACK TO NATURE

The tidal inlet, saltmarsh and dunes at Aberlady Bay Nature Reserve, east of Aberlady, attract great numbers of waders. Regular reports are posted of bird observations: hundreds of sandwich terns, for instance, and godwits, dunlin and plover.

▶ *Leave Aberlady on the **A198** as for Edinburgh, then straight ahead on the **B1348**. Turn left on the **A199** then right on the **A6094** through Dalkeith. Turn right on the **A772** and return to Edinburgh.*

BACK TO NATURE

On the return towards Edinburgh, Dalkeith Park nature trails link the River North Esk and the South Esk through extensive estate woodlands.

SCENIC ROUTES

The B7062, past Kalizie Gardens, and the A72 follow the Tweed as it winds among woodlands, farms and hillside forests.
You can follow a tree-lined road on the B7060 over the shoulder of a hill between two stretches of the Tweed.

Along the
Smugglers' Coast

Mountains, forests and beautiful stretches of coastline are the accompaniment to this tour from Dumfries. The huge Galloway Forest Park offers walks and trails, exhibitions, nature reserves and fishing waters. Along the coast, the Solway smugglers once brought contraband from the Isle of Man.

2/3 DAYS • 119 MILES • 191.5KM

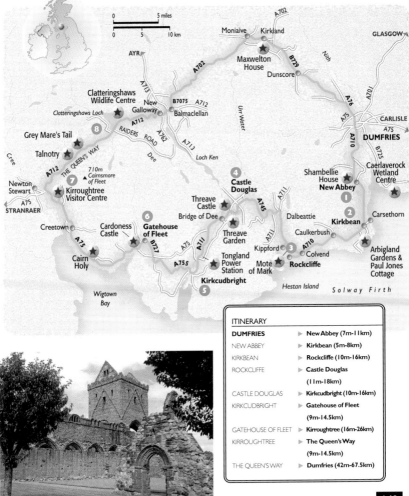

ITINERARY		
DUMFRIES	▶	**New Abbey** (7m-11km)
NEW ABBEY	▶	**Kirkbean** (5m-8km)
KIRKBEAN	▶	**Rockcliffe** (10m-16km)
ROCKCLIFFE	▶	**Castle Douglas** (11m-18km)
CASTLE DOUGLAS	▶	**Kirkcudbright** (10m-16km)
KIRKCUDBRIGHT	▶	**Gatehouse of Fleet** (9m-14.5km)
GATEHOUSE OF FLEET	▶	**Kirroughtree** (16m-26km)
KIRROUGHTREE	▶	**The Queen's Way** (9m-14.5km)
THE QUEEN'S WAY	▶	**Dumfries** (42m-67.5km)

ℹ️ *Whitesands, Dumfries*

BACK TO NATURE

The Wildfowl and Wetlands Trust reserve at Caerlaverock provides some of the best opportunities anywhere to observe wild barnacle geese and family parties of whooper swans in the winter. Both the sanctuary of the reserve and the supplementary supply of food attract these species along with wigeon, teal and many more. There is a charge for admission (except to members of the WWT).

New Abbey's 18th-century corn mill restored to working order

▶ *Leave Dumfries on the **A710** to New Abbey.*

❶ New Abbey, Dumfries and Galloway

Here, 'new' is a relative term. It refers to the lovely ruined abbey of mellow red sandstone which stands on the south side of the village. This is Sweetheart Abbey, new in the 13th century when it was founded by the family which also endowed Balliol College at Oxford. New Abbey also has a splendidly restored 18th-century corn mill. Among the pinewoods at the entrance to the village, Shambellie House is the site of Scotland's Museum of Costume.

▶ *Continue on the **A710** to Kirkbean.*

❷ Kirkbean, Dumfries and Galloway

American visitors often come to this attractive village in 'the garden of Galloway' to trace the roots of Paul Jones, organiser and first commander of the US Navy, who was baptised John Paul in the parish church here. His birthplace cottage on the Arbigland estate is a museum of his life and exploits, which included raiding his home coast during the American War of Independence! Arbigland itself has attractive sheltered gardens stretching to the Solway shore, where Paul Jones' father was employed.

Also near Kirkbean, Carsethorn is a Solwayside village with salmon stake-nets out on the treacherous tidal sands. Facing the Cumbrian shore, it was built to house the men of a 19th-century coast-guard station, in the days when the coastguards' major work was stopping the smugglers.

▶ *Continue on the **A710**. Turn left off it, first to Rockcliffe and then to Kippford.*

❸ Rockcliffe and Kippford, Dumfries and Galloway

These are the principal villages of the Colvend coast, the most beautiful stretch of the Solway Firth. Rockcliffe, with its rock flakes in a curving bay, was a Victorian sea-bathing resort.

Kippford, near the mouth of the River Urr, used to make its living from boat-building and quarrying. Now it is the main sailing centre on the Solway. Almost all the land between the villages is owned by the National Trust for Scotland. Both offer outstanding views over the wooded peninsulas around Rough Firth.

Above Rockcliffe stands the Mote of Mark, site of a 6th-century settlement and now a fine viewpoint.

ℹ️ *Colvend Post Office, Colvend (A710)*

RECOMMENDED WALKS

For one of the most beautiful walks in Scotland, leave Rockcliffe by the Jubilee Path, with its gorgeous views over the estuary.
At Kippford, turn left by the post office along the shore road, then return to Rockcliffe by grassy pathways.
Except in May and June when the terns and oystercatchers are nesting, you can extend the walk – with care – along the tidal causeway to Rough Island.

FOR CHILDREN

Take the children for a boat trip from the floating jetty at Kippford, and let their imaginations run riot as they sail the smugglers' waters around Rough Firth and Hestan Island, a place honeycombed with 'brandy holes' and contraband hideaways.

▶ *Continue on the **A710**, then follow signs for Castle Douglas on the **A711** and **A745**. Turn left at a roundabout and go through the town centre, 11 miles (18km).*

4 Castle Douglas, Dumfries and Galloway

A light and lively market town, Castle Douglas is lucky in having, as its principal public park, the land around Carlingwark Loch. Here you can hire a rowing boat to potter round the wooded islets and reed-beds where swans and great crested grebes nest and raise their young.

West of the loch, watch for the road on the left to Threave Garden. A property of the National Trust for Scotland, it features springtime daffodil displays as well as herbaceous borders, peat, woodland and rock gardens. Threave House is the Trust's School of Horticulture, and the whole 60 acres (24 hectares) are impeccably kept.

i Market Hill Car Park

FOR HISTORY BUFFS

At the roundabout after Castle Douglas, take the second exit for the walk and short ferry trip across the Dee to Threave Castle, the ruined island fortress of the Black Douglases, rebels against the crown.

▶ *Turn left at a roundabout, go along the A75, then turn left on to the A711 to Kirkcudbright.*

5 Kirkcudbright, Dumfries and Galloway

Built as the county town, this is a place of elegantly proportioned and colour-washed Georgian houses. It attracted turn-of-the-century artists, and their successors still live and work here. Broughton House, an 18th-century mansion, was presented to the town by the painter E A Hornel. It hosts art exhibitions and is well furnished with a fine antiquarian library and features such as a 1920s-style laundry. Outside, you may be surprised to find a Japanese garden; Hornel was influenced by Oriental themes.

Maclellan's Castle, now an ancient monument, is the ruin of a grander and earlier town mansion. The Stewartry Museum holds a fascinating local collection, including a room devoted to Kirkcudbright shipping, in which Paul Jones features strongly.

i Harbour Square

▶ *Leave Kirkcudbright on the A755 then follow the B727 through Gatehouse of Fleet.*

The estuary of the Dee in Kirkcudbright at dusk

SPECIAL TO...

Phone Kirkcudbright 330114 to book a place on the tour – starting from Kirkcudbright – of Tongland power station, with its audio-visual presentation on the Galloway hydro-electric scheme, followed by visits to the spotless turbine hall and the salmon ladder in the ravine behind.

6 Gatehouse of Fleet, Dumfries and Galloway

Gatehouse by the River Fleet is one of the most intriguing country towns in Scotland, full of restored buildings from its brief heyday – from 1790 onwards – as a cotton town. Robert Burns visited Gatehouse during the boom years, and it was in a room at the Murray Arms Hotel that he wrote what was to become Scotland's unofficial anthem, *Scots, wha hae*. The town is surrounded by delicious woodland country. Try the Fleet Oakwoods interpretative trail. A shorter open ground stroll leads to the field-top viewpoint on Venniehill, which identifies the features of Gatehouse and its surroundings. Beyond

Grey Mare's Tail waterfall

Venniehill, Cardoness Castle is an imposingly situated 15th-century tower which was the home of the notoriously hot-tempered McCullochs.

i *The Car Park, High Street*

▶ *Turn right on to the **A75** (heading west) and in Palnure watch for a right turn to Kirroughtree Visitor Centre.*

FOR HISTORY BUFFS

Turn right off the A75 for the standing stones of Cairn Holy, overlooking the Solway. On the return to Dumfries, Maxwelton House, on the B729, was the birthplace of the heroine of Scotland's famous love song, *Annie Laurie*.

---

7 Kirroughtree Forest,
Dumfries and Galloway
The oldest South of Scotland plantations of the Forestry Commission cover a landscape of hills and a river valley over-looked by the great bulk of Cairnsmore of Fleet. An audio-visual presentation explains the workings of the forest, and

outdoor attractions include a forest garden with plots of more than 60 tree species, from redwoods and monkey puzzles to cypress and rarities such as the Englemann spruce. Four trails explore the upper parts of the forest, visiting hill lochs and viewpoints, and you should follow the separate Papy Ha'bird trail above the Palnure Burn, habitat of warblers, woodpeck-ers, dippers, goosanders, shel-duck, jays and ravens.

i *Kirroughtree Visitor Centre*

▶ *Rejoin the **A75**, then go right on to the **A712**.*

8 The Queen's Way,
Dumfries and Galloway
Several visitor areas of the Galloway Forest Park are concentrated along the stretch of A712 known as the Queen's Way. The start is signalled by the hilltop obelisk at Talnotry commemorating Alexander Murray, a local shepherd's son who became the greatest Oriental linguist in early 19th-century Britain.

Look out for the Grey Mare's Tail waterfall. Further on there is a visitor centre, by the side of Clatteringshaws Loch, where

you'll find information on the Red Deer Range and Wild Goat Park. Close by is 'Bruce's Stone', where Robert the Bruce is supposed to have rested after defeating the English in 1307.

RECOMMENDED WALKS

At Talnotry, on the Queen's Way, marked trails explore the steep forested hills. Do not be misled by the wide path at the start; much of this is roughish going. The trails go to viewpoints and an old lead mine, and follow the 'lost' 18th-century Edinburgh-Wigtown coach road.

FOR CHILDREN

Turn off the Queen's Way after the Red Deer Range for the Raiders Road forest drive, an old cattle-rustlers' trail which runs beside the Black Water of Dee. Children love the bronze otter sculpture at a picnic pool with rocky islets.

▶ *Continue on the **A712** through New Galloway. Turn right on the **A713**, left on the **A712**, left on the **B7075** and right on the **A702** through Moniaive. In Kirkland, turn right on the **B729** and return to Dumfries.*

SCENIC ROUTES

Beyond Dumfries, the A710 gradually comes within sight of the wide Solway sands and, across the water, the faraway Lakeland hills.
After Gatehouse, the A75 offers beautiful high-level views over the bird-watcher's paradise of Wigtown Bay. After Moniaive, the A702 and B729 follow the Cairn Valley through a fine landscape of farms, woods and stone-dyked fields.

The Beautiful
Western Highlands

4 DAYS • 246 MILES • 396KM Some of the most striking seascapes, mountains, forests and moorland scenery in the West Highlands form the landscape of this tour, based on the firmly Lowland town of Dumbarton.

ITINERARY

DUMBARTON	▶ Helensburgh (8m-13km)
HELENSBURGH	▶ Inveraray (40m-64km)
INVERARAY	▶ **Crinan Canal** (27m-43km)
CRINAN CANAL	▶ Kilmartin (7m-11km)
KILMARTIN	▶ Easdale (29m-47km)
EASDALE	▶ Oban (16m-26km)
OBAN	▶ **Barcaldine Castle** (11m-18km)
BARCALDINE CASTLE	▶ Port Appin (14m-23km)
PORT APPIN	▶ Ballachulish (18m-29km)
BALLACHULISH	▶ Glen Coe (5m-8km)
GLEN COE	▶ Loch Lomond (50m-80km)
LOCH LOMOND	▶ Dumbarton (21m-34km)

☐ *Milton, by Dumbarton*

▶ *Leave Dumbarton on the A814 through Cardross, Helensburgh, Rhu and Shandon.*

❶ Helensburgh, Strathclyde
Think of this residential town rising from the estuary of the River Clyde when you switch on your television. John Logie Baird, the television pioneer, was born here in 1888. Another inventive Helensburgh man was Henry Bell, whose *Comet*, launched in 1812, was the world's first sea-going steamboat. Both men are commemorated in the town.

Charles Rennie Mackintosh, the most famous of Scotland's 20th-century architects, completed Hill House in 1902. You may share the feelings of many visitors that the elegant interiors, showing Mackintosh's amazing attention to detail, seem to become more rather than less modern as the decades pass by.

The cone-topped towers of Inveraray Castle

In summer, ferries sail across the Clyde from Helensburgh. There are sailing races, and dozens of yachts lie moored off Rhu – where the garden of Glenarn is an early-season attraction – and Shandon. After Shandon the road passes the Clyde Submarine Base, home port of Britain's nuclear fleet.

☐ *The Clock Tower*

▶ *Take the third exit from the roundabout, follow the A814 to Arrochar and turn left on the A83. Ignore a left turn for the A815, bear left on an unclassified road through Cairndow, and rejoin the A83 for Inveraray.*

❷ Inveraray, Strathclyde
Once the county town of Argyll, this gem of 18th-century architecture is reflected in the waters of Loch Fyne near Inveraray Castle, home of the 12th Duke of Argyll. The castle's public rooms include an imposing armoury hall, a tapestry drawing room and a state dining room with elaborate plasterwork. In the grounds, Cherry Park houses

a Combined Operations Museum recalling how a quarter of a million troops were trained at Inveraray for seaborne landings of World War II. There are also pleasant woodland walks. If you are fit and sure-footed, try the steep climb through roe deer territory to the viewpoint summit of Dun na Cuaiche.

The town's 20th-century bell tower acts as the Clan Campbell war memorial; and Inveraray Gaol is one of the finest theme museums in Scotland. In the courtroom, sitting among lifelike figures of lawyers and jurymen, you can hear the tape-recorded transcript of an actual trial held in 1850.

☐ *Front Street*

▶ *Continue on the A83 to Lochgilphead. Turn right on the A816, bear left on the B841 to cross the Crinan Canal, then go right at Bellanoch on the B8025.*

❸ Crinan Canal, Strathclyde
Built to avoid the risky journey round the Mull of Kintyre, this 9-mile (14.5m) waterway is now

used mostly by yachts and motor cruisers. To the south of the summit level, spruce plantations clothe the hills where reservoirs store the canal's water supply. From the picnic site at Dunardry a forest walk looks down on the canal, its locks and towpath, and an attractive tree-backed lagoon.

FOR HISTORY BUFFS

Beside the A83, Auchindrain is a farming museum. In and around a cluster of restored cottages once lived in by MacCallums, MacCoshams, MacNicols and Munros you can see furnishings and displays of agricultural techniques of generations long gone by.

SPECIAL TO…

South of Furnace, on the A83 is the spectacular Crarae Garden; acres of shrubs and woodland that give the steep-sided Crarae Burn the feel of a Himalayan valley. Since acquiring it in 2001, the National Trust for Scotland plantings have included wild rhododendrons.

▶ Bear left on the **A816** to Kilmartin.

4 Kilmartin, Strathclyde

The lovely Kilmartin valley was the heartland of the 6th-century kingdom of Dalriada, which expanded to become the kingdom of Scotland. The valley also contains Bronze-Age burial cairns and standing stones, some set out in a straight linear alignment.

Kilmartin church and churchyard house many medieval grave slabs, and Carnassarie Castle, high above the village, offers a magnificent view, unobtainable from road level, into the narrow canyon which swings down from Loch Awe.

▶ Continue on the **A816**, then left on the **B844** and follow signs to Easdale.

Crinan Canal was opened in 1801

FOR HISTORY BUFFS

Few places are as atmospheric, for Scots or descendants of Scots, as Dunadd, south of Kilmartin. This hilltop fortress enjoys panoramic views and was once the capital of the kingdom of Dalriada and the coronation site of the first Scottish kings.

5 Easdale, Strathclyde

The steeply arched 'bridge over the Atlantic' to Seil joins one of Argyll's Slate Islands to the mainland. Easdale is the name both of the old quarry village on the west side of Seil, and of the smaller offshore island facing it. A deep quarry at Easdale village, breached by the sea during a ferocious storm in November 1881, survives as an open bay.

The village retains its rows of whitewashed quarriers' cottages. In contrast, high walls and a wooded cliff protect the garden of An Cala – with its gentle stream, ponds, herbaceous borders and flowering shrubs – from the salt-laden wind.

Across the narrow sound on Easdale Island, the workings of a now vanished trade and the way the quarry communities created their own lively social life are explained in a fascinating museum.

ⓘ *Easdale Island Folk Museum*

▶ Return to the **A816** and turn left for Oban.

6 Oban, Strathclyde

Oban is a major car-ferry port and hosts several important yacht races. St Columba's, the 20th-century cathedral with carved oak panels showing scenes from the life of the famous Celtic saint, is the heart of the Roman Catholic diocese of Argyll and the Isles.

Elsewhere in the town you can watch glass-blowers and paper-weight makers at work, and visit the distillery founded in the 18th century. Footpaths climb to outstanding viewpoints such as McCaig's Tower, built in the style of the Colosseum at Rome. Gallanach Road leads south to the little ferry slip for Kerrera, where you can enjoy an exhilarating island walk round a 7-mile (11km) circuit of paths and farm roads.

ⓘ *Argyll Square*

▶ Leave Oban on the **A85**. At Connel, turn right on the **A828** as it swings over Connel Bridge.

7 Barcaldine Castle, Strathclyde

This 16th-century home of the Campbells of Barcaldine, set in magnificent scenery with views

Fishing boats at Oban harbour

FOR CHILDREN

Two miles (3km) outside Oban
is the Oban Rare Breeds Farm
Park. The 35-acre site is the
only Rare Breeds Survival
Trust-approved centre in
Scotland. Many of the animals
are very tame; look out for
Tamworth pigs and Castlemilk
Moorit sheep.

---

towards Glencoe, is also known
as the Black Castle because of
the colour of the stone. It was
built by Black Duncan, and is
associated with the Appin
Murder and Glencoe Massacre.
The castle now offers bed and
breakfast accommodation, and is
closed to the public.

▶ *Continue on the A828 into
Appin village then turn left for
Port Appin.*

RECOMMENDED
WALKS

The most spectacular of the
Forestry Commission walks
around Barcaldine on the A828
starts from Sutherland's Grove.
Paths lead up Glen Dubh – the
Dark Glen – to a footbridge
over the ravine where the river
rampages down.

---

8 Port Appin, Strathclyde
On one of the finest stretches of
the coast of Argyll, this little
village looks out to the long
island of Lismore and, beyond it,
to the lonely hills of Kingairloch.
There is a peninsula walk past a
natural archway in the cliffs, and
another excursion could start
with a ferry trip to the north end
of Lismore. Walks there include
one to the former limeworkers'
village of Port Ramsay. North of
Port Appin, look for Castle
Stalker, romantically located on a
tidal islet.

▶ *Return to the A828 and turn
left. Pass Ballachulish Hotel
and turn left on the A82.*

9 Ballachulish, Strathclyde
The 'Village at the Narrows'
used to be well known for its
ferry across Loch Leven, which
has been replaced with a
modern bridge. A flight of steps
after the Ballachulish Hotel
climbs to a memorial marking
the site of the gibbet where, in
1755, James Stewart of the Glen
was hanged for the murder –
which he did not commit – of
government agent Colin
Campbell. After he was dead,
Stewart's body was left hanging
for three years. The mystery of
who really did commit the
Appin Murder is still discussed,
and Robert Louis Stevenson
made it the central theme of his
novel *Kidnapped*.

Extensive landscaping has
disguised the fact that between
1697 and 1955 Ballachulish was
a major centre of the slate industry. A comprehensive display in
the visitor centre describes its
rise and decline.

ⁱ *Albert Road*

SPECIAL TO...

Railway enthusiasts often trace
the old line from Oban via
Connel Bridge to Ballachulish.
It features handsome turn-of-
the-century stations, one of
which is the Holly Tree Hotel
at Kentallen.

▶ *Continue on the A82, diverting
left into Glencoe village, then
return to the main road for
Glen Coe itself.*

**10 Glen Coe and the Black
Mount,** Strathclyde
Now the tour heads into its most
dramatic phase. At the village of
Glencoe the informative local
museum recalls how, one night

in February 1692, the MacDonalds of Glencoe were slaughtered in their homes by troops billeted on them – an atrocity which has never been forgotten. The story of the massacre is retold in a National Trust for Scotland Visitor Centre a little way up the glen. It also features the wildlife and geology of the district. The northern wall of Glen Coe is a forbidding mountain ridge, while a glorious succession of towers, buttresses, gullies and hanging valleys marches along its southern side. Beyond the isolated Kings House Hotel, desolate Rannoch Moor stretches away to the left.

RECOMMENDED WALKS

After the river bridge at Glencoe village, turn left for the Lochan Trail, which circles an ornamental lake backed by Corsican pines. On a calm day it reflects like a mirror the striking outline of Ben Vair – the Peak of the Thunderbolt.

Further on there are tremendous views into the corries of the Black Mount.

[i] *National Trust for Scotland Visitor Centre, A82*

▶ *Continue on the A82.*

🄸🄸 Loch Lomond,
Strathclyde

Having swooped down Glen Falloch, the route reaches Ardlui at the head of Loch Lomond. In the north, the loch fills a narrow glacial trough between crammed-in mountains. Luss, with its low sandstone cottages and fine Victorian church, lies where Loch Lomond broadens out to become part of a gentler Lowland scene with lovely wooded islands. Like Ardlui, Inveruglas, Tarbert, Inverbeg and Balloch, Luss is a port of call for ferries. You can cruise through the islands or cross the loch, walk on the West Highland Way through spruce, larch, birch and oakwoods under the shoulder of Ben Lomond, and sail back to the western shore.

Glen Coe, the most infamous glen in Scotland

[i] *Harbour Street, Tarbet*

SPECIAL TO...

The most famous but most elusive fish for Loch Lomond anglers is the powan, unique to Scotland. This freshwater herring had to adapt to life away from the sea after glacial debris blocked out the tidal waters.

▶ *Continue on the A82 and return to Dumbarton.*

BACK TO NATURE

Queen Elizabeth Forest Park, near to Loch Lomond, harbours woodland birds, including woodcock and wood warbler, while on the higher ground of Ben Lomond there are golden eagles, ptarmigan and mountain flowers.

MOTORING IN BRITAIN

Driving is one of the best ways to discover Britain. The routes recommended in this book have been designed to maximise the enjoyment of discovering some of Britain's prettiest scenery and famous sights.

Roads are generally good, but busy; if possible, aim to travel outside the rush hours of 8–9.30am and 4.30–6pm, especially in built-up areas.

British drivers are in the main courteous, but try to minimise frustration for other drivers by keeping pace with the traffic, signalling promptly and driving positively.

ACCIDENTS

In the event of an accident, move the vehicle off the carriageway wherever possible. If your vehicle is fitted with hazard warning lights, they should be used and, if available, a red triangle should be placed on the same side of the road at least 165ft (50m) before the vehicle.

If damage or injury is caused to any other person or vehicle you must stop, give your own and the vehicle owner's name and address and the registration number of the vehicle to anyone who has reasonable grounds for having them. If you do not do this, you must report the accident to the police as soon as reasonably practicable, and in any case within 24 hours.

BREAKDOWNS

Visitors who are members of a recognised automobile club in their own country may benefit from the services provided free by the AA.

Car rental companies normally provide cover with one of the major motoring organisations.

On motorways there are emergency telephones beside the hard shoulder every mile (1.6km). In the event of a breakdown, see **accidents** above.

CAR HIRE

Drivers must have a valid national licence, held for at least one year, or an International Driving Permit. The minimum age for hiring a car ranges from 18 to 25. With some companies, there is a maximum age limit of 70. You can arrange to pick up your car in one town and return it in another.

Rental rates usually include free unlimited mileage. The well-established car rental companies have offices in most major conurbations throughout Britain. Smaller, local companies may offer better deals; look up telephone numbers in the *Yellow Pages*.

It is important to ensure that you have some form of personal insurance along with Collision Damage Waiver (CDW). Many companies also offer Damage Excess Reduction (DER) and Theft Protection for an additional premium.

Find out what equipment is standard: air-conditioning is not always available.

Most cars use unleaded fuel; make sure you know what's required (unleaded or diesel) before filling the tank.

Check that rear seat belts are fitted and arrange for a car seat if you have small children.

CLAMPING AND TOWING AWAY

If your car is parked illegally it may be clamped; the notice posted on your windscreen explains how to get it released. Vehicles are usually released within one hour of payment. If your vehicle is removed it will cost at least £125 to get it back. Vehicles must be collected in person and you must produce at least one form of identification, such as your drivers' licence.

CRASH HELMETS

Visiting motorcyclists and their passengers must wear crash or safety helmets.

DOCUMENTS

You must have a valid driver's licence or an International Driving Permit.

Holders of permits written in a foreign language are advised to obtain an official translation from an embassy or recognised automobile association.

Non-EC nationals must have Green Card insurance.

DRINKING AND DRIVING

The laws regarding drinking and driving are strict and the penalties severe. A blood alcohol level of 80mg/100ml is permitted, but the best advice is – if you drink don't drive.

DRIVING CONDITIONS

Traffic drives on the left (it goes clockwise at roundabouts [traffic circles], of which there are many).

Never overtake on the left (see **Motorways**). It is illegal for cars to use bus lanes. Speed-limit and destination signs use miles (one kilometre is roughly ⅝ of a mile).

Motorways link most major cities; service areas are indicated well in advance. On some motorway stretches, however, there aren't many stopping places, eg the M25 (London's busy orbital route), the M11, M20 and M40.

Roads in parts of Wales, the West Country and in the north-west of Scotland are sometimes narrow. On single-track roads, pull into passing places only if they are on your left. Stop level with those on your right – oncoming traffic will make the detour.

FUEL

Petrol (gas) and diesel are widely available, and outlets for LGP are increasing. Unleaded petrol has a minimum octane rating of 95; super octane has around 98. Leaded petrol has been replaced by LRP (Lead Replacement Petrol).

Petrol stations are plentiful on motorways and major roads. Those on motorways, and some on busy major roads and in large towns, are open 24 hours, or at least until late at night. Most accept credit cards.

Most large petrol stations are self-service. If driving a rental car, make sure you know what fuel is required (petrol or diesel) before filling the tank; leaded fuel is being phased out.

Higher octane fuel is more expensive than lower octane. Diesel, once cheaper, is now the most expensive.

Prices vary throughout the country, with supermarket petrol stations usually being the most competitive.

INSURANCE

Fully comprehensive insurance, covering some of the expenses incurred after a breakdown or an accident, is advisable.

LIGHTS

Front and rear sidelights and rear registration plate lights must be lit at night. Headlights must be used when visibility is poor and at night on unlit roads and those where the street lights are more than 185m (600 feet) apart.

MOTORWAYS

The routes in this book are largely based on main and secondary roads, rather than motorways, but motorways may be used to reach the start point of a tour.

The major arteries are the M1 (north/south), the M6 (north-west), M2 (southeast), M3 (south), M4 (west), and M5 (southwest). There are no tolls to pay, with the exception of Britain's first toll road, the M6 Toll, opened in 2003 (see **Tolls**).

Major considerations when using motorways are:
• Electronic information panels warn of problems ahead, such as accidents, fog, snow or ice.

• When joining the motorway, give priority to the traffic already on the motorway.

• Do not overtake on the inside unless the queue you are in is moving faster than the queue on the right.

• Keep a safe distance from the vehicle in front, and increase the gap in wet, windy, icy or snowy conditions.

• Do not exceed the 70mph (112kph) speed limit.

• Do not drive on the hard shoulder except in an emergency or when directed to do so.

PARKING

Parking is very difficult, especially in large towns and cities. Parking on the street is limited, and usually for short periods only. Always check for parking restrictions; never park if you do not understand the signs or regulations, and do not take spaces reserved for doctors, ambulances or the disabled.

Traffic wardens patrol streets and issue parking fines where illegal parking is taking place; the fixed penalty of £40 should be paid promptly – many carry a discount if paid within 14 days.

Common parking restrictions are:
• A single yellow line indicates parking restrictions; a notice should explain what these are.

• No parking is allowed at any time on a double yellow line

• A broken yellow line indicates limited restrictions.

• A single red line indicates a clearway, where stopping is not permitted at any time.

• Many inner-city streets are reserved for permit-holding residents only.

Follow car park signs and always carry small change to feed ticket machines (Pay-and-Display) and parking meters; ensure your ticket is clearly displayed. Car parks and meters may be free after 7pm on Mondays to

Saturdays, and sometimes all day on Sundays, but always check the notices.

Hotels usually have their own car parks, or can arrange overnight parking for you. Enquire about car parking and book a space if possible, while arranging your accommodation.

ROUNDABOUTS (TRAFFIC CIRCLES)

Traffic moves clockwise around roundabouts (traffic circles). Cars already on the roundabout (coming from the right) have priority unless indicated otherwise by signs, road markings or traffic lights.

If the roundabout is on a dual carriageway, stay in the left lane if you are turning off left; stay in the right lane if you are going straight ahead or turning right to exit the roundabout. but watch out for the many drivers who don't follow this rule and go straight ahead from the left-hand lane. Use mini-roundabouts in the same way.

ROUTE DIRECTIONS

These abbreviations are used for British roads:
A – main roads
B – local roads
M – motorways
unclassified roads – minor roads.

SEAT BELTS

Seat belts are compulsory for drivers and front seat passengers, and for those in rear seats where belts are fitted.

SPEED LIMITS

Speed limits for cars are:
motorways and dual carriageways 70mph (112kph);
other roads 60mph (96kph);
built-up areas 30mph (48kph), unless otherwise indicated.

TOLLS

Since December 2003 car drivers have had to pay a £4 toll to use a stretch of the M6, from junction 4a to 11a around Birmingham at peak times. It's Britain's first toll road. The rate is £3 between 11pm and 6am.

ACCOMMODATION AND RESTAURANTS

ACCOMMODATION AND RESTAURANTS

The following hotels (◇) and restaurants (◉) can be found along the routes of each tour.

It is worth booking hotels as early as possible, particularly for the peak holiday period from the beginning of June to the end of September. Bear in mind that Easter and other public holidays may be busy, too, and in some parts of Scotland, the ski season is a peak holiday period. Some hotels may ask for a deposit or full payment in advance.

Full listings of British and Irish hotels and B&Bs available through the service can be found and booked at the AA's Internet site: www.theAA.com.

Hotel prices

Hotels are divided into three price brackets based on a nightly rate for a double room with breakfast:
Expensive £££ – over £110
Moderate ££ – £60–£110
Budget £ – up to £60

Restaurant prices

Restaurants are divided into three price brackets based on the cost of a set-price dinner, excluding drink:
Expensive £££ – over £25
Moderate ££ – £15–£25
Budget £ – up to £15

TOUR I
PENZANCE Cornwall
◉ **Harris's Restaurant £££**
46 New Street, TR18 2LZ.
Tel: 01736 364408;
www.landsendhotel.co.uk
Innovative seafood dishes.

LANDS END Cornwall
◇ **The Land's End Hotel ££**
TR19 7AA.
Tel: 01736 871844. 33 rooms.

ST IVES Cornwall
◉ **Alba Restaurant £££**
Old Lifeboat House, TR26 1LF.
Tel: 01736 797222.
Successful modern eatery.

TRURO Cornwall
◇ **Carlton ££**
Falmouth Road, TR1 2HL.
Tel: 01872 272450;
www.carltonhotel.co.uk
29 rooms.

ST MAWES Cornwall
◉ **Rising Sun Hotel £££**
St Mawes, TR2 5DJ.
Tel: 01326 270233;
www.risingsunstmawes.co.uk
Popular, with a picturesque harbour setting.

FALMOUTH Cornwall
◇ **Royal Duchy £££**
Cliff Road, TR11 4NX.
Tel: 01326 313042; www.brend-hotels.co.uk/duchy/imdex.cfm
43 rooms.

MULLION Cornwall
◇ **Mullion Cove Hotel ££–£££**
TR12 7EP.
Tel: 01326 240328;
www.mullioncove.com
30 rooms.

TOUR 2
ST AUSTELL Cornwall
◉ **Carlyon Bay Hotel £££**
Sea Road, Carlyon Bay, PL25 3RD.
Tel: 01726 812304.
Modern fare with marvellous views.

BODMIN Cornwall
◇ **Westberry ££**
Rhind Street, PL31 2EL.
Tel: 01208 72772;
www.westberryhotel.net
21 rooms.

TINTAGEL Cornwall
◇ **Bossiney House £**
Bossiney, PL34 0AX.
Tel: 01840 770240;
www.bossineyhouse.com
19 rooms.

LYDFORD Devon
◉ **Dartmoor Inn ££**
Lydford, EX20 4AY.
Tel: 01822 820221.
Welcoming gastro pub.

MORETONHAMPSTEAD Devon
◇ **Bovey Castle £££**
North Bovey, TQ13 8RE.
Tel: 01647 445016;
www.boveycastle.com
65 rooms.

TAVISTOCK Devon
◇ **Bedford Hotel £££**
1 Plymouth Road, PL19 8YG.
Tel: 01822 613221;
www.bedford-hotel.co.uk
30 rooms.

LISKEARD Cornwall
◉ **Well House Hotel £££**
St Keyne, PL14 4RN.
Tel: 01579 342001.
Traditional cuisine.

TOUR 3
LYNMOUTH Devon
◉ **Rising Sun Hotel ££**
Harbourside, EX35 6EG.
Tel: 01598 753223.
Seafood a speciality.

PORLOCK Somerset
◉ **Andrews on the Weir £££**
Porlock Weir, TA24 8PB.
Tel: 01643 863300.
European cooking with local ingredients.

MINEHEAD Somerset
◇ **Channel House Hotel ££**
Church Path, TA24 5QG.
Tel: 01643 703229;
www.channelhouse.co.uk
8 rooms.

WINSFORD Somerset
◉ **Karslake House £££**
Halse Lane, TA24 7JE.
Tel: 01643 851242.
Home cooking in a country house.

SIMONSBATH Somerset
◇ **Simonsbath House ££**
Exmoor National Park, TA24 7SH.
Tel: 01643 831259;
www.simonsbathhouse.co.uk
10 rooms.

SOUTH MOLTON Devon
🍴 **The Corn Dolly £**
115a East Street, EX36 3DB.
Tel: 01769 574249.
Real Devon cream tea.

BARNSTAPLE Devon
◇ **Park Hotel ££**
Taw Vale, EX32 9AE.
Tel: 01271 372166;
www.brend-hotels.co.uk/park
39 rooms.

TOUR 4
BRIDGWATER Somerset
◇ **Walnut Tree Hotel ££**
North Petherton, TA6 6QA.
Tel: 01278 662255;
www.bw-walnuttreehotel.co.uk
33 rooms.

TAUNTON Somerset
◇ **Corner House Hotel £**
Park Street, TA1 4DQ.
Tel: 01823 284683;
www.corner-house.co.uk
28 rooms.
🍴 **Farthings Hotel & Restaurant £££**
Hatch Beauchamp, TA3 6SG.
Tel: 01823 480664.
British cuisine at its best.

BRIDPORT Dorset
🍴 **Riverside Restaurant ££**
West Bay, DT6 4EZ.
Tel: 01308 422011.
Friendly seaside eatery.

DORCHESTER Dorset
🍴 **Yalbury Cottage £££**
Lower Bockhampton, DT2 8PZ.
Tel: 01305 262382.
British food in a cosy cottage setting.

BEAMINSTER Dorset
🍴 **Bridge House Hotel £££**
3 Prout Bridge, DT8 3AY.
Tel: 01308 862200.
Country cooking in a lovely setting.

YEOVIL Somerset
◇ **Yeovil Court ££–£££**
West Colker Road, BA20 2HE.
Tel: 01935 863746;
www.yeovilhotel.com
30 rooms.

TOUR 5
SALISBURY Wiltshire
◇ **Milford Hall £££**
206 Castle Street, SP1 3TE.

Tel: 01722 417411;
wwwmilfordhallhotel.com
35 rooms.

WARMINSTER Wiltshire
🍴 **Angel Inn ££**
Upton Scudamore, BA12 0AG.
Tel: 01985 213225.
Good pub meals.

WELLS Somerset
◇ **White Hart ££**
Sadler Street, BA5 2RR.
Tel: 01749 672056;
www.whitehart-wells.co.uk
15 rooms.

BRUTON Somerset
🍴 **Bruton House £££**
2–4 High Street, BA10 0AA.
Tel: 01749 813395; no website
Fine dining, contemporary style.
🍴 **Truffles £££**
95 High Street, BA10 0AR.
Tel: 01749 812255.
Modern cooking in ivy-clad cottages.

SHAFTESBURY Dorset
🍴 **Wayfarers Restaurant £££**
Sherborne Causeway, SP7 9PX.
Tel: 01747 852821.
Good food in family-run inn.

TOUR 6
TUNBRIDGE WELLS Kent
◇ **Royal Wells Inn ££**
Mount Ephraim, TN4 8BE.
Tel: 01892 511188;
www.royalwells.co.uk
25 rooms.
◇ **The Spa Hotel £££**
Mount Ephraim, TN4 8XJ.
Tel: 01892 520331;
wwwspahotel.co.uk
69 rooms.
🍴 **Right on the Green £££**
15 Church Road, Southborough, TN4 0RX.
Tel: 01892 513161.
Top British cooking using quality local ingredients.

EDENBRIDGE Kent
🍴 **Haxted Mill & Riverside Brasserie £££**
Haxted Road, TN8 6PU.
Tel: 01732 862914.
Riverside brasserie with international flavours.

SISSINGHURST Kent
🍴 **Rankins £££**
The Street, TN17 2JH.
Tel: 01580 713964.
Closed lunch Wed–Sat, dinner Sun–Tue.

TENTERDEN Kent
◇ **London Beach Hotel and Golf Club ££–£££**
Ashford Road, TN30 6HX.
Tel: 01580 766279;
www.londonbeach.com
24 rooms.

TOUR 7
CANTERBURY Kent
🍴 **Café Belge ££**
89–90 St Dunstans Street, CT2 8AD.
Tel: 01227 768222.
Traditional Belgian cuisine.
◇ **Swallow Falstaff Hotel ££**
8–10 St Dunstan's Street, CT2 8AF.
Tel: 01227 462138; www.english-inns.co.uk/Falstaff-Canterbury
25 rooms.

ASHFORD Kent
🍴 **Eastwell Manor £££**
Boughton Lees, TN25 4HR.
Tel: 01233 213000.
Classic cooking in historic building.

RYE East Sussex
◇ **Mermaid Inn £££**
Mermaid Street, TN31 7EY.
Tel: 01797 223065;
www.mermaidinn.com
31 rooms.

FOLKESTONE Kent
◇ **Harbourside Hotel ££**
14 Wear Bay Road, CT19 6AT.
Tel: 01303 256528.;
www.harboursidehotel.com
17 rooms.

DEAL Kent
◇ **Royal Hotel ££**
Beach Street, CT14 6JD.
Tel: 01304 375555;
www.theroyalhotel.com
18 rooms.

DOVER Kent
🍴 **Walletts Court Country House Hotel £££**
West Cliff, CT15 6EW
Tel: 01304 852424.
Country house with nice atmosphere.

TOUR 8
SOUTHAMPTON
Hampshire
◇ **Elizabeth House £**
42–44 The Avenue, SO17 1XP.
Tel: 02380 224327;
www.elizabethhousehotel.com
27 rooms.

WINCHESTER Hampshire
🍽 **Café de Paris ££**
5 Jewry Street, SO23 8RZ.
Tel: 01962 860006.
Classic French brasserie.
◇ **Mercure Wessex £££**
Paternoster Row, SO23 9LQ.
Tel: 01962 861611;
www.mercure.com
94 rooms.

STOCKBRIDGE Hampshire
🍽 **The Greyhound £££**
High Street, SO20 6EY.
Tel: 01264 810833.
Riverside gastro-pub.

ROMSEY Hampshire
🍽 **Bertie's ££**
80 The Hundred, SO51 8BX.
Tel: 01794 830708.
French food in a converted pub.

TOUR 9
BOURNEMOUTH Dorset
◇ **Chine Hotel £££**
Boscombe Spa Road, BH5 1AX.
Tel: 01202 396234;
www.bestwestern.co.uk
65 rooms.
🍽 **Bistro on the Beach ££**
Solent Promenade, Southbourne
Coast Road, BH6 4BE.
Tel: 01202 431473.
Bistro overlooking the beach.

BROCKENHURST
Hampshire
◇ **Cloud £££**
Meerut Road, SO42 7TD.
Tel: 01590 622165;
www.cloudhotel.co.uk
18 rooms.
🍽 **New Park Manor £££**
Lyndhurst Road, SO42 7QH.
Tel: 01590 623467.
Modern British fare.

LYMINGTON Hampshire
🍽 **The Mill at Gordleton £££**
Silver Street, Hordle, SO41 6DJ.
Tel: 01590 682219.
Dining in a converted watermill.

BEAULIEU Hampshire
🍽 **Montagu Arms Hotel**
£££
Palace Lane, SO42 7ZL.
Tel: 01590 612324.
Modern British cooking.

FORDINGBRIDGE
Hampshire
🍽 **Hour Glass ££**
Burgate, SP6 1LX.
Tel: 01425 652348.
Thatched cottage, modern interior.

TOUR 10
CHEPSTOW Monmouthshire
◇ **Castle View Hotel ££**
16 Bridge Street, NP6 5EZ.
Tel: 01291 620349;
www.hotelchepstow.co.uk
13 rooms.
🍽 **Wye Knot Restaurant ££**
The Back, NP16 5HH.
Tel: 01291 622929.
Honest cooking in a friendly cottage.

ROSS-ON-WYE
Herefordshire
🍽 **Glewstone Court ££**
Glewstone, HR9 6AW.
Tel: 01989 770367.
*British, French cooking in an
elegant manor.*

SKENFRITH Monmouthshire
🍽 **The Bell at Skenfrith £££**
NP7 8UH.
Tel: 01600 750235.
*Innovative Welsh cuisine. Closed
Mon Nov–Mar.*

BRECON Powys
◇ **Castle of Brecon ££**
Castle Square, LD3 9DB.
Tel: 01874 624611;
www.breconcastle.co.uk
43 rooms.

TALYBONT-ON-USK
Powys
🍽 **The Usk Inn ££**
Station Road, LD3 7JE.
Tel: 01874 676251.
Bistro-style British and European.

ABERGAVENNY
Monmouthshire
◇ **Llansantffraed Court ££**
Llanvihangel Gobion, NP7 9BA.
Tel: 01873 840678;
www.llch.co.uk
21 rooms.

USK Monmouthshire
🍽 **Three Salmons Hotel ££**
Bridge Street, NP15 1RY.
Tel: 01291 672133.
Fresh food, friendly atmosphere.

TOUR 11
TENBY Pembrokeshire
◇ **Atlantic £**
The Esplanade, SA70 7DU.
Tel: 01834 842881;
www.atlantic-hotel.uk.com
42 rooms.
◇ 🍽 **Panorama Hotel and
Restaurant £–££**
The Esplanade, SA70 7DU.
Tel: 01834 844976;
www.tenby-hotel.co.uk
7 rooms.
*Tempting international menu
featuring seafood.*

HAVERFORDWEST
Pembrokeshire
◇ **Lower Haythog Farm £**
Spittal, SA62 5QL.
Tel: 01437 731279;
www.lowerhaythogfarm.co.uk
4 rooms.
🍽 **Wolfscastle Country
Hotel ££**
Wolf's Castle, SA62 5LZ.
Tel: 01437 741225.
*British cooking using the best local
produce.*

ST DAVID'S Pembrokeshire
🍽 **Morgan's Brasserie ££**
20 Nun Street, SA62 6NT.
Tel: 01437 720508.
Homely modern British bistro.

CARDIGAN Ceredigion
◇ **Cliff Hotel ££**
Gwbert-on-Sea, SA43 1PP.
Tel: 01239 613241;
www.cliffhotel.com
70 rooms.

CARMARTHEN
Carmarthenshire
🍽 **Falcon Hotel ££**
Lammas Street, SA31 3AP.
Tel: 01267 234959.
Friendly family-run restaurant.

LAUGHARNE
Carmarthenshire
🍽 **The Cors Restaurant ££**
Newbridge Road, SA33 4SH.
Tel: 01994 427219.
Exciting food in a vibrant setting.

TOUR 12
ABERYSTWYTH Ceredigion
◇ **Four Seasons ££**
50–54 Portland Street, SY23 2DX.
Tel: 01970 612120;
www.fourseasonshotel.uk.com
15 rooms.
|◎| **Harry's ££**
40-46 North Parade, SY23 2NF.
Tel: 01970 612647.
Classic bistro, sound dining.

MACHYNLLETH Powys
◇ **Wynnstay £**
Maengwyn Street, SY20 8AE.
Tel: 01654 702941;
www.wynnstay-hotel.com
23 rooms.

BUILTH WELLS Powys
|◎| **Caer Beris Manor Hotel ££**
LD2 3NP.
Tel: 01982 552601.
European fare in good dining room.

LLANWRTYD WELLS Powys
|◎| **Carlton House £££**
Dolycoed Road, LD5 4RA.
Tel: 01591 610248.
Modern cuisine. Closed Sun dinner.

TOUR 13
BARMOUTH Gwynedd
◇|◎| **Tŷ'r Graig Castle Hotel ££**
Llanaber Road, LL42 1YN.
Tel: 01341 280470;
www.tyr-graig-castle.co.uk
12 rooms.
Welsh eclectic cooking.

HARLECH Gwynedd
|◎| **Castle Cottage £££**
Pen Llech, LL46 2YL.
Tel: 01766 780479.
Modern cooking in a fine setting.

BALA Gwynedd
◇ **Plas Coch ££**
High Street, LL23 7AB.
Tel: 01678 520309;
www.plascoch.com
10 rooms.

ABERDYFI Gwynedd
|◎| **Penhelig Arms Hotel £££**
Terrace Road, LL35 0LT.
Tel: 01654 767215.
Seafood overlooking the harbour.

DOLGELLAU Gwynedd
|◎| **Dolserau Hall ££**
LL40 2AG.
Tel: 01341 422522.
Traditional cooking in Snowdonia.

TOUR 14
BANGOR Gwynedd
◇ **Garden Hotel £**
1 High St, LL57 1DQ.
Tel: 01248 362189.
12 rooms.

CAERNARFON Gwynedd
◇ **Menai Bank House £**
North Road, LL55 1BD.
Tel: 01286 673297;
www.menaibankhotel.co.uk
15 rooms.
|◎| **Seiont Manor £££**
Llanrug, LL55 2AQ.
Tel: 01286 673366.
Welsh specialities.

LLANBERIS Gwynedd
◇ **Royal Victoria Hotel ££–£££**
LL55 4TY.
Tel: 01286 870253;
www.royal-victoria-hotel.co.uk
106 rooms.
|◎| **Y Bistro ££**
Glandwr, 43–45 Stryd Fawr (High Street), LL55 4EU.
Tel: 01286 871278.
Modern Welsh dishes.

PORTMEIRION Gwynedd
|◎| **Hotel Portmeirion £££**
LL48 6ET.
Tel: 01766 770000.
Creative menu using local produce.

BETWS-Y-COED Conwy
|◎| **Royal Oak Hotel ££**
Holyhead Road, LL24 0AY.
Tel: 01690 710219.
Good food and friendly service.

COLWYN BAY Conwy
|◎| **Café Nicoise ££**
124 Abergele Road, LL29 7PS.
Tel: 01492 531555.
Modern European food. Closed dinner Sun, Mon.

CONWY Conwy
◇ **Castle Hotel Conwy £££**
High Street, LL32 8DB.
Tel: 01492 582800;
www.castlewales.co.uk
28 rooms.

TOUR 15
LINCOLN Lincolnshire
◇ **Branston Hall £££**
Branston Park, LN4 1PD.
Tel: 01522 793305;
www.branstonhall.com
50 rooms.
◇ **Edward King House £–££**
The Old Palace, Minster Yard, LN2 1PU.
Tel: 01522 504050;
www.ekhs.org.uk
17 rooms.
|◎| **Wig & Mitre ££**
30–32 Steep Hill, LN2 1TL.
Tel: 01522 535190.
International fare, cathedral views.

WOODHALL SPA Lincolnshire
◇ **Eagle Lodge £**
The Broadway, LN10 6ST.
Tel: 01526 353231;
www.4hotels.co.uk
23 rooms.

SLEAFORD Lincolnshire
|◎| **Carre Arms £**
1 Mareham Lane, NG34 7JP.
Tel: 01529 303156.
Bar meals or smart brasserie.

NEWARK-ON-TRENT Nottinghamshire
◇ **Grange Hotel ££**
73 London Road, NG24 1RZ.
Tel: 01636 703399;
grangenewark.co.uk
19 rooms.

TOUR 16
KING'S LYNN Norfolk
◇ **Congham Hall Country House ££**
Lynn Road, PE32 1AH.
Tel: 01485 600250;
www.conghamhallhotel.co.uk
14 rooms.

ELY Cambridgeshire
|◎| **Anchor Inn ££**
Sutton Gault, CB6 2BD.
Tel: 01353 778537.
Traditional British cooking in a riverside inn.

FAKENHAM Norfolk
◇ **Crown ££**
6 Market Place, NR21 9BP.
Tel: 01328 851418; www.crown-hotelfakenham.co.uk
14 rooms.

WELLS-NEXT-THE-SEA
Norfolk
🍽️**The Crown Restaurant**
£££
The Buttlands, NR23 1EX.
Tel: 01328 710209.
Pacific Rim and seafood.

HOLKHAM Norfolk
🍽️ **The Victoria at Holkham**
££
Park Road, NR23 1RG.
Tel: 01328 711008.
Modern brasserie wtih colonial feel.

BURNHAM MARKET
Norfolk
🍽️ **Fishes £££**
Market Place, PE31 8HE.
Tel: 01328 738588.
Seafood specials.

TOUR 17
IPSWICH Suffolk
◇ **Claydon Country House**
££
16–18 Ipswich Road, Claydon,
IP6 0AR. Tel: 01473 830382;
www.bestwestern.co.uk
36 rooms.
🍽️ **Il Punto ££**
Neptune Quay, IP4 1AX.
Tel: 01473 289748.
French-style cooking on a boat.

CAMBRIDGE Cambridgeshire
◇ **Arundel House ££–£££**
Chesterton Road, CB4 3AN.
Tel: 01223 367701;
www.arundelhousehotels.co.uk
103 rooms.
◇ **Gonville Hotel £££**
Gonville Place, CB1 1LY.
Tel: 01223 366611;
www.gonvillehotel.co.uk
73 rooms.
🍽️ **Midsummer House £££**
Midsummer Common, CB4
1HA.
Tel: 01223 369299.
French cuisine in a country setting.

LONG MELFORD Suffolk
🍽️ **The Black Lion Hotel ££**
Church Walk, The Green, CO10
9DN.
Tel: 01787 312356.
Stylish dining near village green.

LAVENHAM Suffolk
◇ **Lavenham Priory £££**
Water Street, CO10 9RW

Tel: 01787 247404;
www.lavenhampriory.co.uk
6 rooms.

TOUR 18
OXFORD Oxfordshire
◇ **Victoria ££**
180 Abingdon Road, OX1 4RA.
Tel: 01865 724536;
http://victoriahotelox.com
22 rooms.
🍽️ **Gee's Restaurant ££**
61 Banbury Road, OX2 6PE.
Tel: 01865 553540.
British food in a light conservatory.

WOODSTOCK Oxfordshire
🍽️ **Macdonald Bear Hotel**
££
Park Street, OX20 1SZ.
Tel: 0870 4008202.
Historic inn, modern cooking.

BANBURY Oxfordshire
◇ **Banbury House ££**
Oxford Road, OX16 9AH.
Tel: 01295 259361;
www.banburyhouse.co.uk
64 rooms.

DEDDINGTON Oxfordshire
🍽️ **Deddington Arms**
££–£££
Horsefair, OX15 0SH.
Tel: 01869 338364.
Continental food with British tones.

BICESTER Oxfordshire
🍽️ **Bignell Park Hotel ££**
Chesterton, OX26 1UE.
Tel: 01869 326550.
Creative cooking in a rustic setting.

TOUR 19
GLOUCESTER
Gloucestershire
◇ **Hatherley Manor**
££–£££
Down Hatherley Lane, GL2
9QA.
Tel: 0870 194 2126;
www.macdonaldhotels.co.uk
52 rooms.

LEDBURY Hereford and
Worcester
◇ **Feathers Hotel £££**
High Street, HR8 1DS.
Tel: 01531 635266;
www.feathers-ledbury.co.uk
19 rooms.

EVESHAM Worcestershire
◇ **Northwick Hotel ££**
Waterside, WR11 1BT.
Tel: 01386 40322;
www.northwickhotel.co.uk
29 rooms.
◇ **Wood Norton Hall £££**
Wood Norton, WR11 4YB.
Tel: 01386 425780.
45 rooms.

STRATFORD-UPON-AVON
Warwickshire
🍽️ **Fox and Goose ££**
Armscote, CV37 8DD.
Tel: 01608 682293.
Blackboard choices in a country inn.

CHELTENHAM
Gloucestershire
🍽️ **Parkers £££**
The Hotel on the Park, GL52
2AH.
Tel: 01242 518898.
Modern international cuisine.

TOUR 20
SHREWSBURY Shropshire
◇ **Albright Hussey £££**
Ellesmere Road, SY4 3AF.
Tel: 01939 290571;
www.albrighthussey.co.uk
26 rooms.

CHURCH STRETTON
Shropshire
🍽️ **The Studio ££**
59 High Street, SY6 6BY.
Tel: 01694 722672.
Modern British menus.

LUDLOW Shropshire
◇ **Bromley Court ££**
73 Lower Broad Street, SY8
1PQ.
Tel: 01584 876 996;
www.ludlowhotels.com
3 rooms.
◇ **Feathers Hotel £££**
The Bull Ring, SY8 1AA.
Tel: 01584 875261.
Innovative modern food.

KIDDERMINSTER
Worcestershire
◇ **The Granary Hotel and**
Restaurant ££
Heath Lane, Shenstone, DY10
4BS.
Tel: 01562 777535.
18 rooms.

BRIDGNORTH Shropshire
◇ **Parlors Hall £**
Mill Street, WV15 5AL.
Tel: 01746 761931;
www.4hotels.co.uk
15 rooms.

MUCH WENLOCK
Shropshire
◇ **Raven Hotel £££**
Barrow Street, TF13 6EN
Tel: 01952 727251; www.raven-
hhotel.com
15 rooms.

TOUR 21
CARLISLE Cumbria
◇ **Crown Hotel £££**
Wetheral, CA4 8ES.
Tel: 01228 561888;
www.crownhotelwetheral.co.uk
51 rooms.

KESWICK Cumbria
◇ **Horse & Farrier Inn £**
Threlkeld, near Keswick, CA12
4SQ.
Tel: 017687 79688;
www.horseandfarrier.com
9 rooms.
◎ **Underscar Manor £££**
Applethwaite, CA12 4PH.
Tel: 017687 75000.
Formal French and English dining.

GRASMERE Cumbria
◎ **Rothay Garden Hotel
£££**
Broadgate, LA22 9RJ.
Tel: 015394 35334.
Modern British food.

WINDERMERE Cumbria
◎ **Holbeck Ghyll £**
Holbeck Lane, LA23 1LU.
Tel: 015394 32375.
Classic cuisine.

PENRITH Cumbria
◎ **Edenhall Country Hotel
££**
Edenhall, CA11 8SX.
Tel: 01768 881454.
Traditional fine dining.

TOUR 22
RIPON North Yorkshire
◇ **Ripon Spa £££**
Park Street, HG4 2BU.
Tel: 01765 602172;
www.bw-riponspahotel.co.uk
40 rooms.

MASHAM North Yorkshire
◇ **Swinton Park £££**
Masham, Ripon, HG4 4JH.
Tel: 01765 680900; www.swin-
tonpark.com 30 rooms.

RICHMOND North Yorkshire
◇ **King's Head £££**
Market Place, DL10 4HS.
Tel: 01748 850220;
www.kingsheadrichmond.com
30 rooms.

BARNARD CASTLE
Durham
◇ **Morritt Arms Hotel and
Restaurant ££**
Greta Bridge, DL12 9SE.
Tel: 01833 627232;
www.themorritt.co.uk
27 rooms.

HAWES North Yorkshire
◇ ◎ **Simonstone Hall Hotel
£££**
Hawes, DL8 3LY.
Tel: 01969 667255.
Dinner only. 18 rooms.

AYSGARTH North Yorkshire
◎ **George and Dragon Inn
£££**
DL8 3AD.
Tel: 01969 663358.
Beamed restaurant with real ales.

TOUR 23
MORECAMBE Lancashire
◇ **Clarendon ££**
76 Marine Road West, LA4 4EP.
Tel: 01524 410180;
www.mitchellshotels.co.uk
29 rooms.

KIRKBY LONSDALE
Cumbria
◇ **Pheasant Inn ££**
LA6 2RX. Tel: 015242 71230;
www.pheasantinn.co.uk
10 rooms.

SKIPTON North Yorkshire
◎ **The Coniston ££**
Coniston Cold, BD23 4EB.
Tel: 01756 748080.
Traditional British cuisine.

CLITHEROE Lancashire
◎ **Café Caprice £**
6–8 Moor Lane, BB7 1BE.
Tel: 01200 422034.
Award-winning teas.

BLACKPOOL Lancashire
◎ **Kwizeen ££**
47–49 Kings Street, FY1 3EJ.
Tel: 01253 290045.
Modern food combinations.

TOUR 24
MACCLESFIELD Cheshire
◇ **Shrigley Hall £££**
Pott Shrigley, SK10 5SB.
Tel: 01625 575757;
www.paramount-hotels.co.uk
150 rooms.

ROWSLEY Derbyshire
◎ **East Lodge Hotel £££**
DE4 2EF.
Tel: 01629 734474.
Modern cooking, country house style.

MATLOCK Derbyshire
◎ **Riber Hall £££**
DE4 5JU. Tel: 01629 582795.
Modern cuisine.

BAKEWELL Derbyshire
◇ **Hassop Hall Hotel ££**
Hassop, DE45 1NS.
Tel: 01629 640488;
www.hassophallhotel.co.uk
13 rooms.

BUXTON Derbyshire
◎ **Best Western Lee Wood
Hotel ££**
The Park, SK17 6TQ.
Tel: 01298 23002.
International cuisine.

TOUR 25
YORK North Yorkshire
◇ **Royal York ££**
Station Parade, YO24 1AA.
Tel: 01904 653681;
www.principal-hotels.com
165 rooms.
◎ **Blue Bicycle £££**
34 Fossgate, YO1 9TA.
Tel: 01904 673990.
European menu in a former brothel.

PICKERING North Yorkshire
◇ **White Swan £££**
Market Place, YO18 7AA.
Tel: 01751 472288;
www.white-swan.co.uk
12 rooms.

◇ **Fox & Hounds Country
Inn £**
Main Street, Sinnington,
YO62 6SQ.

Tel: 01751 431577; www.thefox
andhoundsinn.co.uk
10 rooms.

ROSEDALE ABBEY North
Yorkshire
🍽 **Blacksmith's Country Inn
££**
Hartoft End, YO18 8EN.
Tel: 01751 417331.
Bar or restaurant meals.

HELMSLEY North Yorkshire
◇ **Feversham Arms £££**
1 High Street, YO62 5AG
Tel: 01439 770766;
www.fevershamarmshotel.com
20 rooms.

TOUR 26
INVERNESS Highland
◇ **Loch Ness House ££**
Glenurquhart Road, IV3 6JL.
Tel: 01463 231248;
www.lochnesshousehotel.com
21 rooms.

APPLECROSS Highland
🍽 **Applecross Inn ££**
Shore Street, IV54 8LR.
Tel: 01520 744262.
Varied seafood menu.

TORRIDON Highland
🍽 **Loch Torridon Country
House Hotel £££**
Achnasheen, IV22 2EY.
Tel: 01445 791242.
Shooting lodge with malt bar.

GAIRLOCH Highland
◇ **Myrtle Bank ££**
Low Road, IV21 2BS.
Tel: 01445 712004;
www.myrtlebankhotel.co.uk
12 rooms.

CONTIN Highland
🍽 **Coul House Hotel ££**
IV14 9ES.
Tel: 01997 421487.
Contemporary Scottish cuisine.

TOUR 27
ABERDEEN Aberdeenshire
◇ **Macdonald Ardoe House
£££**
South Deeside Road, AB12 5YP.
Tel: 0870 194 2104;
www.mercure.com
109 rooms.

BANCHORY Grampian
🍽 **Banchory Lodge Hotel
££**
AB31 5HS.
Tel: 01330 822625.
Traditional Scottish dishes.

BALLATER Aberdeenshire
◇ **Balgonie Country House
£££**
Braemar Place, AB35 5NQ.
Tel: 013397 55482; www.balgo-
nie-hotel.co.uk
9 rooms.

TOUR 28
EDINBURGH Lothian
◇ **Carlton ££**
North Bridge, EH1 1SD.
Tel: 0131 4723000;
www.paramount-hotels.co.uk
189 rooms.

PEEBLES Borders
◇ **Cringletie House £££**
Edinburgh Road, EH45 8PL.
Tel: 01721 725750;
www.cringletie.com
13 rooms.

INNERLEITHEN Borders
◇ **Traquair Arms Hotel
£–££**
Traquair Road, EH44 6PD.
Tel: 01896 830229;
www.traquairarmshotel.co.uk
14 rooms.

KELSO Borders
🍽 **The Roxburghe Hotel
£££**
Heiton, TD5 8JZ.
Tel: 01573 450331.
Fine Scottish dining.

HADDINGTON East Lothian
🍽 **Maitlandfield House
£**
24 Sidegate, EH41 4BZ.
Tel: 01620 826513.
Scottish and Portuguese food.

TOUR 29
DUMFRIES Dumfries and
Galloway
◇ **Station Hotel ££**
49 Lovers Walk, DG1 1LT.
Tel: 01387 254316; www.best-
western.co.uk
32 rooms.
🍽 **Cairndale Hotel ££**
English Street, DG1 2DF.

Tel: 01387 240289.
Traditional and modern food.

CASTLE DOUGLAS
Dumfries & Galloway
◇ **Douglas Arms ££**
King Street, DG7 1DB.
Tel: 01556 502231;
www.douglasarmshotel.com
23 rooms.

KIRKCUDBRIGHT Dumfries
& Galloway
◇ **Selkirk Arms £££**
Old High Street, DG6 4JG.
Tel: 01557 330402;
www.selkirkarmshotel.co.uk
17 rooms.

GATEHOUSE OF FLEET
Dumfries & Galloway
◇ **Murray Arms ££**
DG7 2HY.
Tel: 01557 814207;
www.murrayarmshotel.co.uk
12 rooms.

TOUR 30
INVERARAY Argyll & Bute
◇ **The Argyll ££**
Front Street, PA32 8XB.
Tel: 01499 302466.
36 rooms.

CAIRNDOW Argyll & Bute
🍽 **Cairndow Stagecoach
Inn ££**
PA26 8BN.
Tel: 01499 600286.
*Bar food, served all day, or
spacious restaurant.*

OBAN Argyll & Bute
◇ **Lancaster ££**
Esplanade, PA34 5AD.
Tel: 01631 562587;
www.lancaster.oban.com
27 rooms.

PORT APPIN Argyll & Bute
🍽 **Airds £££**
PA38 4DF.
Tel: 01631 730236.
Lochside gastronomic treat.

BALLACHULISH Highland
◇ **Ballachulish Hotel £££**
Near Fort William, PH49 4JY.
Tel: 0871 222 3415;
www.ballachulishhotel.com
54 rooms.

PRACTICAL INFORMATION

TOUR 1

[i] Station Road, Penzance. Tel: 01736 362207.
[i] The Guildhall, Street-an-Pol, St Ives. Tel: 01736 796297.
[i] Pydar House, Pydar Street, Truro. Tel: 01872 322900.
[i] Prince of Wales Pier, Falmouth. Tel: 01326 312300.

1 Newlyn
Newlyn Art Gallery
Newlyn, Penzance.
Tel: 01736 363715;
www.newlynartgallery.co.uk
Open daily in summer; Tue–Sat in winter.

3 Porthcurno
The Minack Theatre
Porthcurno, Penzance.
Tel: 01736 810181;
www.minack.com
Open all year, daily. Closed to visitors during performances.

4 Land's End
Last Labyrinth
Land's End, Sennen.
Tel: 0870 4580099;
www.landsend-landmark.co.uk
Open all year, daily.

5 St Just
Geevor Tin Mine
Pendeen, Penzance.
Tel: 01736 788662;
www.geevor.com
Open all year, Sun–Fri.

6 Zennor
Wayside Folk Museum
Zennor. Tel: 01736 796945;
www.stone-circles.org.uk
Open Apr–Oct, daily.

7 St Ives
Barbara Hepworth Museum and Sculpture Garden
Barnoon Hill, St Ives.
Tel: 01736 796226.
Open Mar–Oct, daily; Nov–Feb, Tue–Sun.
Leach Pottery
Higher Stennack, St Ives.
Tel: 01736 796297;
www.leachpottery.com

9 Hayle
Paradise Park
Hayle, near St Ives.
Tel: 01736 753365;
www.paradisepark.org.uk
Open all year, daily.
Cheney Mill Farm Park
Battery Mill Lane, St Erth.
Tel: 01736 759555;
www.cheneymill.co.uk
Open all year, daily.

12 Truro
Royal Cornwall Museum
River Street, Truro.
Tel: 01872 272205;
www.royalcornwallmuseum.org.uk
Open all year, Mon–Sat.

13 St Mawes
St Mawes Castle
St Mawes. Tel: 01326 270526; www.english-heritage.org.uk
Open Apr–Oct, Sun–Fri; Nov–Mar, Fri–Mon.
Trelissick Garden
Feock, Truro.
Tel: 01872 862090;
www.nationaltrust.org.uk
Open daily; restricted opening in Dec.

14 Penryn
Pendennis Castle
Castle Drive, Falmouth.
Tel: 01326 316594;
www.english-heritage.org.uk
Open Apr–Oct, daily; restricted rest of year.

15 Gweek
The National Seal Sanctuary
Gweek, near Helston.
Tel: 01326 221361;
www.sealsanctuary.co.uk
Open all year, daily.

16 Cadgwith
Lizard Point Lighthouse
Lizard Point. Tel: 01326 290202.
Open Jul–Sep, daily; Mar–Jun, Sat–Wed; tel for winter info.

18 Helston
The Flambards Experience
Culdrose Manor, Helston.
Tel: 01326 573404;
www.flambards.co.uk
See website for details.

19 Marazion
St Michael's Mount
The Manor Office, Marazion. Tel: 01736 710507; www.stmichaelsmount.co.uk
Open Apr–Oct, Sun–Fri

TOUR 2

[i] Southbourne Road, St Austell. Tel: 01726 879500.
[i] Shire Hall, Mount Folly, Bodmin. Tel: 01208 76616.
[i] North Cornwall Museum, The Cleave, Camelford. Tel: 01840 212954.
[i] 3 West Street, Okehampton. Tel: 01837 53020.
[i] Town Hall, Bedford Square, Tavistock. Tel: 01822 612938.

1 Bodmin
China Clay Country Park
Carthew, St Austell.
Tel: 01726 850362.
Open all year, daily.
Pencarrow House
Pencarrow, Bodmin.
Tel: 01208 841369;
www.pencarrow.co.uk
Open Apr–late Oct, Sun–Thu.

2 Camelford
North Cornwall Museum
The Cleave, Camelford.
Tel: 01840 212954.
Open Apr–Sep, Mon–Sat.

3 Tintagel
Tintagel Castle
Tintagel Head.
Tel: 01840 770328;
www.english-heritage.org.uk
Open all year, daily.
Old Post Office
Tintagel. Tel: 01840 770024.
Open Apr–Oct, Sun–Fri.

5 Launceston
Launceston Steam Railway
St Thomas Road, Launceston.
Tel: 01566 775665;
www.launcestonsr.co.uk
Open Jun–late Sep, Sun–Fri.
Tamar Otter and Wildlife Centre
North Petherwin, Launceston.
Tel: 01566 785646;
www.tamarotters.co.uk
Open Apr–Oct, daily.

7 Okehampton
The Museum of Dartmoor Life
West Street, Okehampton.
Tel: 01837 52295;
www.museumofdartmoorlife.eclipse.co.uk
Open Easter–Oct, Mon–Sat.

8 Moretonhampstead
Castle Drogo
Drewsteignton.
Tel: 01647 433306;
www.nationaltrust.org.uk
Open mid-Mar–Oct, Wed–Mon.

9 Princetown
The Miniature Pony Centre
Moretonhampstead, Princetown
Tel: 01647 432400;
www.miniaturepony centre.com
Open Easter–Oct, daily.

11 Morwellham Quay
Near Tavistock.
Tel: 01822 833808;
www.morwellham-quay
Open all year, daily.

12 Liskeard
Paul Corin's Magnificent Music Machines
St Keyne Station, Liskeard.
Tel: 01579 343108.
Open May–Oct, daily.

13 Dobwalls
Dobwalls Family Adventure Park
Dobwalls. Closed 2007.
Tel: 01579 320325
www.dobwalls.com;

14 Lostwithiel
Restormel Castle
Lostwithiel.
Tel: 01208 872687;
www.english-heritage.org.uk
Open Apr–Oct, daily.
Shipwreck and Heritage Centre
Quay Road, Charlestown,
St Austell. Tel: 01726 69897.
Open Mar–Oct, daily.

TOUR 3

i Town Hall, Lee Road,
Lynton. Tel: 0845 6603232.
i 17 Friday Street,
Minehead.
Tel: 01643 702624.
i 1 East Street, South
Molton. Tel: 01769 574122.
i Castle Hill, Torrington.
Tel: 01805 626140.
i Victoria Park, The Quay,
Bideford. Tel: 01237 477676.
i The Square, Barnstaple.
Tel: 01271 375000.

3 Porlock
Exmoor Falconry and Animal Farm
Allerford, near Porlock.
Tel: 01643 862816;
www.exmoorfalconry.co.uk
Open Apr–Oct, daily.

5 Minehead
West Somerset Railway
The Station, Minehead.
Tel: 01643 706349;
www.west-somerset-railway.co.uk

Butlin's Holiday Park
Minehead.
Tel: 01643 700517;
www.butlinsonline.co.uk
Dunster Castle & Garden
Minehead.
Tel: 01643 821314;
www.nationaltrust.org.uk
*Open: Castle, late Mar–Oct,
Fri–Wed; gardens daily.*

6 Watchet
Tropiquaria
Washford Cross, Watchet.
Tel: 01984 640688;
www.tropiquaria.co.uk
*Open Apr–Oct, daily; tel for
winter info.*
Cleeve Abbey
Abbey Road, Washford,
near Watchet.
Tel: 01984 640377;
www.english-heritage.org.uk
Open Apr–Oct, daily.
Combe Sydenham Country Park
Monksilver, Watchet.
Tel: 01984 656284.
Open Mar–Sep, daily.

10 South Molton
Cobbaton Combat Collection
Chittlehampton, Umberleigh, near Barnstaple.
Tel: 01769 540740.
*Open Jul–Aug, daily; Apr–Oct,
Sun–Fri; tel for winter info.*

11 Great Torrington
Dartington Crystal
School Lane, Great
Torrington.
Tel: 01805 626242;
www.dartington.co.uk
Open all year, daily.
Rosemoor Garden
Great Torrington.
Tel: 01805 624067.
Open all year, daily.
The Gnome Reserve
West Putford. Tel: 01409 241435.
Open 21 Mar–Oct, daily.

12 Bideford
Tapeley Park
Instow. Tel: 01271 860897.
*Open late March–Oct,
Sun–Fri.*
The Big Sheep
Bideford. Tel: 01237 472366
Open all year, daily.

North Devon Maritime Museum
Odun Road, Appledore.
Tel: 01237 422064.
Open Easter–Oct, pm.

13 Barnstaple
Museum of Barnstaple and North Devon
The Square, Barnstaple.
Tel: 01271 346747.
Open all year, Mon–Sat.

14 Arlington
Arlington Court
Arlington, Barnstaple.
Tel: 01271 850296.
Open late Mar–Oct, Sun–Fri.

15 Blackmoor Gate
Exmoor Zoological Park
South Stowford, Bratton
Fleming, near Barnstaple.
Tel: 01598 763352.
Open all year, daily.

TOUR 4

i Bridgwater House,
Kings Square, Bridgwater.
Tel: 01278 436438.
i Paul Street, Taunton.
Tel: 01823 336344.
i The Guildhall, Fore
Street, Chard.
Tel: 01460 65710.
i 47 South Street,
Bridport.
Tel: 01308 424901.
i Unit 11, Antelope
Walk, Dorchester.
Tel: 01305 267992.
i 3 Tilton Court, Digby
Road, Sherborne.
Tel: 01935 815341.
i Heritage and Visitor
Centre, Hendford, Yeovil.
Tel: 01935 345946.

1 Taunton
County Museum
Castle, Taunton. Tel: 01823 320201.
Open all year, Tue–Sat.
Somerset Cricket Museum
7 Priory Avenue, Taunton.
Tel: 01823 275893.
Open Apr–Oct, Mon–Fri.
West Somerset Railway
The Station, Minehead.
Tel: 01643 704996;
www.west-somerset-railway.co.uk

*Open mid-Mar to Oct, most
days; rest of year,
occasional opening.*

2 Ilminster
Perry's Cider Mills
Dowlish Wake, near
Ilminster. Tel: 01460 55195;
www.perryscider.co.uk
Open all year, daily.
Barrington Court
Barrington, near Ilminster.
Tel: 01460 241938.
Open Mar–Oct, Thu–Tue.

3 Chard
Chard Museum
Godworthy House, High
Street, Chard.
Tel: 01460 65091;
www.wessex.me.uk
*Open May–Oct, Mon–Sat;
Jul and Aug, daily.*
Wildlife Park at Cricket St Thomas
Near Chard. Tel: 01460 30111; www.cstwp.co.uk
Open all year, daily.

7 Abbotsbury
Abbotsbury Swannery
Nr Weymouth. Tel: 01305 871858; www.abbotsbury-tourism.com
Open late Mar–Oct, daily.
Hardy Monument
Black Down, Portesham.
Tel: 01297 561900.
Open Apr–Sep, Sat–Sun.

8 Dorchester
Dinosaur Museum
Icen Way, Dorchester.
Tel: 01305 269880;
www.thedinosaurmuseum.com
Open all year, daily.
The Keep Military Museum
Bridport Road, Dorchester.
Tel: 01305 264066;
www.keepmilitarymuseum.org
*Open Apr–Sep, Mon–Sat;
Oct–Mar, Tue–Sat.*
Dorset County Museum
High West Street,
Dorchester.
Tel: 01305 262735;
www.dorsetcountymuseum.org
*Open Jul–Sep, daily, Mon–Sat
rest of year.*

[10] Sherborne
Sherborne Old Castle
Sherborne.
Tel: 01935 812730;
www.theheritagetrail.co.uk
Open Apr–Oct, daily.

[12] Montacute
Montacute House
Montacute.
Tel: 01935 823289.
*Open mid-Mar–Oct,
Wed–Mon.*

Tintinhull House and
Garden
Near Yeovil.
Tel: 01935 823289.
*Open mid-Mar to Oct,
Wed–Sun.*

TOUR 5

[i] Fish Row, Salisbury.
Tel: 01722 334956.
[i] Central Car Park,
Warminster.
Tel: 01985 218548.
[i] The Round Tower,
Bridge Street, Frome.
Tel: 01373 467271.
[i] Town Hall, Market
Place, Wells.
Tel: 01749 672552.
[i] The Gorge, Cheddar.
Tel: 01934 744071.
[i] The Tribunal, 9 High
Street, Glastonbury.
Tel: 01458 832954.
[i] 8 Bell Street,
Shaftesbury.
Tel: 01747 853514.

[2] Stonehenge
Nr Amesbury.
Tel: 0870 333 1181;
www.english-heritage.org.uk
Open all year, daily.

[3] Warminster
Longleat House and Safari
Park
Longleat, Warminster.
Tel: 01985 844400;
www.longleat.co.uk
Open all year, daily.

[5] Wells
Wookey Hole Caves
Wells. Tel: 01749 672243;
www.wookey.co.uk
Open all year, daily.

[6] Cheddar
Gough's and Cox's Caves
Cheddar.
Tel: 01934 742343;
www.cheddarcaves.co.uk
Open all year, daily.
King John's Hunting Lodge
The Square, Axbridge.
Tel: 01934 732012;
www.nationaltrust.org.uk
Open Apr–Sep, pm.

[7] Glastonbury
Somerset Rural Life
Museum
Chilkwell Street,
Glastonbury.
Tel: 01458 831197;
www.somerset.gov.uk
*Open Apr–Oct, Tue–Fri and
weekend afternoons;
Nov–Mar, Tue–Sat.*

[9] Stourhead
Stourhead Garden and
House
Stourton, Warminster.
Tel: 01747 841152;
www.nationaltrust.org.uk
*Garden: daily. House: late
Mar–late Oct, Fri–Tue.*

[10] Shaftesbury
Shaftesbury Abbey
Museum
Gold Hill, Shaftesbury.
Tel: 01747 852157;
www.theheritagetrail.co.uk
Open Apr–Oct, daily.

[11] Wilton
Wilton House
Estate Office, Wilton,
Salisbury.
Tel: 01722 746714;
www.wiltonhouse.co.uk
Open Apr–Sep, daily.

TOUR 6

[i] The Old Fish Market,
The Pantiles, Royal
Tunbridge Wells.
Tel: 01892 515675.
[i] Buckhurst Lane,
Sevenoaks.
Tel: 01732 450305.
[i] Vestry Hall, Stone
Street, Cranbrook.
Tel: 01580 715686.
[i] Town Hall, High Street,
Tenterden. Tel: 01580
763572. May–Sep.

[1] Penshurst
Penshurst Place and
Gardens
Penshurst, Tonbridge.
Tel: 01892 870307;
www.penshurstplace.com
Open late Mar–Oct, daily.

[2] Hever
Hever Castle and Gardens
Hever, Edenbridge.
Tel: 01732 865224;
www.hever-castle.co.uk
Open Apr–Oct, daily.
Chiddingstone Castle
Chiddingstone, Edenbridge.
Tel: 01892 870347;
www.chiddingstone-
castle.org.uk
Closed for refurbishment
Haxted Watermill
Riverside
Edenbridge. Tel: 01732
862914;
www.haxtedmill.co.uk
*Easter–Sep, Tue–Sun;
Oct–Easter, most Sun.*

[3] Limpsfield
Quebec House
Westerham.
Tel: 01732 868381;
www.nationaltrust.org.uk
*Open mid-Mar to Oct,
Wed–Sun pm.*
Squerryes Court
Westerham.
Tel: 01959 562345;
www.squerryes.co.uk
*Open Apr–Sep, Wed, Thu
and Sun pm.*
Chartwell
Westerham.
Tel: 01732 868381;
www.nationaltrust.org.uk
*Open mid-Mar to Oct,
Wed–Sun; Jul and Aug, Tue
also.*

[4] Sevenoaks
Knole
Sevenoaks.
Tel: 01732 462100;
www.nationaltrust.org.uk
*Open Apr–Oct, Wed–Sun
and Bank Holidays.*

[5] Ightham
Ightham Mote
Ivy Hatch, Sevenoaks.
Tel: 01732 810378;
www.nationaltrust.org.uk
*Open Mar–Oct, Mon, Wed,
Thu, Fri and Sun.*

[6] Mereworth
The Hop Farm
Paddock Wood, Tonbridge.
Tel: 0870 0274166;
www.thehopfarm.co.uk
Open all year.

[7] Lamberhurst
Bayham Abbey
Lamberhurst, Royal
Tunbridge Wells.
Tel: 01892 890381;
www.english-heritage.org.uk
Open Apr–Sep, daily.
Scotney Castle Garden
Lamberhurst, Royal
Tunbridge Wells.
Tel: 01892 893868;
www.nationaltrust.org.uk
Open Apr–Oct, Wed–Sun.

[8] Cranbrook
Cranbrook Windmill
Mill Hill, Cranbrook.
Tel: 01580 712256;
www.unionmill.org.uk
*Open Apr–Sep, Sat pm; mid-
Jul–Aug, also Sun pm.*
Bedgebury National
Pinetum
Goudhurst, Cranbrook.
Tel: 01580 879820;
www.forestry.gov.uk
Open all year.
Sissinghurst Castle
Sissinghurst, Cranbrook.
Tel: 01580 710700;
www.nationaltrust.org.uk
Open late Mar–Oct, Fri–Tue.

[9] Tenterden
Smallhythe Place
Ellen Terry Memorial
Museum, Smallhythe,
Tenterden. Tel: 01580
762334.
*Open Apr–Oct, Sat–Wed
pm.*
Kent and East Sussex
Railway
Town Station, Tenterden.
Tel: 0870 606074;
www.kesr.org.uk
*Open Apr–Sep, daily; other
times throughout year.*

[10] Northiam
Great Dixter House and
Gardens
Northiam, Rye.
Tel: 01797 252878;
www.greatdixter.co.uk
*Open Apr–Oct, Tue–Sun and
Bank Holiday Mon.*

11 Bodiam
Bodiam Castle
Bodiam, Robertsbridge.
Tel: 01580 830436;
www.nationaltrust.org.uk
*Open mid-Feb–Oct, daily;
Sat–Sun rest of year.*

12 Burwash
Bateman's
Burwash, Etchingham.
Tel: 01435 882302;
www.nationaltrust.org.uk
*Open mid-Mar to Oct,
Sat–Wed.*

TOUR 7

i The Buttermarket, 12
Sun Street, Canterbury.
Tel: 01227 378100.
i 18 The Churchyard,
Ashford.
Tel: 01233 629165.
i The Heritage Centre,
Strand Quay, Rye.
Tel: 01797 226696.
i Lydd, New Romney,
Hythe. Tel: 01303 852555.
i 103 Sandgate Road,
Folkestone.
Tel: 01303 258594.
i Biggin Street, Dover.
Tel: 01304 205108.
i Landmark Centre, High
Street, Deal.
Tel: 01304 369576.
i The Guildhall, Market
Square, Sandwich.
Tel: 01304 613565.
Open Apr–Oct.

3 Ashford
Godinton House and
Gardens
Ashford.
Tel: 01233 620773;
www.godinton-house-
gardens.co.uk
*House open early Apr–early
Oct, Fri–Sun pm. Gardens
open late Mar–late Oct,
Thu–Mon.*

5 New Romney
Romney, Hythe and
Dymchurch Railway
New Romney Station,
New Romney. Tel: 01797
362353; www.rhdr.org.uk
*Open Apr–Sep, daily;
Oct–Mar, school hols and
weekends.*

6 Lympne
Port Lympne Wild Animal
Park
Port Lympne, Lympne.
Tel: 01303 264647;
www.portlympne.co.uk
Open all year, daily.

7 Folkestone
Museum and Art Gallery
2 Grace Hill, Folkestone.
Tel: 01303 850123;
www.kent.gov.uk
Open all year, daily.
Metropole Galleries
The Leas, Folkestone.
Tel: 01303 255070;
www.metropole.org.uk
Open Tue–Sun.

8 Hawkinge
Kent Battle of Britain
Museum
Hawkinge Airfield,
Hawkinge, Folkestone.
Tel: 01303 893140;
www.kbobm.org
Open Easter–Sep, Tue–Sun.

9 Dover
Roman Painted House
New Street, Dover.
Tel: 01304 203279;
www.romans-in-
britain.org.uk
*Open Apr–Sep, Tue–Sun;
Jul–Aug, daily.*
Dover Castle
www.english-heritage.org.uk
*Open all year, daily; closed
Tue–Wed Nov–Jan.*

**10 St Margaret's
at Cliffe**
Pines Garden
Beach Road, St Margaret's
Bay, Dover.
Tel: 01304 851737;
www.baytrust.org.uk
Open all year, daily.

11 Walmer
Walmer Castle
Kingsdown Road, Walmer,
Deal. Tel: 01304 364288.;
www.english-heritage.org.uk
*Open Apr–Sep, daily; Mar,
Oct, Wed–Sun; closed when
occupied.*
Deal Castle
Victoria Road, Deal.
Tel: 01304 372762;
www.english-heritage.org.uk
Open Apr–Sep, daily.

Time Ball Tower
Victoria Parade, Deal.
Tel: 01304 360897.
*Open Apr–Sep, Tue week-
ends.*
Deal Maritime and Local
History Museum
St George's Road, Deal.
Tel: 01304 373684.
Open May–Oct, Mon–Sat.

12 Sandwich
White Mill Rural Heritage
Centre
Ash Road, Sandwich.
Tel: 01304 612076.
*Open Easter to mid-Sep, Tue
and Fri am, and Sun.*
Royal St George's Golf
Club
Sandwich.
Tel: 01304 613090;
www.royalstgeorges.com
Open all year, daily.

13 Wingham
Wingham Wildlife Park
Rusham Road, Wingham,
Canterbury. Tel: 01227
720836; www.wing-
hamwildlifepark.co.uk
Open all year, daily.

TOUR 8

i The Guildhall, The
Broadway, Winchester.
Tel: 01962 840500.
i 13 Church Street,
Romsey. Tel: 01794 512987.
i Marwell Zoological
Park (see **5**)
i Queen Elizabeth
Country Park (see **9**)

1 Stockbridge
Andover Museum
(Museum of Iron Age)
6 Church Close, Andover.
Tel: 01264 366283.
Open all year, Tue–Sat.

2 Middle Wallop
Museum of Army Flying
Middle Wallop.
Tel: 01264 784421;
www.flying-museum.org.uk
Open all year, daily.

3 Mottisfont Abbey
Mottisfont Abbey
Mottisfont, Romsey.
Tel: 01794 340757;
www.nationaltrust.org.uk

*House open mid-Mar to Oct,
Sat–Wed; Jul–Aug, Thu; Jun,
daily. Garden open late
Mar–May, Jun, daily; Jul–Aug,
Sat–Thu; Sep–Oct, Sat–Wed.*

4 Romsey
Broadlands
Romsey. Tel: 01794 505010;
www.broadlands.net
Open Jul–Aug weekday pm.
Sir Harold Hillier Gardens
and Arboretum
Jermyns Lane, Ampfield,
Romsey.
Tel: 01794 369317;
www.hillier.hants.gov.uk
Open all year, daily.
Paultons Park
Ower, Romsey.
Tel: 023 8081 4442;
www.paultonspark.co.uk
*Open mid-Mar–Oct, daily;
Nov–Dec, weekends.*

5 Marwell Zoo
Marwell Zoological Park,
Colden Common,
Winchester.
Tel: 01962 777407;
www.marwell.org.uk
Open all year, daily.

6 Bishop's Waltham
Museum
Brook Street, Bishop's
Waltham, Southampton.
Tel: 01489 892460.
Open May–Sep, Sun–Fri.

7 Portsdown Hill
Fort Nelson
Tel: 01329 233734;
www.royalarmouries.org
Open all year, daily.

**9 Queen Elizabeth
Country Park**
Gravel Hill, Horndean,
Waterlooville. Tel: 023
9259 5040;
www.hants.gov.uk/qecp
Open all year, daily.
Butser Ancient Farm
Horndean. Tel: 02392
598838; www.butser.org.uk
*Open Mar–Sep, weekend
events.*

10 New Alresford
Watercress Line
Alresford Station, Alresford.
Tel: 01962 733810.
Open all year, most days.

TOUR 9

ⓘ Westover Road, Bournemouth.
Tel: 08450 511700.
ⓘ 49 High Street, Christchurch.
Tel: 01202 471780.
ⓘ The Furlong, Ringwood. Tel: 01425 470896.
ⓘ St Barb Museum and Visitor Centre, New Street, Lymington.
Tel: 01590 689000.
ⓘ John Montagu Building, Beaulieu, Brockenhurst.
Tel: 01590 612123.
ⓘ New Forest Museum and Visitor Centre, Main Car Park, Lyndhurst.
Tel: 023 8028 2269.
ⓘ 29 High Street, Wimborne Minster.
Tel: 01202 886116.

❶ Christchurch
Place Mill
Quay, Christchurch.
Tel: 01202 487626.
Open Apr–Sep, Tue–Sun.

❻ Bucklers Hard
Bucklers Hard Village and Maritime Museum
Beaulieu, Brockenhurst.
Tel: 01590 616203;
www.bucklershard.co.uk
Open all year, daily.

❼ Exbury
Exbury Gardens
Exbury Estate Office, Exbury, Southampton.
Tel: 023 8089 1203.
Open mid-Mar to Nov, daily.
Lepe Country Park
Lepe, Exbury, Southampton. Tel: 02380 899108;
www3.hants.gov.uk/lepe
Open all year, daily.
Hurst Castle
Keyhaven, Lymington.
Tel: 01590 642344;
www.hurst-castle.co.uk
Open Apr–Oct, daily; weekends in winter..

❽ Beaulieu
National Motor Museum
Beaulieu, Brockenhurst.
Tel: 01590 612345;
www.beaulieu.co.uk
Open all year, daily.

❾ Lyndhurst
New Forest Museum
High Street, Lyndhurst.
Tel: 023 8028 3444; www.
newforestmuseum.org.uk
Open all year, daily.

⓫ Wimborne Minster
Rockbourne Roman Villa
Rockbourne, Fordingbridge. Tel: 01725 518541;
www.hants.gov.uk
Open Apr–Sep, daily.

TOUR 10

ⓘ The Castle Car Park, Bridge Street, Chepstow.
Tel: 01291 623772.
ⓘ Shire Hall, Agincourt Square, Monmouth.
Tel: 01600 713899.
ⓘ Swan House, Edde Cross Street, Ross-on-Wye. Tel: 01989 562768.
ⓘ Cattle Market Car Park, Brecon.
Tel: 01874 622485.
ⓘ Beaufort Chambers, Beaufort Street, Crickhowell.
Tel: 01873 812105.
ⓘ Swan Meadow, Monmouth Road, Abergavenny.
Tel: 01873 857588.

❶ Monmouth
The Castle and Regimental Museum
The Castle, Monmouth.
Tel: 01600 772175;
www.monmouthcastlemuseum.org.uk
Open Apr–Oct, daily pm.
The Kymin Naval Temple
Monmouth. Tel: 01600 719241.
Open all year, daily.
Tintern Abbey
Tintern, near Chepstow.
Tel: 01291 689251;
www.castlewales.com/tintern
Open all year, daily.

❷ Symonds Yat
Museum of Mazes
Jubilee Park, Symonds Yat West, Ross-on-Wye.
Tel: 01600 890360;
www.mazes.co.uk
Open all year, daily.

❸ Goodrich
Goodrich Castle
Goodrich, near Ross-on-Wye. Tel: 01600 890538;
www.english-heritage.org.uk
Open Mar–Oct, daily; Wed–Sun, Nov–Feb.

❼ Hay-on-Wye
Hay Cinema Bookshop
The Old Cinema, Castle Street, Hay-on-Wye, via Hereford.
Tel: 01497 820071.
Open all year, daily.

❾ Brecon
The Brecknock Museum
Captain's Walk, Brecon.
Tel: 01874 624121;
www.powys.gov.uk
Open Apr–Sep, daily; Oct–Mar, Tue–Sat.
South Wales Borderers Army Museum
The Barracks, The Watton, Brecon. Tel: 01874 613310;
www.rrw.org.uk
Open Apr–Sep, Mon–Sat; Oct–Mar, Mon–Fri; closed mid-Dec to mid-Jan.
The Mountain Centre
Libanus, Brecon.
Tel: 01874 623366;
Open all year, daily.

❿ Pontsticill
Brecon Mountain Railway
Pant Station, Merthyr Tydfil.
Tel: 01685 722988; www.breconmountainrailway.co.uk
Open Apr–Oct, most days.

⓮ Raglan
Raglan Castle
Raglan. Tel: 01291 690228.;
www.cadw.wales.gov.uk
Open all year, daily.

⓯ Usk
Usk Rural Life Museum
The Malt Barn, New Market Street, Usk.
Tel: 01291 673777;
www.uskmuseum.org.uk
Open Apr–Oct, daily.

⓰ Caerleon
Caerleon Fortress Baths, Amphitheatre and Barracks
High Street, Caerleon.
Tel: 01633 422518
Open all year, daily.

National Roman Legion Museum
High Street, Caerleon, Newport. Tel: 01633 423134; www.museumwales.ac.uk
Open all year, Mon–Sat and some Sun pm.

⓱ Penhow
Penhow Castle
Closed to the public.
Caldicot Castle, Museum and Countryside Park
Caldicot. Tel: 01291 420241.
Open Apr–Sep, daily.

TOUR 11

ⓘ The Croft, Tenby.
Tel: 01834 842402.
ⓘ Visitor Centre, Commons Road, Pembroke.
Tel: 01646 622388.
ⓘ Old Bridge, Haverfordwest.
Tel: 01437 763110.
ⓘ National Park Visitor Centre, The Grove, St David's. Tel: 01437 720392.
ⓘ The Library, High Street, Fishguard.
Tel: 01348 873484.
ⓘ Theatr Mwldan, Bath House Road, Cardigan.
Tel: 01239 613230.
ⓘ 113 Lammas Street, Carmarthen.
Tel: 01267 231557.
ⓘ The Barbecue, Harbour Car Park, Saundersfoot.
Tel: 01834 813672.

❶ Manorbier
Manorbier Castle
Near Tenby.
Tel: 01834 871394;
www.manorbiercastle.co.uk
Open Apr–Sep, daily.

❷ Lamphey
Bishop's Palace
Lamphey. Tel: 01646 672224.
Open all year, daily.

❸ Pembroke
Pembroke Castle
Main Street, Pembroke.
Tel: 01646 684585; www.pembroke-castle.co.uk
Open all year, daily.

Practical • Information

[4] Haverfordwest
Town Museum
Castle House,
Haverfordwest. Tel: 01437
763087; www.haverford-
west-town-museum.org.uk
Open Easter–Oct, Mon–Sat.
Scolton Manor
Haverfordwest. Tel: 01437
731328.
*Gardens open all year, daily;
house Apr–Oct, daily.*

[5] Solva
Middle Mill
The Woollen Mill, Solva,
Haverfordwest. Tel: 01437
721112; www.solvawool-
lenmill.co.uk
*Open Jul–Sep, daily; Mon–Fri
rest of year.*

[6] St David's
St David's Cathedral
The Close, St David's.
Tel: 01437 720060; www.st
davidscathedral.org.uk
Open all year, daily.
Bishop's Palace
St David's. Tel: 01437
720517.
Open all year daily.
**Thousand Islands
Expeditions**
Cross Square, St David's.
Tel: 01437 721721;
www.thousandislands.co.uk
Trips run Apr–Oct, daily.

[8] Fishguard
Tregwynt Woollen Mill
Castle Morris,
Haverfordwest.
Tel: 01348 891225;
www.melintregwynt.co.uk
Mill open all year, Mon–Fri.

[9] Newport
**Pembrokeshire Candle
Centre**
Trefelin, Cilgwyn, Newport.
Tel: 01239 820470.
*Open daily; winter, telephone
for times.*
Pentre Ifan Cromlech
Newport.
Open all year, daily.

[10] Cardigan
Cilgerran Castle
Cilgerran.
Tel: 01239 621339;
www.nationaltrust.org.uk
Open all year, daily.

Welsh Wildlife Centre
Cilgerran, Cardigan.
Tel: 01239 621212;
www.welshwildlife.org
Open Easter–Dec, daily.
**National Coracle Centre
and Cenarth Mill**
Cenarth, Cardigan.
Tel: 01239 710980/710507;
www.coracle-centre.co.uk
Open Easter–Oct, daily.

[11] Dre-fach and
Felindre
Teifi Valley Railway
Henllan Station, Henllan,
near Newcastle Emlyn.
Tel: 01559 371077;
www.teifivalleyrailway.com
*Open Apr–Oct most days;
check before visiting.*
**Museum of the Welsh
Woollen Industry**
Dre-Fach Felindre,
Llandysul.
Tel: 01559 370929;
www.museumwales.ac.uk
*Open Apr–Sep, daily;
Oct–Mar, Tue–Sat.*

[12] Carmarthen
Gwili Steam Railway
Bronwydd Arms Station,
Bronwydd.
Tel: 01267 238213;
www.gwili-railway.co.uk
Open May–Sep..

[13] Laugharne
**Dylan Thomas' Boat
House**
Dylan's Walk, Laugharne.
Tel: 01994 427420;
www.dylanthomas-
boathouse.com
Open all year, daily.
Laugharne Castle
King Street, Laugharne.
Tel: 01994 427906;
www.cadw.wales.gov
Open Apr–Sep, daily.

TOUR 12

[i] Terrace Road,
Aberystwyth.
Tel: 01970 612125.
[i] Royal House, Penrallt
Street, Machynlleth.
Tel: 01654 702401.
[i] 54 Longbridge Street,
Llanidloes.
Tel: 07824 550821.
[i] The Leisure Centre,

North Street, Rhayader.
Tel: 01597 810591.
[i] Groe Car Park, Builth
Wells. Tel: 01982 553307.

[1] Borth
**Ynyslas National Nature
Reserve**
Information Centre.
Tel: 01970 872901.
Open Easter–Sep, daily.

[2] Machynlleth
**Centre for Alternative
Technology**
Machynlleth. Tel: 01654
705950; www.cat.org.uk
Open all year, daily.

[4] Rhayader
**Welsh Royal Crystal Glass
Factory**
5 Brynberth, Rhayader.
Tel: 01597 811005;
www.welshcrystal.co.uk
Open all year, daily.
Gigrin Farm
South Street, Rhayader.
Tel: 01597 810243;
www.gigrin.co.uk
Open all year, daily.
**Elan Valley Visitor
Centre**
Ellen Valley, Rhayader. Tel:
01597 810898/810880;
www.elanvalley.org.uk
Open mid-Mar–Oct, daily.

[6] Builth Wells
Wyeside Arts Centre
Castle Street, Builth Wells.
Tel: 01982 552555;
www.wyeside.co.uk
Open all year, Mon–Sat.

[9] Tregaron
Cors Caron
Countryside Council
for Wales, Neuaddlas.
Tel: 08451 306229;
www.stayinginwales.com
Kite Centre
Dewi Road.
Tel: 01974 298977.
*Open Apr–Sep, daily; week-
ends in winter.*

[10] Pontrhydygroes
Strata Florida Abbey
Pontrhydfendigaid,
Tregaron.
Tel: 01974 831261;
www.cadw.wales.gov.uk
Open all year, daily.

[11] Devil's Bridge
Vale of Rheidol Railway
Park Avenue, Aberystwyth.
Tel: 01970 625819;
www.rheidolrailway.co.uk
Open Easter–Oct, most days.

[12] Ponterwyd
**Llywernog Silver Lead
Mining Museum and
Caverns**
Llywernog Mine, Ponter-
wyd. Tel: 01970 890620;
www.silverminetours.co.uk
*Open Easter–Oct, Sun–Fri;
Jul–Aug, daily.*
**Nant-yr-Arian Visitor
Centre**
Ponterwyd.
Tel: 01970 890694;
www.forestry.gov.uk
Open all year, daily.

TOUR 13

[i] The Station, Station
Road, Barmouth.
Tel: 01341 280787.
[i] Llys y Graig, Harlech.
Tel: 01766 780658.
[i] Penllyn, Pensarn Road,
Bala. Tel: 01678 521021.
[i] Craft Centre, Corris.
Tel: 01654 761244.
[i] The Wharf Gardens,
Aberdyfi.
Tel: 01654 767321.
[i] High Street, Tywyn.
Tel: 01654 710070.
[i] Tŷ Meirion, Eldon
Square, Dolgellau.
Tel: 01341 422888.

[1] Llanbedr
**Chwarel Hên Llanfair
Slate Caverns**
Llanfair, near Harlech.
Tel: 01766 780247.
Open Easter–Oct, daily.

[2] Harlech
Harlech Castle
Harlech. Tel: 01766 780552;
www.harlech.com
Open all year, daily.

[3] Trawsfynydd
Holiday Village
Bronaber, Trawsfynydd.
Tel: 01766 540219;
www.logcabins-
skiwales.co.uk
Open Dec–Oct.

i Tourist Information Centre
12 Number on tour

4 Bala
Bala Lake Railway
The Station, Llanuwchllyn.
Tel: 01678 540666; www.
bala-lake-railway.co.uk
Open Apr–Sep, most days.

5 Lake Vyrnwy
Vyrnwy Visitor Centre
and RSPB Reserve
Bryn Awel, Llanwddyn,
Oswestry. Tel: 01691
870278.
Open 1 Apr–24 Dec, daily;
Jan–Mar, weekends.

7 Corris
Corris Craft Centre
Machynlleth. Tel: 01654
761584; www.cat.org.uk
Open Apr–Oct, daily.
King Arthur's Labyrinth
Tel: 01654 761584.
Open Apr–Oct, daily.

9 Tywyn
Talyllyn Railway
Wharf Station, Tywyn.
Tel: 01654 710472;
www.talyllyn.co.uk
Open Apr–Oct, daily.

11 Fairbourne
Fairbourne Railway
Beach Road, Fairbourne,
Dolgellau. Tel: 01341
250362;
www.fairbournerailway.com
Open May–Sep, most days.

TOUR 14

i Town Hall, Deiniol
Road, Bangor.
Tel: 01248 352786.
i Oriel Pendeitsh, Castle
Street, Caernarfon.
Tel: 01286 672232.
i 41b High Street,
Llanberis.
Tel: 01286 870765.
i Canolfan Hebog,
Beddgelert.
Tel: 01766 890615.
i High Street,
Porthmadog.
Tel: 01766 512981.
i Unit 3, High Street,
Blaenau Ffestiniog.
Tel: 01766 830360.
i Royal Oak Stables,
Betws-y-Coed.
Tel: 01690 710426.

i Prince's Drive, Colwyn
Bay. Tel: 01492 530478.
i Mostyn Street,
Llandudno.
Tel: 01492 876413.
i Conwy Castle Visitor
Centre, Castle Street,
Conwy. Tel: 01492 592248.

1 Menai Bridge
Oriel Tegfryn Gallery
Tegfryn, Cadnant Road,
Menai Bridge, Anglesey.
Tel: 01248 715128;
www.orieltegfryn.com
Open all year, daily.

2 Caernarfon
Caernarfon Air World
Dinas Dinlle, Caernarfon.
Tel: 01286 830800;
www.air-world.co.uk
Open Apr–Oct, daily.
Caernarfon Castle
Tel: 01286 677617;
www.cadw.wales.gov.uk
Open all year, daily.
Segontium Roman Fort
and Museum
Beddgelert Road, Caer-
narfon. Tel: 01286 675625;
www.segontium.org.uk
Open all year, Tue–Sun pm.

3 Llanrug
Bryn Bras Castle and
Gardens
Llanrug, near Caernarfon.
Tel: 01286 870210;
www.brynbrascastle.co.uk
Open by appointment only.

4 Llanberis
Llanberis Lake Railway
Llanberis.
Tel: 01286 870549;
www.lake-railway.co.uk
Open Easter–Oct.
Padarn Country Park
Quarry Hospital, Llanberis,
Caernarfon. Tel: 01286
870892.
Open all year, daily.
Electric Mountain
Dinorwig, Llanberis.
Tel: 01286 870636; www.
electricmountain.co.uk
Open Feb–Dec, daily.
Dolbadarn Castle
Llanberis.
www.llanberis.com
Open all year, daily.

Snowdon Mountain
Railway
Llanberis. Tel: 0870
4580033; www.snowdon-
railway.co.uk
Open late Mar–early Nov,
daily.
National Slate Museum
Gilfach Ddu, Padarn
Country Park, Llanberis.
Tel: 01286 870630;
www.museumwales.ac.uk
Open Easter–Oct, daily;
Nov–Mar, Sun–Fri.

5 Beddgelert
Sygun Copper Mine
Tel: 01766 890595; www.
syguncoppermine.co.uk
Open mid-Mar to Oct, daily.

6 Porthmadog
Ffestiniog Railway
Harbour Station,
Porthmadog.
Tel: 01766 516000;
www.ffestiniograilway.co.uk
Open late Mar–early Nov,
daily.
Welsh Highland Railway
Tremadog Road,
Porthmadog;
www.whr.co.uk
Tel: 01766 513402.
Open Apr–Oct, most days.

7 Portmeirion
Portmeirion Village
Tel: 01766 770000; www.
portmeirion-village.com
Open all year, daily.

8 Blaenau Ffestiniog
Llechwedd Slate Caverns
Blaenau Ffestiniog.
Tel: 01766 830306.
Open all year, daily.
Ffestiniog Visitor Centre
Tan-y-Grisiau, Blaenau
Ffestiniog.
Tel: 01766 830310.
Open Jun–Sep, Tue–Sun;
Jul–Aug, daily.
Trawsfynydd Holiday
Village
Bronaber, Trawsfynydd.
Tel: 01766 540219.
Closed Nov.

9 Betws-y-Coed
Motor Museum
Betws-y-Coed. Tel: 01690
710760.
Open Easter–Oct, daily.

10 Llanrwst
Trefriw Wells Roman Spa
Trefriw. Tel: 01492 640057.
Open Easter–Sep, daily;
Oct–Easter, Mon–Sat.
Trefriw Woollen Mills
Trefriw. Tel: 01492 640462;
www.t-w-m.co.uk
Open Easter–Oct, Mon–Fri;
Shop open all year, daily.

11 Tal-y-Cafn
Bodnant Garden
Tal-y-Cafn, Colwyn Bay,
Conwy. Tel: 01492 650460.
Open mid-Mar–Oct, daily.

12 Colwyn Bay
Welsh Mountain Zoo
Colwyn Bay.
Tel: 01492 532938; www.
welshmountainzoo.org
Open all year, daily.

13 Llandudno
The Great Orme Summit
Complex
Llandudno. Tel: 01492
876819.
Open Apr–Oct.
Alice in Wonderland
Visitor Centre, The Rabbit
Hole
3 and 4 Trinity Square,
Llandudno.
Tel: 01492 860082.
Open Easter–Oct, daily;
Nov–Easter, Mon–Sat.

14 Conwy
Conwy Castle
Conwy. Tel: 01492 592358;
www.cadw.wales.gov.uk
Open all year, daily.
Conwy Butterfly Jungle
Bodlondeb Park, Conwy.
Tel: 01492 593149;
www.conwy-butterfly.co.uk
Open Mar–Oct, Wed–Mon.

TOUR 15

i 9 Castle Hill, Lincoln.
Tel: 01522 873213.
i Iddesleigh Road,
Woodhall Spa.
Tel: 01526 353775.
i Pearoom Craft Centre,
Heckington (see **3**)
i Carre Street, Sleaford.
Tel: 01529 414294.
i The Gilstrap Centre,
Castlegate, Newark-on-
Trent. Tel: 01636 655765.

ⓘ Sherwood Heath, Newark. Tel: 01623 824545.

② Woodhall Spa
Tattershall Castle
Tattershall, Lincoln.
Tel: 01526 342543;
www.nationaltrust.org.uk
Open Mar–Nov, Sat–Sun; Apr–Oct, Sat–Wed.
Dogdyke Pumping Station
Bridge Farm, Tattershall, Lincoln. Tel: 01636 707642.
Open Apr–Oct, first Sun of month.

③ Heckington
Heckington Windmill
Pocklington's Yard, Heckington. Tel: 01529 461919.
Telephone for details.

④ Sleaford
The Hub, National Centre for Craft & Design
Carre Street, Sleaford.
Tel: 01529 308710;
www.thehubcentre.org
Open all year, daily.

⑧ Edwinstowe
Sherwood Forest Country Park and Visitor Centre
Edwinstowe. Tel: 01623 823202/824490.
Open all year, daily.

⑨ North Leverton
Sundown Adventureland
Treswell Road, Rampton, Retford. Tel: 01777 248274;
www.sundownadventureland.co.uk
Open mid-Feb–Dec, daily.

TOUR 16

ⓘ The Custom House, Purfleet Quay, King's Lynn. Tel: 01553 763044.
ⓘ 2–3 Bridge Street, Wisbech.
Tel: 01945 583263.
ⓘ Oliver Cromwell's House, 29 St Mary's Street, Ely. Tel: 01353 662062.
ⓘ Staithe Street, Wells-next-the-Sea.
Tel: 01328 710885.
ⓘ The Green, Hunstanton. Tel: 01485 532610.

❶ Wisbech
Wisbech and Fenland Museum
Museum Square, Wisbech.
Tel: 01945 583817; www.wisbechmuseum.org.uk
Open all year, Tue–Sat.
Aviation Museum
Old Lynn Road, West Walton, Wisbech.
Tel: 01945 461771.
Open Mar–Oct, weekends.
Peckover House
North Brink, Wisbech.
Tel: 01945 583463;
www.peckoverhouse.co.uk
Garden: Apr–Oct, Sat–Wed. House: Apr–Oct, Sat–Wed afternoons.

❹ Grime's Graves
Near Weeting.
Tel: 01842 810656;
www.english-heritage.org.uk
Open Apr–Sep, daily; Mar–Oct, Thu–Mon.

❺ Thetford
Euston Hall
Thetford. Tel: 01842 766366.
Open mid-Jun to mid-Sep, Thu and occasional Sun pm.
Ancient House Museum
White Hart Street, Thet-ford. Tel: 01842 752599.
Open Apr to mid-Mar, Mon–Sat.

❻ Dereham
Bishop Bonner's Cottage Museum
St Withburga Lane, Dereham. Tel: 01362 850293.
Open May–Sep, Tue, Thu–Sat pm.
Gressenhall Museum of Norfolk Life
Beech House, Gressenhall, Dereham. Tel: 01362 860563; www.museums.norfolk.gov.uk
Open Apr–Oct, daily.

❼ Fakenham
Fakenham Museum of Gas and Local History
Hempton Road, Fakenham.
Tel: 01328 863150.
Telephone for details.

Pensthorpe Waterfowl Park
Pensthorpe, Fakenham.
Tel: 01328 851465;
www.pensthorpe.com
Open all year, daily.

❾ Wells-next-the-Sea
Wells & Walsingham Railway
Stiffkey Road, Wells-next-the-Sea. Tel: 01328 711630;
www.wellswalsinghamrailway.co.uk
Open Easter–Oct, daily.
Cley Marshes Nature Reserve
Coast Road, Cley-next-the-Sea, Holt. Tel: 01263 740008; www.norfolk-wildlifetrust.org.uk
Reserve open all year, daily; Visitor Centre open late Mar–early Dec, daily.

❿ Holkham
Holkham Hall and Bygones Museum
Wells-next-the-Sea.
Tel: 01328 710227;
www.holkham.co.uk
Open May–Sep, Thu–Mon pm.

🇮🇲 Hunstanton
Sea Life Centre
Southern Promenade, Hunstanton. Tel: 01485 533576.
Open all year, daily.
Norfolk Lavender
Caley Mill, Heacham, King's Lynn. Tel: 0870 2430147;
www.norfolk-lavender.co.uk
Open all year, daily. Guided tours May–Sep.
Oasis Leisure Centre
Central Promenade, Hunstanton. Tel: 01485 534227.
Open Jan–Nov.

🇮🇲 Sandringham
Sandringham Estate
Sandringham, King's Lynn.
Tel: 01553 612908; www.sandringhamestate.co.uk
Open Apr–mid-Jul (not open Good Fri), Aug–Oct, daily.
Castle Rising
Castle Rising, King's Lynn.
Tel: 01553 631330.

Open Nov–Mar, Wed–Sun; Apr–Oct, daily.

TOUR 17

ⓘ St Stephen's Church, St Stephen's Lane, Ipswich.
Tel: 01473 258070.
ⓘ Town Hall, Market Hill, Sudbury.
Tel: 01787 881320.
ⓘ 1 Market Place, Saffron Walden. Tel: 01799 510444.
ⓘ The Old Library, Wheeler Street, Cambridge. Tel: 0871 2268006.
ⓘ Palace House, Palace Street, Newmarket.
Tel: 01638 667200.
ⓘ Lady Street, Lavenham.
Tel: 01787 248207.

❶ East Bergholt
Flatford Mill
Field Studies Council.
Tel: 01206 298283;
www.theheritagetrail.co.uk
Dedham Art and Craft Centre
High Street, Dedham, Colchester. Tel: 01206 322666; www.dedhamartandcraftcentre.co.uk
Open all year, daily.

❷ Sudbury
Gainsborough's House
46 Gainsborough Street, Sudbury.
Tel: 01787 372958;
www.gainsborough.org
Open all year, Mon–Sat.
Quay Theatre
Quay Lane, Sudbury.
Tel: 01787 374745;
www.quaytheatre.org.uk
Open all year, daily.

❸ Castle Hedingham
Hedingham Castle
Hal-stead. Tel: 01787 460261; www.hedingham-castle.co.uk
Open Apr–Oct, Sun–Thu.
Colne Valley Railway
Yeldham Road, Castle Hedingham. Tel: 01787 461174; www.colnevalleyrailway.co.uk

❺ Thaxted
John Webb's Windmill
Mill Row, Thaxted.
Tel: 01371 830285;

www.thaxted.co.uk
*Open Easter–Sep, weekends
and Bank Holidays.*
Thaxted Guildhall
Town Street, Thaxted.
Tel: 01371 831281;
www.thaxted.co.uk
*Open Easter–Sep,
Sun pm and Bank Holidays.*

[5] Saffron Walden
Saffron Walden Museum
Museum Street, Saffron
Walden. Tel: 01799 510333.
*Open all year, Mon–Sat, Sun
pm and Bank Holidays.*
Audley End House
Saffron Walden.
Tel: 01799 522399.
*Open Apr–Sep, Wed–Sun;
Mar and Oct, Sat–Sun.*
Linton Zoo
Hadstock Road, Linton.
Tel: 01223 891308;
www.lintonzoo.com
Open all year, daily.

[7] Duxford
Imperial War Museum
Duxford Airfield, Duxford.
Tel: 01223 835000;
http://duxford.iwm.org.uk
Open all year, daily.

[9] Cambridge
Fitzwilliam Museum
Trumpington Street,
Cambridge.
Tel: 01223 332900;
www.fitzmuseum.cam.ac.uk
*Open all year, Tue–Sat, and
Sun pm.*
**Fowlmere Nature
Reserve**
Manor Farm, High Street,
Fowlmere. Tel: 01763
208978; www.rspb.org.uk
Open all year, daily.

[10] Lode
**Anglesey Abbey, Gardens
and Lode Mill**
Lode, Cambridge.
Tel: 01223 810080.
Open Apr–Oct, Wed–Sun.

[11] Newmarket
National Stud
Wavertree House,
Newmarket.
Tel: 01638 663464;
www.nationalstud.co.uk
*Guided tours twice daily,
Mar–Sep, autumn race days.*

**National Horse Racing
Museum**
99 High Street, New-
market. Tel: 01638 667333;
www.nhrm.co.uk
Open Apr–Oct..

[12] Clare
**Clare Castle Country
Park**
Maltings Lane, Clare,
Sudbury. Tel: 01787
277491.
Open all year, daily.

[13] Long Melford
Melford Hall
Long Melford, Sudbury.
Tel: 01787 379228;
www.nationaltrust.org.uk
*Open Apr and Oct weekend
pm; May–Sep, Wed–Sun pm.*
Kentwell Hall
Long Melford, Sudbury.
Tel: 01787 310207;
www.kentwell.co.uk
Open Apr–Sep, most days.

[14] Lavenham
Lavenham Guildhall
Market Place, Lavenham.
Tel: 01787 247646;
www.nationaltrust.org.uk
*Open Mar–Oct, Tue–Sun;
Nov, Sat–Sun.*

[15] Hadleigh
Guildhall
Market Place, Hadleigh.
Tel: 01473 827752; www.
hadleigh-guildhall.co.uk
Open Tue and Sun pm.

TOUR 18

[i] 15 Broad Street,
Oxford. Tel: 01865 726871.
[i] Oxfordshire Museum,
Park Street, Woodstock.
Tel: 01993 813276..
[i] The Guildhall,
Chipping Norton.
Tel: 01608 644379.
[i] Spiceball Park Road,
Banbury.
Tel: 01295 259855.

[1] Woodstock
Blenheim Palace
Woodstock.
Tel: 08700 602080;
www.blenheimpalace.com
*Open mid-Feb to Oct, daily;
Nov–early Dec, Wed–Sun.*

**Oxfordshire County
Museum**
Fletcher's House, Wood-
stock. Tel: 01993 811456.
*Open all year, Tue–Sat and
Sun pm.*

[4] Broughton
**Wiggington Heath
Waterfowl Sanctuary**
On the road to Broughton.
Tel: 01608 730252; www.
waterfowlsanctuary.co.uk
*Open all year, Tue–Sun; open
daily in school hols.*
Broughton Castle
Banbury.
Tel: 01295 276070;
www.broughtoncastle.com
*Open Easter and May–mid-
Sep, Wed and Sun; also Thu
Jul–Aug.*

[6] Sulgrave
Sulgrave Manor
Manor Road, Sulgrave.
Tel: 01295 760205;
www.sulgravemanor.org.uk
*Open May–Oct, Tue–Thu,
Sat–Sun pm in Apr.*

[9] Steeple Aston
Rousham House
Near Steeple Aston.
Tel: 01869 347110;
www.roushem.org
*House open by
appointment; Gardens open
all year, daily.*

TOUR 19

[i] 28 Southgate Street,
Gloucester.
Tel: 01452 396572.
[i] 3 The Homend,
Ledbury.
Tel: 01531 636147.
[i] 21 Church Street,
Great Malvern.
Tel: 01684 892289.
[i] Out of the Hat, Church
Street, Tewkesbury.
Tel: 01684 295027.
[i] The Almonry, Abbey
Gate, Evesham.
Tel: 01386 446944.
[i] Bridgefoot, Stratford-
upon-Avon.
Tel: 0870 1607930.
[i] Town Hall, High Street,
Winchcombe.
Tel: 01242 602925.
[i] 77 Promenade,

Cheltenham.
Tel: 01242 522878.

[1] Ledbury
Eastnor Castle
Eastnor, Ledbury.
Tel: 01531 633160;
www.eastnorcastle.com
*Open mid-Jul to Aug, Sun–Fri;
mid-Apr to Sep, Sun and
Bank Holiday Mon.*

[2] Great Malvern
**Priory Church of St Mary
and St Michael**
Church Street, Malvern.
Tel: 01684 561020; www.
greatmalvernpriory.org.uk
Open all year, daily.
Malvern Museum
Abbey Road, Malvern.
Tel: 01684 567811.
*Open Apr–Oct; closed Wed
in term time.*

[6] Alcester
Coughton Court
Alcester.
Tel: 01789 762435; www.
coughtoncouort.co.uk
*Open Apr–Jun and Sep,
Wed–Sun; Jul–Aug, Tue–Sun;
Oct, Sat–Sun.*
Ragley Hall
Alcester.
Tel: 0800 0930290;
www.ragleyhall.com
*House and Garden open
late Mar to Sep, Thu, Fri, Sun
(Garden also open daily in
school hols).*

[7] Wilmcote
**Mary Arden's House and
the Shakespeare
Countryside Museum**
Station Road, Wilmcote,
Stratford-upon-Avon.
Tel: 01789 293455.
Open all year, daily.

**[8] Stratford-upon-
Avon**
Shakespeare's Birthplace
Henley Street, Stratford-
upon-Avon.
Tel: 01789 204016;
www.shakespeare.org.uk
Open all year, daily.
**Royal Shakespeare
Company Collection**
Royal Shakespeare Theatre,
Waterside, Stratford-upon-
Avon.

Tel: 01789 262870;
www.shakespeare.org.uk
Open all year, daily.
Harvard House
High Street, Stratford-upon-Avon.
Tel: 01789 204507;
www.shakespeare.org.uk
*Open Jul–Aug, Wed–Sun;
Jun, Sep and Oct, Wed, Sat,
Sun.*
Royal Shakespeare Theatre
Waterside, Stratford-upon-Avon.
Tel: 01789 403444;
www.shakespeare.org.uk
Anne Hathaway's Cottage
Cottage Lane, Shottery,
Stratford-upon-Avon.
Tel: 01789 292100;
www.shakespeare.org.uk
Open all year, daily.
New Place
Chapel Street, Stratford-upon-Avon.
Tel: 01789 292325.
Open all year, daily.

9 Chipping Campden
Hidcote Manor Garden
Chipping Campden.
Tel: 01386 438333;
www.nationaltrust.org.uk
*Open late Mar–Oct,
Sat–Wed (also Fri in Aug).*

10 Buckland
GWR Steam Railway Centre
The Railway Station,
Toddington. Tel: 01242
621405; www.gwsr.com
Open various days through-out year.
Hailes Abbey
Near Winchcombe,
Cheltenham.
Tel: 01242 602398;
www.nationaltrust.org.uk
Open Apr–Oct, daily.
Broadway Tower Country Park
off A44, Broadway.
Tel: 01386 852390; www.
broadway-cotswolds.co.uk
Open Apr–Oct, daily.

11 Winchcombe
Winchcombe Railway Museum
23 Gloucester Street,
Winchcombe. Tel: 01242
602257.
*Open Easter–Oct, Wed–Sun,
Bank Holidays; Aug, daily.*
Winchcombe Folk and Police Museum
Town Hall, High Street,
Winchcombe. Tel: 01242
609151.
Open Apr–Oct, Mon–Sat.
Sudeley Castle and Gardens
Winchcombe.
Tel: 01242 602308;
www.sudeleycastle.co.uk
*Open Apr–Oct, daily; gardens
also Mar.*

12 Cheltenham
Pittville Pump Room
Pittville Park, Cheltenham.
Tel: 01242 523852; www.
pittvillepumproom.org.uk
Open all year, daily.
Holst Birthplace Museum
4 Clarence Road, Pittville,
Cheltenham.
Tel: 01242 524846;
www.holstmuseum.org.uk
Open all year, Tue–Sat.

TOUR 20

$\boxed{i}$ The Music Hall, The
Square, Shrewsbury.
Tel: 01743 281200.
$\boxed{i}$ Castle Street, Ludlow.
Tel: 01584 875053.
$\boxed{i}$ Bewdley Museum,
Load Street, Bewdley.
Tel: 01299 404740.
$\boxed{i}$ The Library, Listley
Street, Bridgnorth.
Tel: 01746 763257.
$\boxed{i}$ The Museum, High
Street, Much Wenlock.
Tel: 01952 727679.
$\boxed{i}$ The Tollhouse,
Ironbridge.
Tel: 01952 884391.

1 Acton Burnell
Acton Burnell Castle
Acton Burnell, Shrewsbury.
www.shropshiretoursim.info
Open all reasonable times.

2 Church Stretton
Acton Scott Historic Working Farm
Wenlock Lodge, Acton
Scott. Tel: 01694 781306.
Open Apr–Oct, Tue–Sun.

3 Craven Arms
Stokesay Castle
Craven Arms. Tel: 01588
672544.
*Open May–Aug, daily;
Mar–Apr, Sep–Oct,
Wed–Sun; Nov–Feb,
Thu–Mon,*

4 Ludlow
Ludlow Castle
Castle Square, Ludlow.
Tel: 01584 873355.
*Open Jun–Aug, daily;
Apr–Sep, Mon–Sat.*
Ludlow Museum
Castle Street, Ludlow.
Tel: 01584 875384.
Open daily in summer, week-days only in winter.

6 Bewdley
Severn Valley Railway
The Railway Station,
Bewdley. Tel: 01299
403816; www.svr.co.uk
*Open May–Sep, daily;
weekends and school hols
rest of year.*
West Midlands Safari and Leisure Park
Spring Grove, Bewdley.
Tel: 01299 402114.
Open Feb–Oct, daily.

7 Bridgnorth
Bridgnorth Castle
West Castle Street, Bridg-north. Tel: 01746 762231.
Open all year, daily.

8 Shipton
Shipton Hall
Shipton. Tel: 01746 785225.
*Open Apr–Sep, Thu pm, and
Bank Hol Sun–Mon.*

9 Much Wenlock
Benthall Hall
Broseley. Tel: 01952
882159.
*Open Apr–Sep, Tue–Wed
pm, and Sun pm Jul–Sep.*

10 Ironbridge
Ironbridge Gorge Museums
Ironbridge. Tel: 01952
433522.
Open all year, daily.
Buildwas Abbey
Tel: 01952 433274;
www.english-heritage.org.uk
Open Apr–Sep, Wed–Sun.

11 Wroxeter
Wroxeter Roman City
Wroxeter. Tel: 01743
761330.
*Open Mar–Oct, daily;
Nov–Feb, Wed–Sun.*
Attingham Park
Atcham. Tel: 01743 708162.
*Gardens open all year, daily;
House, Apr–Oct, Fri–Tue
afternoons.*

TOUR 21

$\boxed{i}$ Carlisle Visitor Centre,
Old Town Hall, Green
Market, Carlisle.
Tel: 01228 625600.
$\boxed{i}$ Moot Hall, Market
Square, Keswick.
Tel: 017687 72645.
$\boxed{i}$ Central Buildings,
Market Cross, Ambleside.
Tel: 015394 32582.
$\boxed{i}$ Ruskin Avenue,
Coniston.
Tel: 015394 41533.
$\boxed{i}$ Glebe Road, Bowness-on-Windermere.
Tel: 015394 42895.
$\boxed{i}$ Victoria Street, Winder-mere. Tel: 015394 46499.
$\boxed{i}$ Main Car Park, Glen-ridding. Tel: 01768 482414.
$\boxed{i}$ Robinson's School,
Middlegate, Penrith.
Tel: 01768 867466.
$\boxed{i}$ Railway Station, Station
Road, Haltwhistle.
Tel: 01434 322002.

3 Buttermere
Whinlatter Forest Park Visitor Centre
Braithwaite, Keswick.
Tel: 017687 78469;
www.forestry.gov.uk
Open all year, daily.

4 Keswick
Cumberland Pencil Museum
Southey Works, Keswick.
Tel: 017687 73626;
www.pencilmuseum.co.uk
Open all year, daily.

5 Grasmere
Dove Cottage and the Wordsworth Museum
Grasmere.
Tel: 015394 35544;
www.wordsworth.org.uk
Open Feb–Dec, daily.

Rydal Mount and Gardens
Ambleside.
Tel: 015394 33002;
www.rydalmount.co.uk
*Open Mar–Oct, daily; Nov
and Feb, Wed–Mon.*

6 Ambleside
Stagshaw Garden
Stagshaw, Ambleside.
Tel: 015394 46027;
www.nationaltrust.org.uk
*Open Apr–Jun, daily; Jul–Oct
by appointment.*

7 Coniston
Beatrix Potter Gallery
Main Street, Hawkshead,
Ambleside.
Tel: 015394 36355;
www.nationaltrust.org.uk
*Open Apr–Oct, Sat–Wed;
Mar, weekends.*

Hill Top
Near Sawrey, Hawkshead,
Ambleside.
Tel: 015394 36269;
www.nationaltrust.org.uk
*Open Apr–Oct, Sat–Wed;
Mar, weekends.*

**8 Bowness and
Windermere**
Windermere Steamboat
Museum
Rayrigg Road, Bowness-on-
Windermere.
Tel: 015394 45565.
Reopens 2008.

Lake District National
Park Visitor Centre
Brockhole, Windermere.
Tel: 015394 46601;
www.lake-district.gov.uk
Open Easter–Oct, daily.

10 Penrith
Eden Ostrich World
Longwathby, Penrith.
Tel: 01768 881771.
Open mid-Feb to Oct, daily.

11 Haltwhistle
South Tynedale Railway
Railway Station, Alston.
Tel: 01434 381696;
www.strps.org.uk
*Open Apr–Oct, most days;
some weekends in Dec.*

Housesteads Fort
Bardon Mill, Hexham.
Tel: 01434 344363;
www.nationaltrust.org.uk
Open all year, daily.

Roman Army Museum
Greenhead.
Tel: 016977 47485;
www.vindolanda.com
*Open mid-Feb to mid-Nov,
daily.*

TOUR 22

[i] Minster Road, Ripon.
Tel: 01765 604625.
[i] Central Chambers,
Railway Street, Leyburn.
Tel: 01969 623069.
[i] Friary Gardens, Victoria
Road, Richmond.
Tel: 01748 850252.
[i] Woodleigh, Flatts Road,
Barnard Castle.
Tel: 01833 690909.
[i] Dales Countryside
Museum (see **8**)
[i] National Park Centre,
Hebden Road, Grassing-
ton. Tel: 01756 751690.
[i] 18 High Street, Pateley
Bridge. Tel: 01423 711147.

1 Masham
Newby Hall & Gardens
Ron. Tel: 0845 4504068;
www.newbyhall.co.uk
*Open Apr–Sep, Tue–Sun
(daily in Jul and Aug)*

Jervaulx Abbey
Masham.
Tel: 01677 460226;
www.jervaulxabbey.com
Open all year, daily.

2 Middleham
Middleham Castle
Middleham.
Tel: 01969 623899;
www.english-heritage.org.uk
Open all year, daily.

4 Richmond
Richmond Castle
Richmond.
Tel: 01748 822493;
www.english-heritage.org.uk
Open all year, daily.

Georgian Theatre Royal
Richmond.
Tel: 01748 823710; www.
georgiantheatreroyal.co.uk
Tours all year, Mon–Sat.

Green Howards Museum
Trinity Church Square,
Market Place, Richmond.
Tel: 01748 826561;
www.greenhowards.org.uk
Open Feb–Nov, most days.

5 Barnard Castle
Barnard Castle
Tel: 01833 638212;
www.english-heritage.org.uk
*Open Apr–Oct, daily;
Nov–Mar, Thu–Mon.*

Bowes Museum
Barnard Castle.
Tel: 01833 690606; www.
bowesmuseum.org.uk
Open all year, daily.

8 Hawes
Dales Countryside
Museum
Station Yard, Hawes.
Tel: 01969 666210;
www.yorkshiredales.org.uk
Open all year, daily.

10 Buckden
Kilnsey Park
Buckden.
Tel: 01756 752150;
www.kilnseypark.co.uk
Open all year, daily.

12 Pateley Bridge
Stump Cross Caverns
Pateley Bridge.
Tel: 01756 752780; www.
stumpcrosscaverns.co.uk
Open Mar–Nov, daily.

Nidderdale Museum
Pateley Bridge.
Tel: 01423 711225; www.
nidderdalemuseum.com
*Open Easter–Oct, daily pm;
Aug am; Nov–Easter, week-
end pm.*

**13 Fountains Abbey
and Studley Royal
Park**
Fountains Abbey. Tel: 01765
608888.
*Open all year, daily; closed Fri
Nov–Jan.*

TOUR 23

[i] Old Station Buildings,
Marine Road, Morecambe.
Tel: 01524 582808.
[i] 24 Main Street, Kirkby
Lonsdale.
Tel: 015242 71437.
[i] Community Centre,
Main Street, Ingleton,
Carnforth.
Tel: 015242 41049.
[i] Town Hall, Cheapside,
Settle. Tel: 01729 825192.

[i] 35 Coach Street,
Skipton. Tel: 01756 792809.
[i] 12–14 Market Place,
Clitheroe.
Tel: 01200 425566.
[i] 1 Clifton Street, Blackpool. Tel: 01253 478222.
[i] 29 Castle Hill,
Lancaster. Tel: 01524 32878.

2 Warton
Leighton Hall
Carnforth.
Tel: 01524 734474;
www.leightonhall.co.uk
*Open May–Sep, Tue–Fri pm
(Sun also in Aug).*

3 Skipton
Skipton Castle
Skipton. Tel: 01756 792442;
www.skiptoncastle.co.uk
Open all year, daily.

Craven Museum
Skipton. Tel: 01756 706407.
*Open Apr–Sep, Wed–Mon;
Oct–Mar, Wed–Sat and
Mon.*

Embsay and Bolton Abbey
Steam Railway
Skipton. Tel: 01756 710614;
www.embsaybolton-
abbeyrailway.org.uk
*Open Apr–Oct, most week-
ends; most days Jul–Aug.*

9 Clitheroe
Clitheroe Castle Museum
Castle Hill, Clitheroe.
Tel: 01200 424635.
*Open Apr–Oct, daily; winter
weekends (closed Jan), Bank
Hols and school hols.*

Browsholme Hall
Clitheroe.
Tel: 01254 826719;
www.browsholme.co.uk
Telephone for opening times.

11 Ribchester
Ribchester Roman
Museum
Riverside, Ribchester.
Tel: 01254 878261; www.
ribchestermuseum.org
Open all year, daily.

12 Blackpool
Blackpool Tower
The Promenade, Blackpool.
Tel: 01253 622242;
www.theblackpooltower.
co.uk
Telephone for opening times.

i Tourist Information Centre
12 Number on tour

Blackpool Pleasure Beach
Ocean Boulevard, Festival Coast, Blackpool. Tel: 0870 4445566; www.blackpool-pleasurebeach.com
Telephone for openiing times.

Sandcastle Waterworld
South Beach, Blackpool. Tel: 01253 343602; www.sandcastle-waterworld.co.uk
Open all year, most days.

Blackpool Sea Life Centre
The Promenade, Blackpool. Tel: 01253 622445; www.sealifeeurope.com
Open all year, daily.

Blackpool Zoo
East Park Drive, Blackpool. Tel: 01253 830830; www.blackpoolzoo.org.uk
Open all year, daily.

13 Lancaster
Lancaster Maritime Museum
Custom House, St George's Quay, Lancaster. Tel: 01524 382264; www.lancashire.gov.uk
Open all year, Easter–Oct. daily; Nov–Mar pm.

Lancaster Castle
Shire Hall, Castle Parade, Lancaster. Tel: 01524 64998; www.lancashire.gov.uk
Open all year, daily

Lancaster City Museum
Market Square, Lancaster. Tel: 01524 64637; www.lancashire.gov.uk
Open all year, Mon–Sat.

Judges' Lodgings Museum
Church Street, Lancaster. Tel: 01524 32808; www.lancashire.gov.uk
Open Apr–Oct, daily.

TOUR 24

i Town Hall, Macclesfield. Tel: 01625 504114/5.
i The Pavilion, Matlock Bath. Tel: 01629 55082.
i Old Market Hall, Bridge Street, Bakewell. Tel: 01629 813227.
i The Crescent, Buxton. Tel: 01298 25106.

1 Castleton
Peveril Castle
Market Place, Castleton. Tel: 01433 620613;

www.english-heritage.org.uk
Open Apr–Oct, daily; Nov–Mar, Thu–Mon.

Peak Cavern
Castleton. Tel: 01433 620285; www.devilsarse.com
Open Easter–Oct, daily; Nov–Easter, weekends.

Treak Cliff Cavern
Castleton. Tel: 01433 620571; www.bluejohnstone.com
Open all year, daily.

Speedwell Cavern
Winnats Pass, Castleton. Tel: 01433 620512; www.speedwellcavern.co.uk
Open all year, daily.

Blue John Cavern and Mine
Buxton Road, Castleton. Tel: 01433 620638/620642; www.bluejohn-cavern.co.uk
Open all year, daily.

3 Chatsworth
Chatsworth House
Chatsworth. Tel: 01246 582204; www.chatsworth.org
Open mid-Mar to mid-Dec, daily.

4 Matlock and Matlock Bath
Peak District Mining Museum
The Pavilion, Matlock Bath. Tel: 01629 583834; www.peakmines
Open all year, daily.

Heights of Abraham
Matlock Bath. Tel: 01629 582365; www.heightsofabraham.com
Open Easter–Oct, daily. Telephone for winter opening information.

National Tramway Museum
Crich. Tel: 01773 854321; www.tramway.co.uk
Open Apr–Oct, daily; winter, Sat–Sun.

5 Bakewell
Old House Museum
Cunningham Place, Bakewell. Tel: 01629 813642; www.oldhouse-museum.org.uk
Open Apr–Oct, daily.

Haddon Hall
Bakewell. Tel: 01629 812855; www.haddonhall.co.uk
Open May–Sep, pm daily; Apr and Oct, Sat–Mon.

7 Buxton
Buxton Spa Water Swimming Pool
St John's Road, Buxton. Tel: 01298 26548; www.peakdistrict-national-park.com
Open all year, daily.

Buxton Opera House
Water Street, Buxton. Tel: 01298 72050; www.buxtonoperahouse.org.uk
Open all year for shows.

Pavilion Gardens
St John's Road, Buxton. Tel: 01298 23114; www.paviliongardens.co.uk
Open all year, daily.

TOUR 25

i York Railway Station, York. Tel: 01904 550099.
i Malton Museum, Market Place, Malton. Tel: 01653 600048.
i The Ropery, Pickering. Tel: 01751 473791.
i The Moors National Park Centre, Danby Lodge, Lodge Lane, Danby. Tel: 01439 772737.
i Helmsley Castle. Tel: 01439 770173.
i Sutton Bank Visitor Centre, Kilburn. Tel: 01439 770657.

1 Malton
Malton Museum
Old Town Hall, Market Place, Malton. Tel: 01653 695136; www.maltonmuseum.co.uk
Open all year, Mon–Sat.

Eden Camp Modern History Museum
Eden Camp. Tel: 01653 697777; www.edencamp.co.uk
Open mid-Jan–23 Dec, daily.

Castle Howard
Castle Howard. Tel: 01653 648333; www.castlehoward.co.uk
Open Mar–Oct, daily.

Flamingo Land Theme Park and Zoo
Kirby Misperton, Malton. Tel: 01653 668287; www.flamingoland.co.uk
Open Apr–Oct, daily.

2 Pickering
North Yorkshire Moors Railway
Pickering Station, Pickering. Tel: 01751 472508; www.nymr.co.uk
Open mid-Mar to Oct.

Pickering Castle
Pickering. Tel: 01751 474989
Open Apr–Sep, daily; Oct, Thu–Mon.

Beck Isle Museum of Rural Life
Pickering. Tel: 01751 473653; www.beckislemuseum.co.uk
Open Apr–Oct, daily.

5 Danby
The Moors National Park Centre
Lodge Lane, Danby. Tel: 01439 772737; www.moors.uk.net
Open Mar–Dec, daily; Jan–Feb, weekends.

7 Hutton-le-Hole
Rydale Folk Museum
Hutton-le-Hole. Tel: 01751 417367; www.ryedalefolk-museum.co.uk
Open mid-Mar–Oct, daily.

9 Helmsley
Helmsley Castle
Helmsley. Tel: 01439 770442; www.english-heritage.org.uk
Open Apr–Sep, daily; Oct–Mar, Thu–Mon.

Rievaulx Abbey
Helmsley. Tel: 01439 798228; www.english-heritage.org.uk
Open Apr–Sep, daily; rest of year, Thu–Mon

11 Coxwold
Shandy Hall
Coxwold. Tel: 01347 868465; www.shandean.org/shandyhall
Open House: May–Sep, Wed and Sun pm; Gardens: May–Sep, Sun–Fri.

i Tourist Information Centre
🔢 Number on tour

Newburgh Priory
Coxwold.
Tel: 01347 868372; www.
newburghpriory.co.uk
Open Apr–Jun, Wed, Sun pm.

🔢 **Wass**
Byland Abbey
Tel: 01347 868614.
*Apr–Sep, Thu–Mon (daily in
Aug)*

🔢 **Sutton-on-the-Forest**
Sutton Park
Sutton-on-the-Forest.
Tel: 01347 811239;
www.statelyhome.co.uk
*Open Apr–Sep, Sun, Wed
and Bank Hol Mon.*

TOUR 26

i Castle Wynd, Inverness.
Tel: 0845 2255121.
i The Car Park,
Drumnadrochit.
Tel: 0845 2255121.
i Main Street,
Lochcarron.
Tel: 0845 2255121.
i NTS Visitor Centre,
Torridon.
Tel: 01445 791368.
i Beinn Eighe Reserve
Visitor Centre, near
Kinlochewe.
Tel: 01445 760258.
i Auchtercairn, Gairloch.
Tel: 0845 2255121.
i The Square,
Strathpeffer.
Tel: 0845 2255121.

1 Culloden
Culloden Visitor Centre
Culloden Moor, Inverness.
Tel: 01463 790607;
www.nts.org.uk
Open all year, daily.

2 Drumnadrochit
The Official Loch Ness
Monster Exhibition
The Drumnadrochit Hotel,
Drumnadrochit. Tel: 01456
450573; www.undiscov-
eredscotland.co.uk
Open all year, daily.

3 Eilean Donan
Eilean Donan Castle
Dornie, Kyle of Lochalsh.
Tel: 01599 555202;

www.eilandonancastle.com
Open Apr–Oct, daily.

6 Beinn Eighe
Beinn Eighe Reserve
Visitor Centre
Kinlochewe.
Tel: 01445 760258;
www.nnr-scotland.org.uk
Open Apr–Oct, daily.

7 Gairloch
Gairloch Heritage
Museum
Achtercairn, Gairloch.
Tel: 01445 712287.
Open Apr–Oct, Mon–Sat.

8 Inverewe Garden
Poolewe.
Tel: 0844 4932225;
www.nts.org.uk
Open Jan–Oct, daily.

TOUR 27

i 23 Union Street,
Aberdeen.
Tel: 0845 2255121.
i Station Square, Ballater.
Tel: 013397 55306.
i Railway Museum,
Station Yard, Alford.
Tel: 0845 2255121.

1 Crathes Castle
Banchory. Tel: 01330
844525; www.nts.org.uk
*Open Apr–Oct, daily;
Nov–Mar, Wed–Sun.*
Storybook Glen
Maryculter, Aberdeen.
Tel: 01224 732941;
www.storybookglenab-
erdeen.co.uk
Open all year, daily.

2 Aboyne
Glen Tanar Visitor Centre
Braeloine.
Tel: 013398 86072;
www.glenatanar.co.uk
*Open Apr–Sep, Wed,
Wed–Mon; Oct–Mar,
Thu–Mon.*

3 Ballater
Royal Lochnagar
Distillery
Crathie, Ballater.
Tel: 01339 742700; www.
discovering-distilleries.com
*Open May–Sep, daily;
Oct–Apr, Mon–Fri.*

4 Balmoral Castle
Balmoral Castle
Balmoral, Ballater.
Tel: 013397 42534;
www.balmoralcastle.com
Open Apr–Jul, daily.

5 Kildrummy Castle
Kildrummy Castle
Gardens
Kildrummy, Alford.
Tel: 019755 71331; www.
kildrummy-castle-
gardens.co.uk
Open Apr–Sep, daily.

6 Alford
Grampian Transport
Museum
Alford. Tel: 019755 62292;
www.gtm.org.uk
Open Apr–Oct, daily.
Alford Valley Railway
Dunnideer, Kingsford Road,
Alford. Tel: 07879 293934.
*Open Apr–May and Sep,
weekends; Jun–Aug, daily.*

8 Drum Castle
Drumoak, Banchory.
Tel: 01330 811204.
*Open Jan–Oct, Sat–Mon,
Wed–Thu (daily in Jul and
Aug)*

TOUR 28

i 3 Princes Street,
Edinburgh.
Tel: 0845 2255121.
i Pentland Hills Ranger
Service Office, Hillend
Country Park, Edinburgh.
Tel: 01968 677879.
i 23 High Street, Peebles.
Tel: 0870 6080404.
i Abbey House, Melrose.
Tel: 0870 6080404.
i Town House, The
Square, Kelso.
Tel: 0870 6080404.

**1 Hillend Country
Park**
Midlothian Snowsports
Centre
Hillend, near Edinburgh.
Tel: 0131 4454433;
www.midlothian.gov.uk
Open all year, daily.
Edinburgh Butterfly and
Insect World
Dobbies Garden World,
Lasswade. Tel: 0131

6634932; www.edinburgh-
butterfly-world.co.uk
Open all year, daily.

2 Peebles
Tweeddale Museum
Chambers Institute, High
Street, Peebles. Tel: 01721
724820.
*Open Nov–Mar, Mon–Fri;
Apr–Oct, also Sat.*
Cornice Museum of
Ornamental Plaster-
work
Innerleithen Road, Peebles.
Tel: 01721 720212.
Open all year, Mon–Fri.
Neidpath Castle
Peebles. Tel: 01721 720333.
*Open May–Sep, Wed–Sat
and Sun pm.*

3 Traquair
Traquair House
Innerleithen.
Tel: 01896 830323;
www.traquair.co.uk
*Open Easter–Oct, daily; Nov,
weekends only.*

4 Innerleithen
Robert Smail's Printing
Works
7–9 High Street,
Innerleithen. Tel: 0844
4932259.
Open Apr–Oct, Thu–Mon pm.
St Ronan's Wells
Interpretive Centre
Wells Brae, Innerleithen.
Tel: 01896 833583.
Open Apr–Oct, daily.
Abbotsford House
Melrose. Tel: 01896
752043.
Open mid-Mar–Oct, daily.

5 Melrose
Harmony Garden
St Mary's Road, Melrose.
Tel: 0844 4932257.
*Open Apr–Oct, Mon–Sat
and Sun pm.*

6 Kelso
Kelso Pottery
The Knowes, Kelso.
Tel: 01573 224027.
Open all year, Tue–Sat.
Floors Castle
Kelso. Tel: 01573 223333;
www.floorscastle.com
Open May–Oct, daily.

🎈 Coldstream
Coldstream Museum
12 Market Square,
Coldstream. Tel: 01890
882630.
*Open Apr–Sep, daily; Oct,
Mon–Sat.*
Hirsel Estate
Estate Office, The Hirsel.
Tel: 01573 224144; www.
hirselcountrypark.co.uk
Open all year, daily.

🎈 Haddington
Lennoxlove House
Lennoxlove Estate,
Haddington.
Tel: 01620 823720;
www.lennoxlove.com
Telephone for information.
**Jane Welsh Carlyle
Museum**
2 Lodge Street,
Haddington. Tel: 01620
823738.
Telephone for details.

🎈 Aberlady
Gosford House
Longniddry. Tel: 01875
870201.
*Open mid-Jun to mid-Aug,
Fri–Sun, pm.*
Dalkeith Country Park
Dalkeith. Tel: 0131 654
1666; www.dalkeithcoun-
trypark.co.uk
Open Apr–Sep, daily.

TOUR 29

ⓘ Whitesands, Dumfries.
Tel: 01387 253862.
ⓘ Colvend Post Office,
Colvend.
Tel: 01556 630228.
ⓘ Market Hill Car Park,
Castle Douglas.
Tel: 01556 502611.
ⓘ Harbour Square,
Kirkcudbright.
Tel: 01557 330494.
ⓘ The Car Park, High
Street, Gatehouse of Fleet.
Tel: 01557 814212.
ⓘ Kirroughtree Visitor
Centre, Palnure.
Tel: 01671 402165.
ⓘ Galloway Forest Park
Clatteringshaws Wildlife
Centre, Castle Douglas.
Tel: 01644 420285.

🎈 New Abbey
Caerlaverock Wetland
Centre
East Park Farm, Dumfries.
Tel: 01387 770200.
Open alll year, daily.
**Shambellie House
Museum of Costume**
New Abbey, Dumfries.
Tel: 01387 850375;
www.nms.ac.uk
Open Apr–Oct, daily.

🎈 Kirkbean
**John Paul Jones Birthplace
Museum**
Arbigland, Kirkbean,
Dumfries.
Tel: 01387 880613;
www.jpj.demon.co.uk
*Open Apr–Jun and Sep,
Tue–Sun; Jul–Aug, daily.*

🎈 Castle Douglas
**Threave Garden and
Estate**
Castle Douglas, Dumfries.
Tel: 0844 4932245;
www.nts.org.uk
Open all year, daily.
Threave Castle
Castle Douglas, Dumfries.
Tel: 07711 223101; www.
historic-scotland.gov.uk
Open Apr–Sep, daily.

🎈 Kirkcudbright
**Broughton House and
Garden**
12 High Street,
Kirkcudbright.
Tel: 0844 4932246;
www.kirkcudbright.co.uk
*Open Jul–Aug, dail; Apr–Jun
and Sep–Oct, Thu–Mon..*
The Stewartry Museum
St Mary Street,
Kirkcudbright. Tel: 01557
331643.
*Open Nov–Apr, Mon–Sat;
May–Oct, daily.*

**🎈 Gatehouse of
Fleet**
Cardoness Castle
Gatehouse of Fleet.
Tel: 01557 814427; www.
historic-scotland.gov.uk
*Open Apr–Sep, daily; Oct,
Sat–Wed; Nov–Mar wknds.*
Maxwelton House
Moniaive, Thornhill.
Tel: 01848 200385.
Open Jun–Sep, Sun–Fri.

**🎈 Kirroughtree
Forest**
Kirroughtree Visitor
Centre
Stronord, Palnure, Newton
Stewart. Tel: 01671
402165.
*Open late Mar–Oct, daily;
some winter weekends.*

🎈 The Queen's Way
Clatteringshaws Wildlife
Centre
New Galloway, Castle
Douglas. Tel: 0860 853351.
Open Apr–Oct,, daily.

TOUR 30

ⓘ Milton, by Dumbarton.
Tel: 01389 742306.
ⓘ The Clock Tower,
Helensburgh.
Tel: 0870 2255121.
ⓘ Front Street, Inveraray.
Tel: 01499 302063.
ⓘ Easdale Island Folk
Museum, Easdale.
(see 🎈)
ⓘ Argyll Square, Oban.
Tel: 01631 563122.
ⓘ Ballachulish Visitor
Centre Albert Road,
Ballachulish (see 🎈).
ⓘ National Trust for
Scotland Visitor Centre,
A82, Glencoe.
Tel: 01855 811307.
ⓘ Harbour Street, Tarbert.
Tel: 01880 820429.

🎈 Helensburgh
Hill House
Upper Colquhoun Street,
Helensburgh.
Tel: 0844 4932208;
www.nts.org.uk
Open Apr–Oct, pm.

🎈 Inveraray
Inveraray Castle
Inveraray.
Tel: 01499 302203.
Open Apr–Oct, daily
Inveraray Gaol
Church Square, Inveraray.
Tel: 01499 302381;
www.inverarayjail.co.uk
Open all year, daily.
**Auchindrain Open Air
Museum**
Inverary. Tel: 01499 500235.
Open Apr–Oct, daily.

Crarae Garden
Minard, Inverary.
Tel: 0844 4932210.

🎈 Kilmartin
Carnassarie Castle
Kilmartin. Tel: 0131
6688800 for information.

🎈 Easdale
**Easdale Island Folk
Museum**
Easdale Island, Oban.
Tel: 01852 300370;
www.slate.org.uk
Open Apr–Oct, daily.

🎈 Oban
Oban Distillery
Stafford Street, Oban.
Tel: 01631 572004; www.
discovering-distilleries.com
*Open Feb to mid-Dec,
Mon–Fri. Also Sat
Easter–Oct., and Jul–Sep.*
**Oban Rare Breeds Farm
Park**
Stafford Street, Oban.
Tel: 01631 572004.
Open mid-Mar to Oct, daily.

🎈 Barcaldine Castle
Barcaldine Connel, Oban.
Tel: 01671 402165.
Closed to the public.

🎈 Ballachulish
Ballachulish Visitor Centre,
Albert Road, Ballachulish.
Tel: 01855 811866;
www.glencoetourism.co.uk
Open all year, daily.

**🎈 Glen Coe and the
Black Mount**
Glencoe and North Lorn
Folk Museum
Glencoe. Tel: 01855
811664.
Open Apr–Oct, Mon–Sat.
Glencoe Visitor Centre
Tel: 01855 811307.
*Open Mar–Oct, daily;
Nov–Feb, Thu–Sun.*

🎈 Loch Lomond
Queen Elizabeth Forest
Park
Aberfoyle. Tel: 01877
382383.
Open all year, daily.

INDEX

Index & Acknowledgements

The Automobile Association
would like to thank the following for their assistance in the preparation of this book.
WOOLSACK COMMITTEE 2.

All remaining pictures are held in the Association's own library (AA World Travel Library)
with contributions from the following photographers:
P AITHIE 77; M ALLWOOD-COPPIN 64, 69; A BAKER 89, 110/1, 137; P BAKER 13, 16/7, 19a, 19b, 25, 26, 32, 40, 44, 86/7, 90/1, 130/1; J BEAZLEY 124, 147, 149, 150, 155; A W BESLEY 7; M BIRKITT 84, 85a, 85b, 88, 94, 95, 96, 97, 129; E A BOWNESS 113, 114, 115; I BURGUM 58/9, 65, 66, 66/7, 72, 107; M BUSSELLE 5, 34; D CORRANCE 146, 148; D CROUCHER 50, 57, 76, 81; R CZAJA 24; S L DAY 29, 99, 103, 106, 116, 127, 153; E ELLINGTON 140/1, 165; P ENTICKNAP 49; D FORSS 33, 35, 42, 46, 47, 48, 51, 54, 55; J GRAVEL 63; V GREAVES 123; S GREGORY 135; J HENDERSON 139, 141; A J HOPKINS 59, 71, 128; C JONES 10, 11, 27, 56, 78, 80, 109; A LAWSON 8, 12, 18; S & O MATHEWS 45, 91, 92, 151; E MEACHER 28/9, 70; C & A MOLYNEUX 60, 61; J MORRISON 120/1, 126, 132; R MOSS 14b, 15; J MOTTERSHAW 134; R NEWTON 22, 130; D NOBLE 36, 37, 38, 39, 41, 43; K PATERSON 145, 154; N RAY 9, 23, 100/1; P SHARPE 117, 156, 156/7; M SHORT 102, 111; R SURMAN 83; D TARN 112, 119, 122b, 125; M TAYLOR 136; T TEEGAN 14a; T D TIMMS 73, 74, 75, 79; W VOYSEY 30, 31, 52/3, 93; R WEIR 142/3, 144; J WELSH 104, 105; L WHITWAM 82, 122a; H WILLIAMS 6, 152.

Contributors
Indexer: Marie Lorimer.   Thanks also to **David Halford** for his updating work on this book.

Atlas

Orkney Islands

Western Isles

Thurso

Shetland Islands

200-201

202-203

Inverness

Isle of Skye

Aberdeen

Orkney Islands

197

Oban

198-199

Edinburgh

Glasgow

Carlisle

Newcastle upon Tyne

Isle of Man

194-195

196

Blackpool

York

IRL

Anglesey

Liverpool

Manchester

Lincoln

Bangor

190-191

Birmingham

192-193

Norwich

Builth Wells

Cambridge

Fishguard

Gloucester

Oxford

LONDON

Cardiff

Bristol

188-189

Dover

Barnstaple

Southampton

186-187

Isle of Wight

Exeter

F

Truro

Isles of Scilly

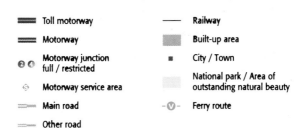

▬▬ Toll motorway		── Railway
▬▬ Motorway		▨ Built-up area
❷ ❹ Motorway junction full / restricted		▪ City / Town
↻ Motorway service area		National park / Area of outstanding natural beauty
═══ Main road		-Ⓥ- Ferry route
═══ Other road		

0   10   20   30   40 km

0   10   20 miles

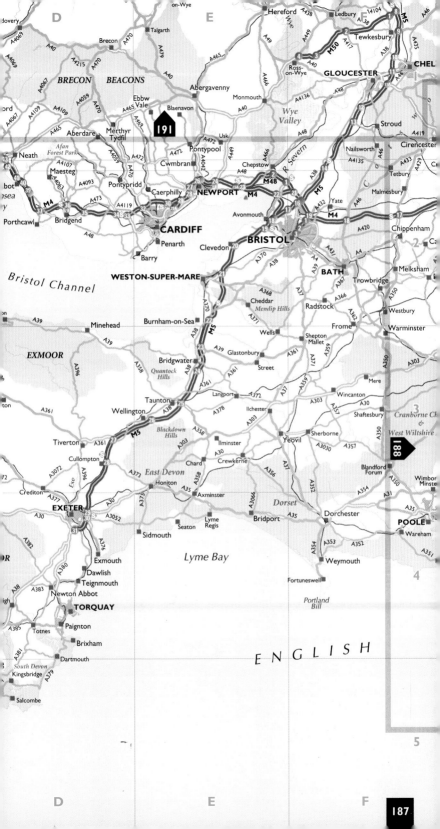

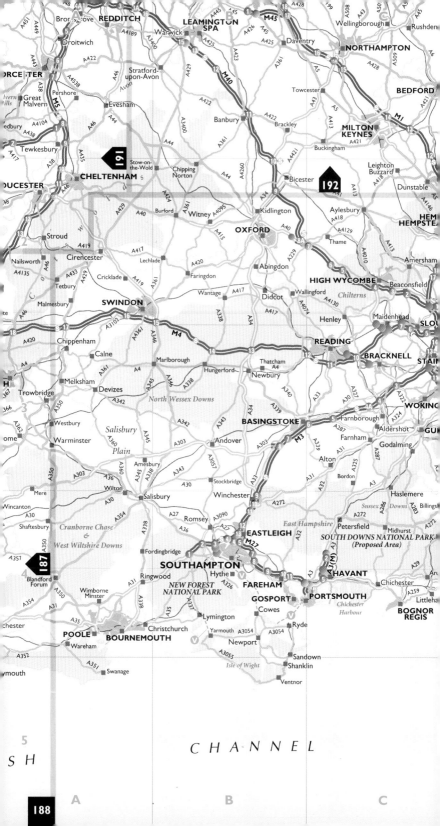

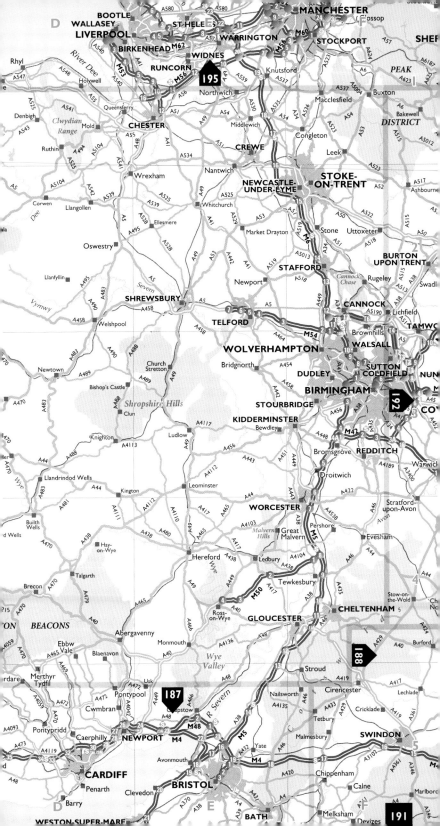

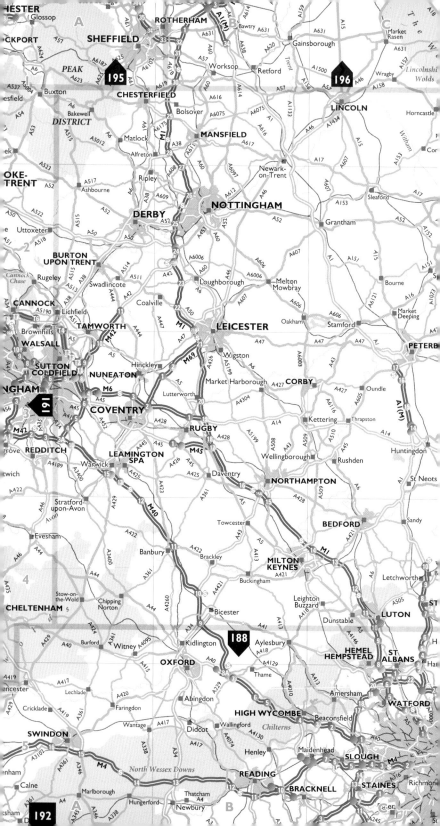

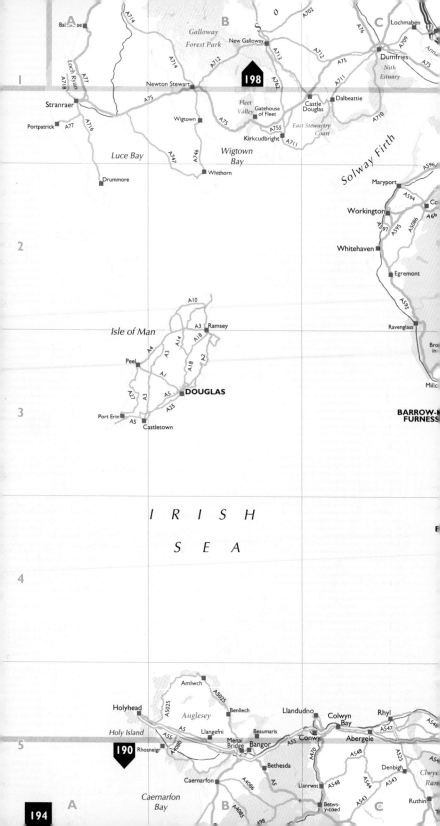

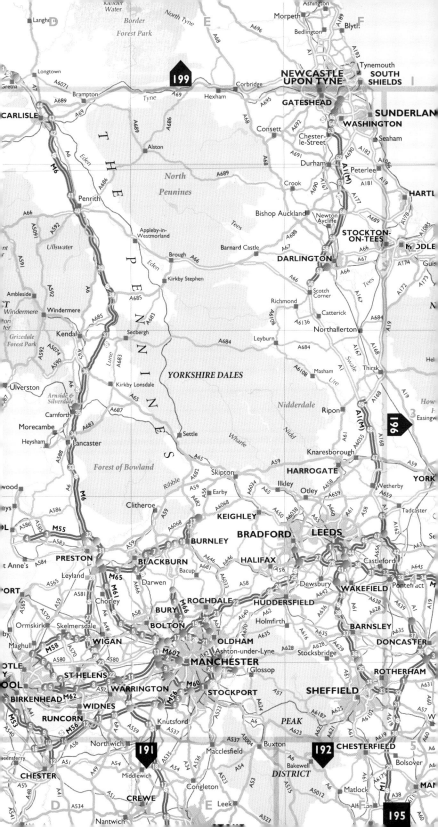

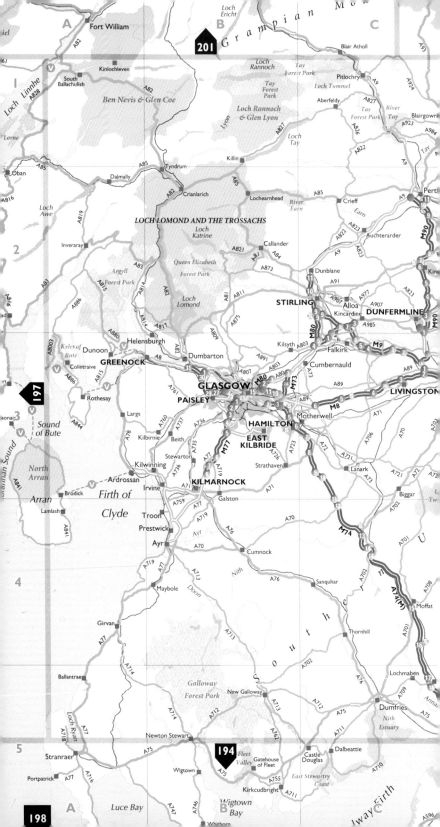

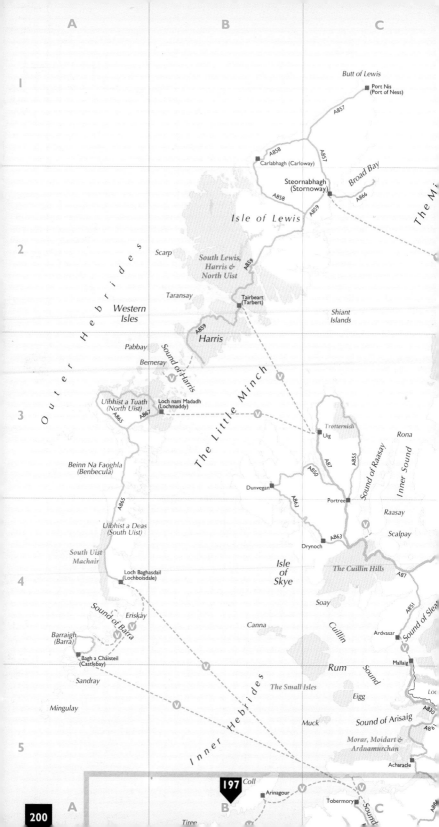

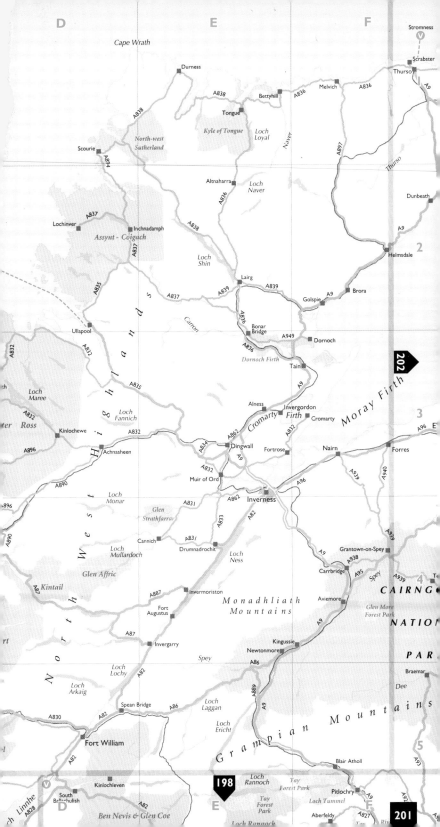

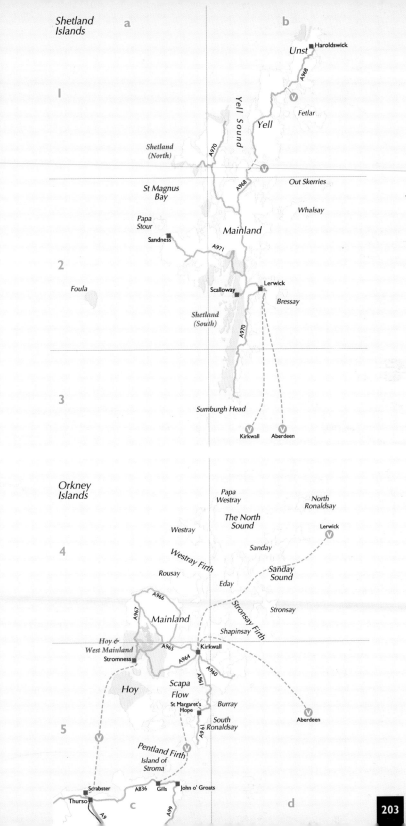

Shetland Islands

a

b

Unst

Haroldswick

A968

V

Yell Sound

Yell

Fetlar

Shetland (North)

1

St Magnus Bay

A970

V

Out Skerries

A968

Whalsay

Papa Stour

Sandness

Mainland

A971

Foula

Scalloway

Lerwick

2

Bressay

Shetland (South)

A970

3

Sumburgh Head

Kirkwall

V

Aberdeen

V

Orkney Islands

Papa Westray

North Ronaldsay

The North Sound

Westray

Lerwick

V

Sanday

4

Westray Firth

Rousay

Sanday Sound

Eday

Stronsay

Stronsay Firth

Mainland

A966

A967

Shapinsay Firth

Hoy & West Mainland

A965

Kirkwall

Stromness

A964

A960

Scapa Flow

Hoy

A961

St Margaret's Hope

Burray

Aberdeen

V

5

South Ronaldsay

A961

V

Pentland Firth

Island of Stroma

Scrabster

A836

Gills

John o' Groats

Thurso

A9

c

A99

d